Dedicated with love to Kiera Llord-Ratcliffe and Joanne Gore.

Acknowledgments

Many praiseworthy contributors made the *Guide* a reality.

At the top of the authors' "without whom this book wouldn't have been possible" list are our technical editor, Stephen Howard, and master illustrator, cartoonist and iconizer, Nevin Berger. In addition to having to live with the absurdly short deadlines we kept giving them they also had to deal with us at *MacWEEK.* Thanks guys! Top-of-the-line kudos also go to our publisher, Michael Mellin. What can we say? Michael took a big chance on two news guys from San Francisco. We hope you enjoyed the process as much as we did, Michael, and will be richly rewarded in this life and the next for giving us our Big Break!

We can't possibly commend Michael without also expressing our gratitude to Jane Mellin, the woman who checked our style, edited our words, and applied generous amounts of lubricant to the production process, keeping graphics and text together and pages flowing in everyone's first effort at "near real-time" book publishing. Also, the folks down at Modern Design, the layout house in L.A., deserve our undying gratitude for getting proofs in our hands as we travelled around the country. Sorry for all the time you guys had to spend downloading files from AppleLink.

Back at *MacWEEK,* we'd like to thank Henry Norr, Raines Cohen, and Rick LePage for moral support and for answering a neverending barrage of little PowerBook questions which had little to do with stories we were working on for *MacWEEK.* And to Daniel Farber, *MacWEEK*'s now-departed editor-and-chief (*PCWEEK*'s gain is our great loss), for his understanding and endorsement of this project, merci, mon ami!

The short list of Apple people we'd like to thank include Bruce Gee, who came in late in the process to save us from our own excesses and flights of fancy and Kate Paisley, for her understanding and help in connecting us with Bruce. We'd also like to thank Bruce Cooper and Peter Fletcher for lending us the 180 and Duo just days after they were introduced; and thanks to all the Apple engineers, salespeople and product managers who made the PowerBooks a success. Our special appreciation to Randy Battat and Neil Selvin (keep them new PowerBooks comin', guys!) and to John Sculley for his words of wisdom.

To the people who made the PowerBook Roadside Assistance Kit a reality, including Kurt Bauman, Mikki Barry, Steve Christensen, Mike Frost, Richard Holzgrafe, Dave Loverink, Michael Paulette, Michael Reeds, Pierre Saine, Jim Sheldon-Dean, Richard Skeie, Brian Smiga, Tony Stayner, and Kim Wilson, mucho appreciato!

And, finally, to all the people who would rather we didn't mention their names, but without whom this book truly wouldn't have been possible, thank you all very, very much!

POWERBOOK™
THE DIGITAL NOMAD'S GUIDE

Everything the Modern Road Warrior
Needs to Turn the Macintosh PowerBook into
the Complete Mobile Habitat

ANDREW GORE & MITCH RATCLIFFE
SENIOR NEWS EDITOR & EDITOR-AT-LARGE OF MacWEEK

RANDOM HOUSE
ELECTRONIC PUBLISHING

New York

PowerBook: A Digital Nomad's Guide

Copyright ©1993 by Andrew Gore and Mitch Ratcliffe

Page xxii Copyright © Serious Productions Ltd. 1993

Random House Electronic Publishing is a division of Random House, Inc., 201 E. 50th St., NY, NY 10022. Published simultaneously in the U.S. by Random House, NY and in Canada by Random House of Canada, Ltd.

The author and publisher have used their best efforts in preparing this book, the disk accompanying this book, and the programs and data contained therein. However, the author and publisher make no warranties of any kind, express or implied, with regard to the documentation or programs or data contained in this book or disk, and specifically disclaim, without limitation, any implied warranties of merchantability and fitness for a particular purpose with respect to the disk, the programs and/or data contained therein, program listings in the book and/or the techniques described in the book. In no event shall the author or publisher be responsible or liable for any loss of profit or any other commercial damages, including but not limited to special, incidental, consequential or any other damages in connection with or arising out of furnishing, performance, or use of this book or the programs or data.

Library of Congress Cataloging-in-Publication Data

Gore, Andrew.
    Powerbook: the digital nomad's guide : everything the modern-day
road warrior needs to turn the Macintosh powerbook into the complete
mobile habitat / Andrew Gore and Mitchell Ratcliffe.
        p.   cm.
    Includes index.
    ISBN 0-679-74588-2
    1. Macintosh PowerBook notebook computers.   I. Ratcliffe,
Mitchell.   II. Title.
QA76.8.M3G68   1993
004.165—dc20   92-40494
                                                        CIP

CONTENTS

This chapter dispels some rumors about sleeping PowerBooks and battery hazards, and it provides an invaluable travel checklist that will ensure you're as well prepared as any good scout. It also tells you how to cope with the power outlet and phone jack obstacles that can stand in your way when you're on the road or in the air.

Power management is a big issue for Digital Nomads. Here you'll find tips for conserving power via system settings and conservative work habits. And, you'll read the facts you need on battery care and feeding.

What should you do if your PowerBook falls ill on the road? How can you keep it in tip-top condition? Find the answers here.

Cyberspace is the telephone network, and this chapter introduces the wonders of electronic mail, online services, and The Internet, as well as your modem options for keeping in touch.

This chapter describes the software you receive with this book: what it is, what it can do for you, and how to install it.

Find out where you can get hardware, software, and online services for your PowerBook. The names, addresses, and phone numbers are here.

At the very end of the book you'll find the all-important registration form for *The Digital Nomads's Guide*, as well as valuable coupons from two major online services. Take a look now!

COMMENTARY

Nomadic computing returns us to our roots.

Thousands of years ago, our ancestors roamed the planet, travelling great distances and inhabiting uncharted territory in search of sustenance and safety from the elements and natural predators. Influenced by the advent of agriculture and the domestication of animals, these nomadic tribes of hunters and gatherers gradually grew into more sedentary cultures. Complex, sophisticated civilizations were carved out of the wilderness, and the roots of our modern communications systems were formed.

The citizens of these early city-states were tethered, or wired, into their society. While they lacked cellular telephones and fax machines, the people of ancient Sumerian, Mayan, or Chinese cultures developed their own, simpler forms of writing and long-distance communication that extended their social and economic world.

In today's world, we have the convenience of modern telecommunications and computers. But until recently, most people had to be tethered to their desks to take advantage of that technology. With liquid crystal displays, low-power components, wireless networks, and miniaturization, notebook computers have helped users cut the cord and gain mobility. We are once again becoming a kind of nomadic—mobile—society, hunting, gathering, and sifting through information on the electronic frontier.

Leading the way in mobile computing is Apple's PowerBook family of notebook computers. The design, remote connectivity, and integration with desktop systems of the PowerBooks have set a new industry standard. And with *PowerBook: The Digital Nomad's Guide*, there is now an essential guidebook for people who are taking up the mobile computing lifestyle.

Co-authors Andrew Gore and Mitch Ratcliffe are well qualified to write on the subject and to bring neophytes into the new world. They are mobile computing pioneers who are intimate with the technical underpinnings of the PowerBooks and experienced twenty-first-century nomads who use their PowerBooks tethered and untethered every day. They have written a book that contains practical advice and technical information written in a straightforward, lively style.

PowerBook: The Digital Nomad's Guide also captures the social significance of mobile computing and confronts the problems that users face in moving away from traditional desktop computing.

For anyone seriously interested in mobile computing or getting the most out of Apple's PowerBooks, *PowerBook: The Digital Nomad's Guide* will be a good companion to take on the road.

—Daniel Farber
Editor in Chief, *MacWEEK*
November 10, 1992

Over the last few years, as Apple has built its business around the world, I often find myself on the road. Sometimes, if I'm walking through an airport and I see somebody using a PowerBook, I might muster the courage to ask them, "What are you doing with it?" Usually, their eyes will light up, and they'll say, "Here, look, this is wonderful! Let me show you…"

To see that experience repeated over and over in different parts of the world gives us the encouragement to want to keep building more iterations of the PowerBook. And one of the reasons why the PowerBook has been so amazingly well-received, is that we began with specific design criteria that we put in place at the very beginning of the product development process.

We wanted to move the PowerBook beyond the "shrunken down desktop" notion of notebook computing, and give people a tool that would positively transform the way they work with information when they're on the road. Of course, we expected people to be using it for the typical kinds of tasks—such as word processing and working on spreadsheets—and with the new functionality of the PowerBooks 160 and 180 and the Macintosh Duo System, people are relying on their PowerBooks for presentation development and delivery.

But we wanted to take the proposition further by incorporating powerful communications capabilities into each and every PowerBook. The AppleTalk remote access capability and built in modem are perfect examples of how the PowerBook is more of a personal communications device than a notebook computer. Using its built-in communications capabilities, individuals can: access their desktop at home or the office, connect to one of their organization's servers, collaborate with a coworker on a project, and send a fax—all from their PowerBook.

But as I've watched the PowerBook phenomenon take off, the most exciting dimension has been the extent to which "pervasive" or "ubiquitous" computing is becoming a regular part of modern life. And this is at the heart of Andrew Gore and Mitch Ratcliffe's book, *PowerBook: The Digital Nomad's Guide.* As they point out in their comprehensive guide, the introduction of the PowerBook has spawned a huge industry based on the notion of "mobile living." I can only add that even though Apple has introduced several implementations of the PowerBook, you can count on us to continue to develop and deliver even more innovative, more personal and more mobile information technology in the future.

—John Sculley
Chairman and CEO, Apple Computer

Ungrateful bunch of louts we are, aren't we? Never satisfied. I've just been rushing round twenty American cities on a book promotion tour (modern writers get to spend more time signing books than actually writing them), and it was the first tour for which I had a Macintosh PowerBook with me. But so far from being in a permanent state of ecstatic gratitude that I had all my work with me, could write on planes, could set up my actual *office* in one hotel room after another, I found that I was continually grumbling over the business of how to connect it to the hotel phone system when there was only one phone line and no dataport, or even in extreme cases of the Mid West, no modular telephone jack or cashew nuts in the minibar (a different problem, I admit, but it bugged me at the time).

Then I had to change my AppleLink and CompuServe access phone numbers in every city. Even—can you imagine the horror of this?—I even sometimes had to change the access number for an outside line from 9 to 8! Just to send a fax or do my e-mail! And sometimes I would run low on battery power in the plane and become utterly incensed that the plane seats didn't deliver 12 volts direct to the arm rest! How, I felt, can someone be expected to live and work under such conditions?

So how did I ever manage without a PowerBook at all? The extraordinary thing is that I simply don't know. I can't remember how we did it, and they've only been around for a couple of years.

We have to remind ourselves that if Charles Babbage had ever seen such a machine as a PowerBook it would have made him gibber and quite possibly go and hide in a tree. Even I, who as recently as fifteen years ago came up with the idea of *The Hitch Hiker's Guide to the Galaxy,* would have found all that the PowerBook *can actually do* in real life to be beyond belief and probably done with mirrors or hallucinogenic drugs or a lethal combination of the two. The future is a wild and crazy place and if we are going to stay on top of it we need better connections for PowerBooks and more cashew nuts in every room.

—Douglas Adams

MANIFESTO

TAMING THE NEW WILDERNESS

I had 30 minutes to recharge my battery and make a connecting flight to Munich. First I had to find an electrical outlet.

I looked frantically around the waiting area, around the brownish indoor/outdoor carpet and the gray plastic pillars with broad, red stripes running up their sides. No matter how exotic the port of call, there are two things all airports share in common: mindlessly cheerful decor and well-camouflaged outlets.

One thing was different about this Flughafen's furnishings—a porcelain Marlboro cowboy that sat astride a life-sized clay-colored horse in the waiting area. His china-white smile and blue glass eyes sparkled as he smoked a cigarette. A red Christmas tree light protruding from the cigarette's tip blinked feebly, a good sign that electricity was flowing somewhere in the vicinity.

And then I spied it behind the last chair in the third row of seats: a gunmetal plate crammed between a bolted-down chair leg and a pillar. These plates hide outlets in almost every airport I've visited; the outlets are intended primarily for use by maintenance staff, not current thieves like me.

I ran over and grabbed the seat next to the outlet just before a large, sweaty businessman could lower himself into it. He grunted at me in German. I'm sure he wasn't being polite.

I reached down and flipped up the plate. Behind it were two round holes in a plastic panel. I studied it for a moment, then rooted around in my black PowerBook bag. I pulled a strange-looking pass-through plug out and tried it in the socket. It fit, not perfectly, but then these foreign current adapters rarely do.

Back into the bag, this time with both hands, I retrieved my slate-gray PowerBook 170, laying it on my lap. I fished again, and pulled out the power supply, which I attached to the adapter.

And finally, I plugged in my computer. I tapped a key, and after a moment was rewarded with a glowing screen and whirring hard drive. The battery icon on the righthand side of the PowerBook's menu bar indicated that there was power flowing to my nearly depleted battery.

I sighed. Plenty of time to get a quick charge. I put the PowerBook back to sleep and gently closed the clamshell.

It was at that moment that I first understood what it was to be a Digital Nomad.

The Age of Mobility is upon us, heralded by the Macintosh PowerBook.

Apple's portables have proven themselves a keystone in the foundation of a society with an ever-increasing wanderlust. They have liberated modern-day nomads, torn down the office walls and made distance inconsequential to productivity.

PowerBook: The Digital Nomad's Guide contains the facts you need to take these small, inexpensive machines and transform the way you and your company work. You'll find information on technologies, telecommunications and user tactics that will help make your Macintosh PowerBook 100, 140, 145, 160, 170, 180, or Duo 210 or 230 the most useful tool in your life.

In the pages that follow you'll get information on turning your Power-Book into the ultimate mobile environment. There are tips on power conservation, system configurations, what software to run, and how to connect to computers and networks where you can communicate with other users and collect information. You'll find information on the products you need to add (telephone) and wireless communications capabilities to your PowerBook, and you'll get the facts about groupware, data access, file-sharing, security, and international standards that will let you keep in touch from across town or across distant continents.

While corporations and hobbyists have built tremendously powerful computing environments at the office and at home, most people continue to work in the realm of the adding machine and paper receipt. That closed, proprietary world demands that you make smart choices about which PowerBook model you buy and the accessories you'll carry along when you enter the world of the digital nomad. Because, if the truth be known, it's a wilderness out there. Once you step away from the tame environs of your office you are cast into a world that is about as computer-savvy as a public toilet. If you're lucky, you might just find a working pay phone next to the loo, but you'll not find a data jack or a clean, dry place to set your computer.

PowerBooks can supply the most important technological creature comforts anywhere a charged battery and a phone line are available, and they can liberate your creativity, so your ideas can flow when you're in the office or on the road. Moreover, a portable like the PowerBook, built from the ground up to perform like a real computer, lets fresh air into the information vacuum most of us live in when we're traveling. It can provide access to online services like CompuServe and Prodigy, or to communities like the worldwide Internet that links more that 10 million users at universities, corporations, and myriad organizations. It can also engage you with games and electronic books, while keeping you productive with spreadsheet, word processor, and database applications.

The best portable to address all these needs, in our opinion and in the opinion of almost a half-million executives, writers, artists, salespeople, producers, accountants, programmers, account representatives, technical support engineers, architects, students, teachers, and God knows what other professionals, is the Macintosh PowerBook. Apple reportedly sold almost 420,000 PowerBooks during the first year they were available, propelling the Cupertino, California-based company from laptop "also-ran" to what Michael Spindler, president of Apple Computer, characterized as the number one manufacturer of portable computers in the world.

Only our computers are smaller.

The world remains a really big place. Despite popular belief, the modern age has not shrunk the globe by one square inch or reduced its mass by one molecule. Instead, we've changed ourselves by transforming our comprehension of distance with faster transportation and innovative tools for gathering, editing, and distributing information. Computer technologies have freed the individual from the strictures of geography and time. In a matter of seconds, an executive using a telephone and a computer can meet and exchange information with colleagues in Tokyo, San Francisco, and Zurich.

A century ago, we never would have embarked on a cross-country trip without first agonizing over the departure: leaving family and friends whom we might never see again, making extensive plans, writing a will, and stocking a covered wagon with the tools necessary to tame the land.

But today, a day's travel can take us halfway around the world. The real trick to life in our fast-moving age is not isolating yourself. Friends, family, and coworkers can be contacted with ease, the tools of our trades are available via the telephone networks, and we can enjoy a little light entertainment anywhere and any time the mood strikes.

However more comfortable we might feel with a covered wagon full of supplies, it's not going to fit in the overhead compartment or under the seat on an airliner (despite what some travelers try to sneak onto the plane). All that's necessary, no matter how naked we might feel jetting off to New York City without an expeditionary force behind us, is an overnight bag, a couple of credit cards, and a portable computer. And a last will and testament, of course (you are going to the wilds of Manhattan, after all).

"You've got yer clothes, some plastic—natch," says the Cosmic Cabby, who measures the fitness of travelers against the perils of the day. "And you got a nice PowerBook there, you're tied in, *connected*. That's a passport to the world you got there, because with plastic and computer, you can get anything you need. Food, clothes, entertainment, and information; you name it, you pay for it, you got it."

Miniaturization and microelectronics chiseled this new traveler from the old pioneer stock. Not only are the circuits in a computer getting smaller, they are becoming more efficient, enabling new battery-powered devices to help us deal with information by collecting, sorting, and storing data for our consumption. Today, when traveling, the processor power of a 1960s NASA mainframe fits neatly into a briefcase. Distance is irrelevant. You're always as close to home as your desktop computer when your PowerBook is linked back to it through a modem.

The evolution of human society is becoming more challenging as the pace of technological innovation accelerates. Despite the protestations that people can take only so much future shock, each decade requires that we recast our understanding of the tools at our disposal. They are seldom the same tools.

Technologies essential to personal productivity today were luxuries—and magic—just a decade ago. Since the appearance of the first IBM Personal Computer, the fax machine, word processors, spreadsheets, electronic Rolodexes, and electronic mail have become integral parts of how people work.

Two kinds of tools are emerging in the Information Age: computers reaching the boundaries of complexity that separate machines from the human mind, like the parallel-processing mainframes from Thinking Machines; and our subject—the small, portable devices that let us conquer time and distance. Eventually, the evolution of high-end computing will bequeath to the average consumer highly intelligent mobile devices that can act as virtual proxies—collecting and sifting information based upon assumptions made by intelligent software agents which learn to anticipate your needs and desires by observing your behavior.

The Vanguard of the Revolution in Coach Class

Until Apple introduced the first PowerBooks on October 21, 1991, portable computers were a rare sight in hotel lounges, at conferences, or on airplanes. Portables of a size and weight conducive to travel, mostly MS-DOS-based laptops, really weren't good for much. They were fine for taking notes. But working on a spreadsheet took up two airline seats—you need a lot of elbow room to operate that external mouse. MS-DOS's limited and complex interface became even more claustrophobic and intimidating on the road. And Microsoft Windows required much more RAM and processor power than DOS, which added bulk and consumed batteries like popcorn.

Besides, no one was prepared to carry DOS and Windows manuals around the country with them, and a team of corporate technical support engineers didn't fit in a set of overnight luggage. Portable computers were stored for the voyage and hauled out in hotel rooms—not exactly the paragon of convenience! Travelers determined that what little productivity they might get from lugging their PC notebook along simply wasn't worth it.

Despairing executives, arms sore from lugging around 15-pound "portables," turned to the Casio B.O.S.S. and Sharp Wizard. But these puny devices inspired claustrophobia and cramped fingers and had interfaces that make DOS look intuitive. And with these anemic computers there was no way for executives in the field to get at important information locked away in the data vaults at corporate headquarters. There was much wailing and gnashing of teeth in the business precincts of the land.

Then came the PowerBook. Sleek and slate-gray, it is the laptop for the fast lane. Even its minor innovations, such as palmrests and an ambidextrous trackball, make it a computer built to perform best on the road. It is equally at home in the tight quarters of a coach class seat or spread out on the desktop.

Adding cause for celebration was the fact that the most lauded user interface in the computer industry didn't lose stature as its packaging shrunk. If anything, the Macintosh operating system is more useful in the Power-Books. System 7's interapplication communications (IAC), file-sharing, and aliasing invite connections never before possible on a laptop (they don't call it System 7-savvy for nothing). Collecting a few important aliases for each network lets users automate access to individual file servers and applications, and with Apple events, which allow the invisible exchange of commands and data, instant updates of collaborative files, calendars, and forms can happen transparently.

During the first few flights out of San Francisco on which we carried our PowerBooks, other passengers crowded around us to see the notebook Macs in action; it was as though we had a baby unicorn in our laps. Shortly thereafter, flights between the Bay Area and the Northeast saw a quick increase in PowerBook populations.

Now the little gray Macs are everywhere. PowerBooks have traveled from oddity to necessity.

Apple didn't anticipate the wild success of a fully-functioning System 7 Macintosh laptop. For the first few months after they were announced, the high-end PowerBook 170s were in such short supply that it was not uncommon to wait eight weeks or more to take delivery. Users recognized that System 7 required more power than available on the PowerBook 100 and 140. The most important memory management and software tricks worked faster and looked better on the 170, and buyers stunned the market analysts and product planners by paying a lot more for the extra power.

The PowerBook 170 took off like a rocket and remains the bestseller of Apple's laptop family. According to *The Hartsook Letter*, an Alameda, California-based Mac market research newsletter, in the first year after introducing the PowerBooks, Apple sold 100,000 PowerBook 100s, 125,000 PowerBook 140s, 15,000 PowerBook 145s, and 175,000 Power-Book 170s worldwide. The PowerBooks' no-compromise look and feel made them the foundation of a billion-dollar-a-year business.

With Apple continuing to crank up PowerBook performance with the recently introduced 160s, 180s, and PowerBook Duo 210s and 230s, all the while pushing down prices, it looks like if you've bought or are planning to buy a PowerBook, you'll have lots of company on your next flight.

PowerBooks and the Evolution of Mobility

When we first thought of doing a series of books about the tools people will use when living and working in the mobile society, the Macintosh PowerBook family of portable computers was the obvious and best place to start. The PowerBook combines the Macintosh user interface and an extensive software library with a complete network environment, all in an ergonomic package. For example, the design incorporates into one sleek chassis the mouse and modem that hang like awkward arms off a DOS- or Windows-based laptop. The PowerBooks are excellent tools for acquiring, managing, and manipulating information, any time, anywhere.

Fundamental changes in the way we communicate, first prophesied by Nicholas Negroponte of the Massachusetts Institute of Technology Media Lab, are now taking place. Wires, which have carried our voices for the past 95 years, now transmit computer data very efficiently. Concurrently, voice communications, like the warm conversations with Grandmother on Saturday afternoons, are becoming the common fare of radio waves via cellular and wireless phones.

As Negroponte predicted, once this transition is complete, network communications will become as integral a part of the computing experience as the graphical user interface and mouse pointing device. At the same time, the networks will be converted from slower, less reliable analog transmission technology to high-speed, digital communications capable of broadcasting the contents of a novel like *Moby Dick* in a matter of seconds.

Extra speed translates into greater network capacity, or "bandwidth," that can be filled with higher-density data types such as sound and video.

The "Negroponte Switch" will change the way people use computers, as it will force those computers to change. More and more, the computer will be the conduit through which we view and communicate with the world. With a computer, users will control their telephones, gather mail, read news, browse the latest novels, and sift through vast libraries of movies and television shows. Therefore, the computer will have to evolve into a form that is both mobile *and* connected, with neither feature compromising the other.

It's not an issue of whether this device will be built but only a matter of who will build it first. Whether it scales down from computers or up from cellular phones, something will eventually evolve to fill this niche.

If you understand how easy it is to update an important statistic before a meeting using a portable, you've taken the first step into the mobile society. A laptop and a spreadsheet application can be a powerful combination when you encounter new data at deadline. What if you didn't get the news that IBM's stock dropped 24 percent in the last minutes of trading today? You could be hanging in the wind when you recommend that your biggest client sink a quarter of her worth into Big Blue! (Don't scoff, situations like this happen every day.)

The PowerBook offers a unique opportunity to leverage one's productivity off this switch because it is the only mobile tool currently available that uses seamlessly integrated communications to open the door to information wherever, whenever.

The PowerBooks are just the beginning, the kick-off in a whole new game. Within five years, an entirely new class of information tools will be common. Handheld, communications-savvy devices will make information access as convenient as telephone communications are today. Many of the strategies for handling PowerBooks in this guide will also apply to the first generations of "personal digital assistants" and "personal communicators" touted by Apple, EO Computer, AT&T Corporation, General Magic, and GO Corporation, which we will cover in three books to follow this one.

The PowerBooks and these other devices can keep you in touch with critical data, at all times. The fact is you don't have to be a Willy Loman, working in the sticks while your fate is decided at headquarters. Information tools will help you deal with more data than you can on your own. You'll be able to tap into and manipulate data, the currency of the mobile society, to fit your vision.

The PowerBook Lifestyle

Already the PowerBooks have spawned a new entertainment industry of their own. Interactive books designed to be read on the PowerBook's monochrome screen are fast becoming the new wave in airport novels.

Work styles are also changing from the advent of PowerBooks. Where you now enjoy the convenience of compiling a spreadsheet on your Macintosh desktop, by mid-1993 PowerBooks using a new Macintosh System 7 extension called the Open Collaboration Environment (OCE) will let you share that data with your coworkers as you are doing an analysis. The added insight available in collaboration with your coworkers, even when working in different cities, will let you make incredible leaps in productivity. The biggest bottleneck in life—the long lag time while you wait for feedback and for revisions to be completed—will be greatly reduced.

Even the fact that a little gray PowerBook can contain thousands of names, addresses, and phone numbers; the interactive, unabridged electronic versions of all the bestsellers on the *New York Times* list (fiction and non-fiction); a full suite of productivity applications; a cellular high-speed send and receive fax/data/voice modem; random access digital answering machine software (plus a dozen digitized messages)—and still have room left over for a game or two—is a hard concept to grasp. While it may sound nifty to automatically translate an incoming fax into editable text or to screen incoming voice calls and route the important ones to you (all without being tied to a wall socket, thanks to cellular transmitters that fit inside the PowerBook), selecting, setting up, and exploiting these technologies can get complex.

For example, combine recently announced products like Applied Engineering's cellular telephony products, a wireless Norris Earphone and Articulate Systems' Voice Navigator software, and suddenly you can have totally hands-off computing. With these products, you can wander around your hotel room as you answer an incoming call from your spouse (while your boss gets routed to a custom message saying you're out working hard on that important contract). You can tell your computer to sign on to the office network and download your e-mail; you can tell it to open a Microsoft Excel spreadsheet and run the third-quarter analysis macro. Some day, with text-to-voice software that Apple has under development, it will be able to read the results of the analysis back to you over the Earphone.

You can even tell it to be quiet and it will listen. (Try to get that kind of obedience from your kids sometime.) And all the while, your PowerBook sits snugly in a bag in the hall closet while you sit comfortably watching the ballgame.

Few people understand the power of these technologies, and even fewer are willing or able to ask for their share of this new power. As a result of the complex maze of options available (and their associated costs) many people feel intimidated and never start down the road toward these richer capabilities. There are a lot of vastly underutilized PowerBooks out there.

Admittedly, this stuff can be pretty daunting. But if it doesn't ultimately benefit you, then you probably won't find this new lifestyle very attractive.

Across the Threshold

You've probably already got or are about to buy a PowerBook and, as a result of job pressures or an intrigue with cutting edge technologies, you want to live fast and loose on the electronic frontier. If the research done by Apple and others on PowerBook purchasing is accurate, then you probably have owned or used a Macintosh before and are probably buying the PowerBook as your primary computing device. Less than a quarter of you have owned any kind of portable computer before buying your Power-Book. So, while you're familiar with Macintoshes and therefore the Power-Book, you probably aren't as familiar with the eccentricities of computing on the road.

This is not a book about System 7. There are several excellent titles available that can help you learn about using the Macintosh operating system. Our efforts are aimed at getting the most from Apple's dynamic laptop. So, if all you want from your PowerBook is a convenient place to take notes, then *The Digital Nomad's Guide* probably isn't for you.

We developed a taxonomy of user types as keys for navigating through the book. Understanding how you will use the PowerBook will let you use *The Digital Nomad's Guide* most effectively. Take a moment to read the descriptions of different kinds of PowerBook users below, then decide into which category or categories your primary usage falls. Special notes throughout the book are broken out and marked with the appropriate icon for each of these usage classifications. These notes help put the *Guide's* information in context for your particular needs.

By the way, there's no reason why one kind of user wouldn't get something out of reading an annotation intended for another user type. These notes are here to help organize the *Guide* not to create a PowerBook caste system. So feel free to read all the sidebars. We won't complain.

Here are the three tribes of digital nomads:

The Intentional Tourist

During the era when PC laptops ruled the skyways, she left her corporate-issue portable under her desk, sticking to the tried and true Day Timer for organizational needs. Now that she has a PowerBook, she runs a calendaring program, takes notes in meetings, and uses an electronic address book that provides ticklers to keep her up-to-date on sales contacts when traveling. She only packs her PowerBook for business or pleasure travel, leaving it at the office most evenings.

Portable is a hard-and-fast conceptual category in her mind. The Intentional Tourist still maintains strong ties to her desktop. When she's at the office, she connects her PowerBook to the local-area network to download data, but that's all. The PowerBook remains her computer for the road.

Her special concerns are how to find the right power outlet and phone connectors, how to conserve power on long plane flights, knowing access rules and numbers for getting online, and how to get things fixed quickly when problems arise.

The Mobile Commuter

This is the largest tribe of digital nomad. With PowerBooks, an interesting trend began to emerge that was seldom seen among PC notebooks. PowerBook users bought systems to use primarily around the home. The key word is "around" the home. These people like the idea of not tying their creativity to one particular room in the house, a requirement the PowerBook fulfills admirably.

See the Mobile Commuter note below.

BIS Strategic Decisions, a computer research company in Norwell, Massachusetts, projects that 45 percent of homes will have some form of office activity taking place in them by 1995. This no doubt means the number of Mobile Commuters will proliferate in the coming years, as PowerBooks make it easy to capture ideas wherever they strike.

The typical Mobile Commuter does most of his work at the office, but the PowerBook is an integral part of his life, because it acts as a lifeline to corporate computing resources—whether that's through access from home or a hotel in Hong Kong. During the average work day, the Mobile Commuter needs to send faxes to coworkers, dial in to his office computer network to grab a few files or leave electronic mail for the boss, and get fast database access when doing research.

The Mobile Commuter needs to work confidently on several hard disks without worrying about accidentally erasing an important file, so he relies on software that takes care of file version reconciliation automatically.

Once a quarter, his patience is tested when he frets over how to squeeze the corporate productivity analysis, a 10,000-cell Microsoft Excel spreadsheet, onto a 10-inch PowerBook screen.

The greatest question in the Mobile Commuter's life is: Will my wife kill me if I bring the PowerBook to bed? The answer is Yes.

If power corrupts, then PowerBooks corrupt absolutely.

Don't come home without it!

According to BIS, in 1992 there were approximately 20.3 million U.S. households that had income-generating businesses operating out of them. Another 18.1 million home offices were used to do work after normal office hours, not specifically to generate additional income.

Of the income-generating home offices, 42.7 percent had desktop computers while only 5.3 percent had laptops. Of after-hours home offices, 37.6 percent had desktop systems and only a minuscule 3.6 percent had laptops.

But here's where it gets interesting. BIS asked these same households what kinds of computers they planned to purchase in the next year, if any. Only 10.5 percent of income-generating and 10.8 percent of after-hours home offices plan to purchase desktop machines. However, 4.7 percent of income-generating and 3.6 percent of after-hours home offices plan to buy laptops in the next year. That means, in terms of how people are looking to outfit their home offices, the desktop versus laptop computer ratio will go from 8-to-1 to 2-to-1 in the next year.

The Road Warrior

She's on the road 22 weeks of the year, and the PowerBook is a godsend. Since she bought her PowerBook 170 (the desktop computer went out with that week's trash), she has outfitted it with extra RAM, a larger hard disk, and an array of software that keeps her in touch and lets her finish any project from an airline seat, a hotel bed, or her home office. The Road Warrior finishes each day at the office, folding the PowerBook under her arm like managers of yore who carried files home to work on late into the night. She can count on one hand the number of hours she has spent separated from her PowerBook.

The Road Warrior scours the trade magazines looking for robust communications capabilities; information on attaching color displays for use in business presentations; and a spacious, comfortable carrying case to replace the one that is bursting at the seems with gadgets, diskettes, and network cables.

All Road Warriors share this in common: whatever the latest hack, trick, gimmick or gadget is, they want it and will probably, eventually, find a way to get it. They want to be on the bleeding edge of mobile technology. They'll invest days writing a HyperCard stack to track the hunting patterns of the Komodo Dragon so that on a once-in-a-lifetime trip to Indonesia, the only place on Earth where you can find a wild Komodo Dragon, they'll be all set if one happens by.

They'll all claim it's in the best interest of improving their lives. But we know better. The Road Warrior is an irretrievable PowerBook addict.

If you took a Road Warrior, her husband and her PowerBook to the edge of a cliff and let her choose which would be tossed into the void, the Road Warrior would never have to wash the dinner dishes again. (No matter how much she's enamored of her PowerBook, she wouldn't waste a perfectly good husband to save it. This book is about keeping you sane in the face of technology, after all.)

The Digital Nomad

Sometimes there will be items of interest to all digital nomads that don't fit in the main text of the *Guide*. You'll find these annotations highlighted by the Digital Nomad icon.

Don't leave home without it!

The PowerBook Roadside Assistance Kit included with this *Guide* contains a handful of useful applications and system extensions that add power to the portable Macs. Many of the software titles on the Roadside Assistance Kit are fully functioning commercial products, and some (like Quic-Keys for Nomads) were designed specifically for this book.

In selecting these programs, we wanted to put together a collection of software that would immediately get you using your PowerBook in a variety of productive ways. Unlike a utility collection, the Roadside Assistance Kit is designed to give you everything you need to do calendaring, list management, note-taking, file synchronization and (with the addition of a modem) get you connected to the outside world. We've also included a couple of helpful freeware utilities which we've found supply some conveniences missing from PowerBooks that have just come out of the box.

Even though we like to think the advice we've collected in the *Guide* is invaluable, we have to admit the disk is one of the best deals going in software today.

(Please stand for the Digital Nomad invocation.)

Part of the PowerBook's appeal is that it instantly distinguishes you as a breed apart, someone who simply won't accept that uncomfortable and ill-equipped environs should force you to compromise your work style. You, the digital nomad folding the wanderer's tent of the Information Age into your carry-on luggage, are a pioneer bringing civilization to the inherently hostile and primitive environments of modern travel and home offices.

Although some may call the PowerBook the latest in a long line of yuppie techno-titillators, we prefer to think of it as better living through hip technology.

Welcome to the Mobile Society. We hope you find this a good introduction to the tools you will be living with. You are joining the world of Digital Nomads—Intentional Tourists, Mobile Commuters and Road Warriors—the people who are turning the few thousand dollars they invested in a PowerBook into hundreds of thousands of dollars worth of productivity. These are the pioneers who started just one year ago to scout the boundaries of the new wilderness.

P.S.—This information won't spoil, it's been irradiated!

We know that during technology's bold march forward some of the information in this book might become dated. If nothing else, that opens all sorts of possibilities for second, third, and so on editions.

But, until we can knock out those updated editions, we want you to feel comfortable that the information you're basing purchasing decisions on is the most current.

That's why the authors are willing to risk jamming the data skyways by inviting you to contact us via e-mail with your questions and comments. We really will try to respond to every letter we get.

You can contact Mitch Ratcliffe at:

> CompuServe: 72511,274
> Internet: coyote@well.sf.ca.us

Andrew Gore is online at:

> CompuServe: 72511,224
> AppleLink: AndyGore
> America Online: MW Andy
> Connect: AndyGore

Also, if you return the registration card included in this book, not only will we let you know about future editions of the *Guide*, you'll also get a complimentary copy of *Nomad Notes*, a quarterly newsletter for digital no-mads. *Nomad Notes* is designed to keep you up to date on the latest Power-Book tips and toys, not to mention the latest PowerBooks.

Thanks for buying our book.

SECTION I

POWERBOOK TECHNICAL READOUTS

PART

1

A BRIEF HISTORY OF EVERYTHING POWERBOOK

"I've never used one of these," said the stylishly dressed executive in the seat next to me, pointing to the cellular phone embedded in the airplane seat in front of him. "I'm not mechanically inclined. It took me forever to work one of those money machines at the bank. Computers are scary."

I looked at him in disbelief. We just spent the last hour comparing notes and trading freeware programs between our two PowerBook 140s. There is a strange sense of community among PowerBook users. This wasn't the first time that opening my portable has been a great conversation starter. This one started with this man saying to me, "I have a 140, too," which he then whipped out of his carry-on bag by way of demonstration.

"If you're scared of computers, why'd you get a PowerBook?" I asked. We'd already established that the 140 was his first and only computer.

"I had one of those Sharp Wizards," he explained. "I figured if I could run that, I could run one of these." He gave the PowerBook a pat.

"I saw an ad that said I could get a PowerBook for $1,000. As it turned out, I've spent over $5,000 on it to date," he said with a smile. All Power-Book addicts know that you never really own your Mac portable, it owns you. Or more precisely, it owns your bank account.

"The ad was for a 100, but the salesman convinced me that it really was a dead-end machine." I grimaced. Yet another example of unfair discrimination against 100s. "So I got a 140 and software and a printer."

After a moment, as if to remove any doubt, he added: "But it was worth it! I got it mostly to do spreadsheets; I travel a lot. Now I use it for my diary and word processing, I couldn't live without it!" He beamed and caressed his 140.

"You ever do any telecommunications with it?" I asked.

"No, what's that?"

"Remember how you were saying you wished there was a way for you to get to play with a lot of different kinds of software without paying for it first? Well, if you get an internal modem... Don't worry they're not too expensive," I added quickly, seeing his face shift to the all-too-familiar "oh no, not more pricey add-ons!" expression.

"With a modem," I continued, "not only can you download programs practically for free, you can also send e-mail and get your technical questions answered and..."

Buying a PowerBook can be a daunting experience. The range of technical terms and acronyms that describe the guts of a portable computer are as clear and easy to understand as a manuscript on Euclidean geometry in the original Greek. If you want to save some money you're probably going to purchase your PowerBook from a discount reseller rather than from a full-service Apple dealer or VAR (Valued Added Reseller). So, you're unlikely to find salespeople capable of delivering an even moderately credible explanation of the differences between models.

Unless you really want to go naked into that new wilderness (and we'd challenge anyone to find a more hostile environment to start your journey than the average discount computer store), you'd better bone up on the basics.

Despite the vacuum of good advice and information you're likely to find when making a purchase, that's no reason for you to try to digest every specification before you buy a PowerBook. It's supposed to be a tool for extending the power of your brain, not for taxing your will to live.

With that in mind, we've included this overview of everything Power-Book and the following technical readouts. They'll help prepare you to ask the right questions when standing at the PowerBook counter of your local dealer and help you decide for yourself which PowerBook best fits your needs so you can take advantage of the low prices available at discounters.

By the time you're done reading through this introduction to Power-Book technology and models, you'll probably know more about Apple's laptops than your average computer salesperson (not a particularly difficult feat). As we said earlier, don't expect to get much help at a discount outlet. The salespeople probably spend more time trying to mimic the dialog from *Wayne's World* than they do reading the latest Apple technical literature. We've overheard salespeople at big discounters make comments like, "This is the latest 386-based Macintosh," and "The big feature of these computers [Macs] is Inter-Office Interlacing!" (We suppose you'd call that IOI networking.) So, unless you want to make your buying decision based on that much-vaunted (and totally fictitious) Mac IOI capability, know what you want and how much you're willing to pay for it before you walk into the store.

Even if you already own a PowerBook, this section may provide interesting reading. Although we have been living with these computers 24 hours a day for over a year now, we still occasionally come across some small detail we hadn't heard of before. We've also included some of the known gotchas of the different models, so if you've been wondering whether those folders really did vanish off your PowerBook desktop or if you're experiencing just another symptom of declining mental capacity, you may find the answer here.

Finally, there is technology's bold march forward. A new family of PowerBooks, the 160, 180, and the Duo 210 and 230, were introduced on October 19, 1992. You'll find what makes these new Macs the latest and greatest here as well. (Of course, if you already own a PowerBook, you might not want to know about Apple's latest and greatest.)

Technophobia

Speaking of last year's fashions, another barrier you have to overcome when buying a computer is the FUD (Fear, Uncertainty, and Doubt) factor. This is a phenomenon born in an age when computer companies routinely preannounced products that promised to obsolete their competition's (and sometimes their own) hardware and software.

Apple has routinely outdated its Macs with newer, cheaper versions. Sometimes those updates have come within months of the original design's introduction. For example, the Quadra 950, which uses a 33MHz version of the Motorola 68040 processor, replaced the 25MHz Quadra 900 just six months after its debut. The 950 came out initially at the same price as the 900 and has since dropped over $1,000 from the 900's original price, all in less than a year.

Far from being ashamed of this behavior, Apple has proudly proclaimed that it is accelerating the obsolescence of current Macs with newer, faster systems. It now introduces new Mac models three times a year, where just a few years ago the company rarely announced new models more than once every twelve months.

Innovation fuels fear among consumers who have been sold, not on a product, but on the idea that they must live on the bleeding edge of technology. They are told that if they don't own the latest hack, they will be left behind. Technology advances so rapidly that many people, hoping for a better deal, succumb to FUD. Rather than buying a computer today and getting down to the work they need to do, FUD sufferers comb trade magazines like *MacWEEK*, devouring product specifications and pricing as diligently as stockbrokers who specialize in short selling. They believe that if they wait just one more month, somehow the computer they buy won't become obsolete.

You can avoid this trap by accepting that computers always become obsolete, sometimes within months of their introduction; it is the Zen of computer usership, just go with the flow. The average time it takes for a computer to fall out the bottom of the obsolescence funnel is between 18 and 24 months. In that time a computer can go from the best the market has to offer to demonstratively inferior in both price and functionality when compared to newer models.

Putting your money down for a PowerBook is a good move, if that PowerBook meets your needs at a price you can justify. We can say with confidence that any PowerBook, including the relatively primitive 100, will live a long, productive life before you'll feel compelled to toss it in favor of something new—if you approach it with the right attitude. Just innovate through improving the way you use your PowerBook, and a Mac laptop can realistically give you three to five years of good service before you'll want to relegate it to the kids' playroom.

The Brains of the Operation

See the
Digital Nomad
note below.

⬇

Think of the Central Processing Unit (CPU) as the brains and the brawn of your computer. These chips are densely packed collections of circuits, and like human muscle, they get stronger as the density of those circuits increases. A Motorola 68000 processor has fewer circuits on it than a Motorola 68030 CPU, making the '030 more powerful than the 68000. You'll sometimes hear this density referred to as chip "geometry." This refers to the space between circuits, which determines how many circuits you can squeeze onto a chip.

The Incredible Shrinking Processor

One of the greatest causes of FUD among seasoned computer users is the constant shrinking of processors, or more precisely, the incredible increase in the number of circuits or transistors chip makers manage to squeeze on to a chip.

For example, a Motorola 68040 processor has about 1.2 million transistors on it, while the 68030 processor, only one generation older, has only 300,000 transistors. As impressive as all those circuits sound, it's nothing compared to how many Intel, the company that builds the 80X86 processors used by MS-DOS and Windows-based computers, is going to press into its next generation processor. The Pentium chip currently under development at Intel contains a whopping 3 million transistors.   *(continued)*

The Incredible Shrinking Processor (continued)

However, more isn't always better. You've probably heard a lot of talk about RISC (Reduced Instruction Set Computing) processors. These CPUs require fewer instructions, and therefore fewer cycles or clock ticks, to do many of the same things as CISC (Complex Instruction Set Computing) processors like the 68040 or Pentium. The first PowerPC RISC chip, on which Apple will base its post-1993 desktop and mobile Macs, will contain only 1 million transistors and yet will be at least three times faster than a 68040. The chip, called the 601, will actually cost considerably less than an '040 does today, allowing Apple to ship 601-based Macs that cost as little as a Mac LC II.

We can only imagine what we'll be able to do when IBM and Motorola come out with later generations of the PowerPC processor, which are supposed to hit densities of 10 million transistors.

Having more circuits in the same space on a processor not only makes the computer faster, it allows it to do things that a computer equipped with an inferior CPU can't do, like address (access) larger amounts of RAM (Random Access Memory).

See the
Intentional
Tourist
note below.

Each circuit on the CPU is like a light switch. It can either be on, with electricity flowing through it, or off, with no current bridging the gap. The state of each circuit is represented as either a *0* (no current) or a *1* (current flowing) which in turn are collected into groups of *1*s and *0*s that represent a character (letter, number, space, or symbol) in the standard U.S. character set. The *0*s or *1*s are known in computer parlance as bits, and each character formed by a collection of bits is known as a byte (although some characters, such as those used in foreign writing systems like Kanji or Arabic, may use two bytes to represent a single character).

The Power of Babel

Even as we speak, changes are being made in the way computers define character sets for different languages.

Under the standard, accepted, and culturally bigoted way of doing things, a single byte is used to define each character in the collection of glyphs the computer uses to define type. This is fine, as long as the character set needed by the user doesn't go beyond the range of the Roman alphabet plus a handful of special symbols.   *(continued)*

The Power of Babel (continued)

For many languages, such as Japanese and Arabic, the character sets go far beyond the relative simplicity of the Roman alphabet, both in the number of glyphs and in the interaction among symbols, which can re-define each symbol's look and meaning.

That's why Apple implemented WorldScript in System 7.1 to add support for two-byte extended character sets such as those required by Japanese and Korean writing systems. All you need to do to localize your PowerBook to the native symbols of another culture is drop a special extension into the System Folder and make sure the appropriate font files are installed.

Intentional Tourists with multilingual skills may find this ability to switch language modalities "on-the-fly" most helpful when they want to print a Russian-language document using Cyrillic characters or prepare documents that mix Kanji and Roman glyphs.

This language of *0*s and *1*s is called binary. The only thing you really need to know about binary is that everything else you see on the computer screen is built up from it.

See the
Road Warrior
note below.

⬇

In addition to packing more circuits onto the processor, you can also boost the performance of a CPU by increasing its clockrate, the speed at which it performs calculations. You can find out the CPU clockrate by asking at how many megahertz (MHz) the chip is running. For instance, while the PowerBook 100 and the Macintosh Classic both run on Motorola 68000 chips, the PowerBook's 16MHz CPU delivers twice the performance of the Classic's 7.8MHz CPU. Applications carry out commands, like reformatting a word processing document, more quickly as a result of having a higher clockrate.

The main drawback to a more powerful CPU is its larger appetite for power. A chip with twice as many circuits that runs at twice the clockrate of another chip can consume four times as much battery power, which is why you'll probably never see the Quadra 950's 68040 CPU in a Power-Book—at least not until battery technology makes some advances.

One last point about the clockrate of processors. Although a Quadra 950's '040 is rated at 33 MHz, it is in fact many times faster than a PowerBook 180, which uses an '030 processor also rated at 33 MHz. This is where circuit density comes into play. The '040 is so much faster because it squeezes more circuits, including a math coprocessor and two 4-Kbyte banks of high-speed cache memory, into the CPU. Cache memory gives the CPU a place to store program code without having to send it out of the processor to RAM. Currently no PowerBooks include CPU cache.

MIPS-Leading

MIPS, or Millions of Instructions Per Second, is another way of expressing the performance of a CPU and is another in a long line of chic methodologies for measuring computer speed. The idea is to find a "median task" and take a snapshot of how fast the computer completes that task. Then, through arcane mathematics, computer scientists produce a number that they believe represents the "objective" speed of the computer. This number can be compared to any other computer's number, and whichever computer has the highest number wins.

The problem is, there are so many variables that affect the performance of computers at the user level, from how much data the application needs to draw off the hard drive to how often it needs to refresh the display or access a serial port, that it is nearly impossible to find a median task for all computers that's a fair test. For example, although the MIPs rating of many 80386-based computers is greater than many 68030-based Macintoshes, the Mac may run the same task in the same application faster than the 386 computer.

The reason for this is that the 386 computer is running MS-DOS, which in turn runs the Microsoft Windows operating system shell. Meanwhile the Mac is running a graphical user interface (sometimes referred to as GUI, pronounced "gooey") that is integrated from the hardware up. This is one of Apple's biggest competitive advantages—it knows exactly what kind of hardware its operating system will be running on because it builds the hardware.

However, performance specs do make interesting fodder for competitive claims made in advertisements. Which, after all, is what they were really invented for.

Our advice to Road Warriors looking for the best-performing Power-Book is to test-drive a unit with your application software. You can do this by bringing to the store an external hard drive with your software on it; the store should have all the correct cables to connect the drive to each model PowerBook you want to test.

The chip at the heart of the PowerBooks 140, 145, 160, and 180, as well as the Duos, is the Motorola 68030, a proven performer that you'll find in all the desktop Macs except the low-end Classic and high-end Quadras. The Mobile Commuter and the Road Warrior will want to look over these machines, taking into account the kinds of applications they'll be running and the kind of performance they're willing to live with. If you will be un-plugged the majority of the time, aim for middle-of-the-road 68030 CPUs, like the 160's 25MHz model; the performance is sufficient for most applications and you'll get a bit more life out of every battery. (You can also "crank-down" the performance of the 145, 160, 170, 180, and the Duos from 25 or 33 MHz to 16 MHz to save even more power.)

The PowerBook 100 was the last Macintosh to rely on the patriarch of the Motorola family, the 68000, a chip that got its start with the very first Macintosh. For the Intentional Tourist, the processor power in the 100 is more than adequate for taking notes and keeping up with the demands of a telecommunications application.

In terms of overall performance, the PowerBook pecking order from slowest to fastest system is: 100, 140, 145, 170, Duo 210, 160, Duo 230, and 180. However, when residing in a Duo Dock with an FPU installed, the Duos will perform better because of the extra boost from the co-processor. According to Apple, the fastest PowerBook you can own is a Duo 230 in a Dock with the FPU installed, although the speed difference between the 230 in a Dock and the 180 is marginal.

As in all things, when choosing a PowerBook you'll need to strike a bal-ance among CPU performance, price, and the inconvenience of carrying extra batteries.

Math in the Fast Lane

FPUs, or Floating Point Units (often referred to as math coprocessors), en-able your PowerBook to offload non-integer math (calculations using numbers with decimal points) to a chip designed specifically to do these calculations. For applications that are math-intensive, such as rendering programs, spreadsheets, and, believe it or not, certain video games, a co-processor is indispensable.

For other kinds of applications an FPU may not be as critical, but it'll still help. Almost any complex application can be helped with the addition of Motorola's 68882 coprocessor.

Unfortunately, only the PowerBook 170 and 180 come with a built-in FPU. It is optionally available for Duos attached to a Duo Dock, where you actually install the FPU—so you don't get FPU performance when working unplugged from a dock! Otherwise, there is no way to add an FPU to any PowerBook that doesn't already come with one.

See the
Intentional
Tourist
note below.

Keep this in mind when evaluating which PowerBook is right for you. If you're a number-crunching, high-performance Road Warrior who likes to push the envelope on any system you use, we'd steer you towards the PowerBook 180.

Fire and Ice

Another thing about processors and coprocessors (and for that matter, hard drives, RAM, and batteries) is they give off a lot of heat. Your PowerBook is designed to dissipate that heat, keeping it from damaging components under normal operating conditions.

According to Apple, normal operating conditions mean using most PowerBooks in temperatures between 50 degrees Fahrenheit (10 degrees Celsius) and 104 degrees Fahrenheit (40 degrees Celsius) with relative humidity between 20 and 80 percent. The place you use it should be between 0 and 10,000 feet (3,048 meters) above sea level (it's okay to use your PowerBook above 15,000 feet, if your airplane has a pressurized cabin). You should store most PowerBooks in temperatures between -13 degrees Fahrenheit (-25 degrees Celsius) and 140 degrees Fahrenheit (60 degrees Celsius) at altitudes between 0 and 15,000 feet (4,722 meters).

The exception to these specifications are the Duos, which can operate in humidity up to 95 percent but can only tolerate being stored in temperatures up to 116 degrees Fahrenheit (47 degrees Celsius). So, forget about keeping your Duo on the oven broiler shelf.

For most Intentional Tourists and Mobile Commuters, these operating conditions are more than generous enough for you to forget about them, unless you use your PowerBook next to a blast furnace or inside a meat locker.

But because Road Warriors use their PowerBooks under a greater variety of conditions, here's a good rule to remember: Only use your PowerBook in conditions you'd feel comfortable in without taking extraordinary measures (wearing a parka or rain slicker count as extraordinary measures). PowerBooks are hearty beasts, so much so that it's easy to forget that under that plastic shell are some pretty exotic and delicate components. *(continued)*

Fire and Ice (continued)

We've used our PowerBooks in some frightfully hostile environments, including running our 140 next to the swimming pool of a hotel in Palm Springs, California for about three hours on a day when it was easily 90 degrees in the shade. The PowerBook survived without incident, and we got a lot of work done on our tans and our writing.

Concerning RAM

Random Access Memory, or RAM, expands your CPU's mind. Adding another Mbyte (megabyte, or enough memory to hold approximately 1 million characters) is like adding another floor to your office building. It provides extra space where more work can be done. A computer can work very quickly when all the information it needs is stored in RAM. When there's not enough, your PowerBook will spend time and vital power loading and unloading sections of application code from the hard drive, which takes a lot more power than if the whole application was stored in RAM. Because RAM consists of no moving parts, it consumes considerably less power than a spinning hard drive.

To work productively on the road, you may want to have several applications open at once. Some Apple events-enabled capabilities, such as finding someone's phone number in your address book and displaying it in your appointment book when you enter that person's name, require that more than one application run in memory simultaneously. In our experience, you'll quickly get comfortable having your Rolodex, calendar, and note-taking program open at once, which is a nearly impossible feat with only 4 Mbytes of RAM.

The first-generation PowerBooks, the 100, 140, 145, and 170, include 2 Mbytes of RAM soldered onto their logic boards. A RAM expansion slot lets you add 2-, 4- or 6-Mbyte expansion cards for up to a total of 8 Mbytes of RAM.

These days, the minimum amount of RAM Apple sells on a PowerBook is 4 Mbytes. This is good and bad. It's good because that's the least you ever want to have available to you when running System 7; it's bad because you're probably going to want to upgrade to 8 Mbytes or more at some point. Although you can trade in the pre-installed 2-Mbyte Apple RAM card to bring a 4-Mbyte PowerBook 100, 140, 145, or 170 up to 8 Mbytes, you're probably going to lose money in the process. Apple's newest models, the 160, 180, and Duo 210 and 230, don't have this problem. The 4 Mbytes they come with is soldered onto the logic board, leaving the expansion slot open for a card.

Another reason to get as much RAM as you can afford is System 7's ability to set up a RAM disk. This allows you to partition the PowerBook's memory, using part of it to store files. The advantage is that the PowerBook will access applications stored in that RAM partition as if it were a hard drive, thus avoiding spinning up the real hard drive and saving even more battery power.

See the
Road Warrior
note below.

The 160 and 180 can handle up to 14 Mbytes of memory, while the Duos, because they use more exotic RAM technology, can support up to a whopping 24 Mbytes of RAM. The Duos' special RAM may make memory expansion cards the province of the big spender for some time to come. Apple is selling 4- and 8-Mbyte expansion cards for the Duos, while third-party vendors are supplying cards that can push Duo memory to 24 Mbytes of RAM.

Be sure when buying RAM for your 100, 140, 145, or 170 that you get the 100-nanosecond (ns) pseudostatic variety. If you've got a 160 or 180, you'll want boards with 85ns chips. Duos require 70ns low-power Dynamic RAM (DRAM).

Pay no attention to the RAM behind the keyboard.

While 24 Mbytes may sound like more than anyone could ever reasonably expect to need, that's what we used to say about the 4-Mbyte limit on the Mac Plus. So, for you Road Warriors always looking for that extra bit of power, here's a tip.

Although you may pay a premium for a 20-Mbyte expansion card, you want to balance the cost against the convenience of extending each battery's life by an hour or more. With 24 Mbytes of RAM, you could create an 18-Mbyte RAM disk and still have plenty of RAM left over for running applications.

You could easily store a couple of programs and related files on the RAM disk and run them without having to spin up the hard drive except when you start up or shut down your PowerBook. This would be especially helpful with databases that need to be saved every time you modify them or with applications that require regular access to a drive, like HyperCard. *(continued)*

Pay no attention to the RAM behind the keyboard. (continued)

Another advantage to running a RAM disk on a PowerBook is the ability to put the Mac notebook to sleep without losing the contents of the RAM disk. Normally, shutting down your Mac clears the RAM disk and all the files stored in it (don't worry, System 7 at least warns you before it dumps your data). However, the PowerBook's sleep mode retains the RAM disk data.

One more RAM disk plus: Not only will a RAM disk save copious amounts of battery power, it can also help kick up the performance of your PowerBook. As we said in the "MIPs-Leading" note above, there are several factors that affect computer performance besides processor speed. Disk access, for example, can really slow a computer down. So, if your PowerBook can get data from RAM instead of from a hard drive, you'll notice a marked improvement in performance, perhaps greater than you'd notice if the CPU clockrate was kicked up a few megahertz.

A RAM rule of thumb is: Try to find third-party memory upgrades in all cases for all PowerBooks. They're cheaper; and besides, everyone—Apple and its third-party developers—gets their memory chips from the same manufacturers.

Some companies don't want to spend money on extra RAM. If you've already fought a pitched battle just to get a PowerBook, don't sweat more RAM now. It's possible to get by on 4 Mbytes (turn to Section II, Part 1, for advice on how to put your system on a diet).

Hard Disk Envy

Great minds are signified by their messy desks and the general disorder of their lives.

Unfortunately, most PowerBook users don't have this luxury. The 2.5-inch internal hard disk drives used by Apple's laptops come in capacities ranging from 20 Mbytes to 120 Mbytes of storage. However, the larger the drive, the greater the additional cost, which has forced many users to opt for less storage space.

The result is, PowerBook users must constantly track the status of their drive, cleaning off their desktop with almost neurotic regularity.

See the Road Warrior note below.

A small hard disk limits every choice you make. After installing System 7, which can take 4.5-Mbytes or more worth of storage, and a couple of key applications, there's hardly room left on a 20-Mbyte drive to store even a handful of data files. An 80- or 120-Mbyte drive is the kind of real estate that lets you spread out and use your portable like a virtual office—there's plenty of room for files that you can dig up later for a critical detail, a great quote, or a telling statistic. If your PowerBook is the only computer you use and you hook it up to a color monitor at home or the office, then you'll want space for an application collection, including storage hogs like Adobe Photoshop, QuarkXPress, or Adobe Premier.

See the
Digital Nomad
note below.

Apple got the message that the 20-Mbyte hard disk configurations of the PowerBook 100 and 140 were ridiculously inadequate and made larger-capacity versions available almost immediately.

Reason prevails in newer PowerBook models. The 145 comes with a 40- or 80-Mbyte drive, the 160 ships with either 40-, 80-, or 120-Mbyte drives, and the 180 ships with either an 80- or 120-Mbyte disk. The Duo 210 comes only with an 80-Mbyte drive while the 230 also offers a 120-Mbyte option. Although 40 Mbytes will prove adequate for Intentional Tourists or Mobile Commuters who only need to run one or two applications on their PowerBooks, the hardened Road Warrior will probably feel cramped without space for lots of programs and a frivolous file or two.

In-Flight Movies

A little-known feature of all PowerBooks, except the 100, is the ability to play QuickTime movies.

There's a good reason for this. The poor fidelity of software-based QuickTime compression combined with a 1-bit screen makes for lousy playback (although it should be noted that QuickTime 1.5 makes some improvements on the quality of movies played on 1-bit screens).

However, the new crop of PowerBooks all feature 16-grayscale screens and built-in or dock-bound color video-out. So, if you're a Road Warrior out to make your PowerBook into your own portable movie studio, we'd make three recommendations. One, buy a 180. The active-matrix screen will make a real difference in playing movies that don't blur, and the 33MHz processor will give you acceptable performance and sound/image synchronization. Two, whatever you think you need in the way of storage, double it. QuickTime is a hog. And three, read Section II, Part 1, "QuickTime: You should be in pictures," for more information on QuickTime and PowerBooks.

There are two solutions to the storage conundrum. The best is to buy your favored PowerBook with the smallest hard drive you can get from Apple and then purchase a third-party replacement drive.

Internal 120-Mbyte and larger capacity drives are available from a variety of sources, or you can opt for a small external drive you can carry along in a briefcase. Some of these drives come with their own batteries, supplying up to three hours of spin time. There are also pocket-sized external hard drives. However, some of these need AC power when connected to a PowerBook.

Free-Market Bingo

While Apple's move to offer PowerBooks with larger capacity internal drives is laudable, it does assume that only Apple makes attractive hard drive solutions for PowerBooks. This, of course, is not the case, and we wish that in addition to offering larger capacity drives Apple had chosen to offer "floppy-only" PowerBook configurations. This would have given users the opportunity to shop for the best deal from third-party suppliers, who like RAM vendors, buy their drives from the same manufacturers Apple does. (Apple doesn't build their own drive mechanisms. In fact, very little of what goes inside your PowerBook is actually fabricated by Apple.)

As it is, if you decide to get a third-party solution, you have to get rid of a perfectly good internal drive or, if some clever company decides to market them, use special mounting kits to set up the internal drive as an external drive. Unfortunately, if you choose to make your internal drive into an external, you throw away the power management features that come with the PowerBook drive.

You could also choose to mount the discarded internal drive in a Duo Dock, with the help of a special mounting bracket, which has a space for an extra internal storage device.

Some third-party hard drive vendors may offer trade-in programs from time to time. With these deals, you get credit for turning in your old drive when you buy a new one. Be careful to compare prices; make sure you aren't paying for the trade-in with a higher drive price.

Another way around sparse storage is the humble compression utility. These applications allow you to selectively shrink the size of your files when they aren't in use; the files are automatically restored to full size when you use them. Some developers claim their compression software can double the capacity of your disk drive, but practically speaking, the percentage of disk space you'll save depends on how many applications you're compressing. This is because programs don't collapse as easily as raw text or spreadsheet figures. A more realistic figure is a 30 percent savings. So, 60 Mbytes' worth of data can probably be compressed onto a 40-Mbyte drive. And the larger your hard drive , the larger the minimum file size can be. If your 120-Mbyte drive has a folder full of e-mail messages or other small files, you'll get next to no space savings from compressing the contents of that folder.

The problem with choosing compression to solve your hard disk worries is that while it may save you space, it will also cost you time. Compressing or decompressing a 1-Mbyte application can take upwards of a minute. Compression also takes a big bite out of your battery power, since compression utilities must run the drive to access files. Compressing a large file can keep the disk spinning for several minutes, and when you need to open several files during a flight from Seattle to Tampa Bay, your batteries are going to take a considerable power hit.

A Public Display of Reflection

So far the difference between various PowerBook models has been as plain as the pixels on their face.

The 1-bit, Film SuperTwist Nematic (FSTN) backlit screen in the 100, 140, and 145 is a bit murky. This might help explain why so many people opted to pay almost $1,500 more for the 170, which sports a crystal-clear backlit active-matrix display. Users were not disappointed either when the 160 and Duo 210 and 230 appeared with a supertwist screen capable of displaying sixteen shades of gray, despite the fact that it still suffers from the motion-blurring and difficult viewing from a distance or an angle typical of all supertwist screens. Without debate the silver screen with the biggest drawing power is the 4-bit grayscale, active-matrix display that puts the sparkle in the 180. This screen not only supports sixteen grays, it also uses a special "shadow mask" to give it deep, rich blacks. The 180 display has a crisp, bluish overall tint which is easier on the eyes than the sickly green cast of the 170 screen.

See the Mobile Commuter note below.

All built-in PowerBook screens display 640 by 400 pixels on their displays. This is slightly smaller than standard 13-inch Macintosh monitors, which display 640 by 480 pixels.

You say "Tomato."

For Mobile Commuters in search of a monitor for their home office who've wondered why 14-inch Macintosh displays don't look bigger than 13-inch Macintosh displays, here's the reason why two screens with exactly the same tube are different sizes:

Apple's new, cheaper series of 14-inch color monitors are measured from bezel-to-bezel diagonally. However, the older Apple 13-inch monitor used to be measured by the size of the maximum image displayed, not the size of the tube. This is also true of the difference between 16- and 17-inch Mac displays.

The reason for the change? Even though you can't do anything with that empty, black frame that runs around the outside of the screen image, it is the way PC monitor manufacturers measure their displays, and Apple decided it was easier to switch than fight.

A pixel is the smallest dot (actually, a square) used to build an image on the screen. PowerBook 100s and both Duos have screens that measure nine inches diagonally, while the rest of the PowerBook lineup measures ten inches diagonally. As a result, the pixels on the 100 and Duo screens are slightly smaller and, therefore, less readable than on their larger brethren.

The screen is one of the most dangerous members of the battery-killer gang, consuming an enormous amount of power when backlighting is turned up. By learning to work in the dark, taking notes or composing letters with backlighting set at the lowest setting, you can extend the life of a battery to four hours with most PowerBooks (and longer with some).

Except for the 100, all the PowerBooks can drive an external color monitor. The problem is getting the video output from the PowerBook to an appropriate display. Since the laptops debuted in 1991, several third parties have delivered a variety of clever internal RAM expansion boards that include video-out and external SCSI connectors that bridge the gap between monitors and the color QuickDraw capabilities stored in most PowerBooks' ROM.

See the
Digital Nomad
note below.

The next-generation PowerBooks solve the video problem without the aid of third-party add-ons. The 160 and 180 come with a standard video-out port that can display up to 8-bit color on a 16-inch monitor. Duos get their video-out capability either from Apple or third-party docking stations. Duo users can add on additional 512 Kbytes of video RAM to the 512 Kbytes already resident in the Duo Dock, allowing them to display up to 16-bit color on a 16-inch display. With the extra VRAM installed, the Duo Dock also supports faster video performance.

A Bit about Bits

You've heard us talk about 8-bit color, 16-grayscale screens, video RAM, and fast video. This is all jargonese for something fairly simple: how many shades of gray or how many colors your PowerBook can display on what size screen and how fast.

1-bit means that two shades, black and white, can be displayed on a screen. This is what 100s, 140s, 145s, and 170s support on their internal screens. 4-bit means sixteen shades of gray (grayscale) or sixteen colors can be displayed. PowerBook 160s, 180s, and Duo 210s and 230s support 4-bit grayscale on their built-in screens.

8-bit means you can display 256 shades of gray or colors on an external monitor (PowerBooks can't display that much detail on their built-in screens without a third-party color screen upgrade). 16-bit means thousands of colors on a display, and 24-bit, also called true color, gets you millions of colors for brilliant, photorealistic images on your monitor. Currently, the only way to get 24-bit output from a PowerBook is by installing a true color board in a Duo Dock NuBus slot. When docked, the Duo would then be able to display 24-bit color on an external monitor.

Video RAM is what your PowerBook uses to process all that color. The more pixels (the bigger the display) you want to paint and the bigger your palette of available colors or grays, the more VRAM it's going to take.

Faster video performance causes the pixels on the screen to get drawn and redrawn more quickly. So when you change an image you don't have to wait as long to see those changes. Apple only recently started saying some of their products have "fast" video. Previously there was plain video and accelerated video, which uses special hardware to increase screen redraw speed. The company has been unclear as to what the exact performance is of fast video, but we suspect it's noticeably, although not substantially, quicker than plain video and still slower than accelerated video.

Apple is also offering the Duo MiniDock, a desktop station built for the company by SuperMac Technology of Sunnyvale, California, which includes 512 Kbytes of VRAM and can display up to 8-bit color on a 16-inch display. E-Machines will offer the PowerLink Presentor, which, in addition to doing 8-bit color on a 16-inch display, can also output NTSC video (the video signal format used by U.S. television) that can put your Power-Book screen on a color TV set. And speaking of non-Mac monitor formats, the 160, 180, and both of Apple's Docks support some of the cheap color VGA and SVGA displays used by many DOS and Windows-based computers. However, you will need a special VGA/SVGA adapter to make the connection.

Along with color video-out, the PowerBook 160 and 180 and the Duos also support dual display and video mirroring. Dual display lets you use your PowerBook screen as extra space on the System 7 desktop when connected to an external monitor. Video mirroring duplicates your Power-Book's screen display (in color, if available) on the external monitor. This is especially useful when you're giving a presentation from your Power-Book and you want to observe the progress of the slideshow without having to constantly refer to the monitor.

Apple Modems Über Alles

You've got to give Apple credit, it is a "no-half-measures" company. When the company blows it, it does so big time.

Case in point: When Apple built its Mac Portable, it seemed the target audience was rich people with biceps like tree trunks. That's the only logical reason someone could have for building a "mobile" computer that was as big as a typewriter, weighed seventeen pounds, and cost a mint.

See the
Digital Nomad
note below.

Fortunately, Apple got it right the second time around with the Power-Books. Yet it seems the company had to make another colossal blunder its first time out with an internal modem.

See the
Road Warrior
note below.

Apple should have made its 2,400-baud (or bits per second) modem an option, not a feature of its first generation of high-end PowerBooks. In fact, they dropped the modem as a standard feature after only six months. Because the engineers in Cupertino played just a little too fast and loose with standard modem specifications, they set sail to a thousand headaches. Most PowerBook 170 users we know have had bad luck with file transfers over the modem Apple included with the first 170s. We've learned from personal experience, too, that those failed transfers always happen when we most needed to get a file delivered from a remote location. More than a couple of *MacWEEK* stories almost didn't make it onto the page because the 170 modem wouldn't cooperate.

We are hoping that the latest version of Apple's internal modems, called the Macintosh PowerBook Express Modems, can solve the telecommunications problem with the same aplomb with which the PowerBooks eclipsed the clunky Mac Portable. Even though the Express modems cost $300, coming out of the starting gate the new models appear headed for a couple of major problems.

The Express modems, which include two versions of the same chipset designed to fit in either the 160 and 180 or the Duos, feature 9,600-bps send-and-receive fax capabilities and can transfer data at a blazing 14.4 Kbps. Both versions "piggyback" on the PowerBook's '030 CPU, using some of the processor's power to handle the conversion of the modem signal into machine language. (This makes the 160/180 Express modem incompatible with the 100, 140, 145, or 170. If you own one of the older PowerBooks, Apple still only offers its flaky 2,400-baud board.) Piggybacking will result in degraded performance of other applications when doing file transfers in the background. According to Apple, the performance degradation is equivalent to running AppleTalk Remote Access on a PowerBook, which can be substantial under certain conditions. CPU performance could drop by as much as 30 percent during high-speed file transfers where a lot of error correction is taking place.

No Baud Dogs

One of the most startling discoveries of the twentieth century is that no civilization can be considered truly "advanced" unless it has invented at least two ways of saying the same thing for all the terms in its language that no one really wanted to know the meaning of in the first place.

At roughly the time this important axiom was uncovered, doctors and lawyers stumbled onto the economic principal that, if in addition you add a third term for that same esoteric verbiage in an altogether different, preferably dead language, you can really flummox the masses into thinking you know what you're talking about. And you can charge them absurd amounts of money for your services, primarily because you know what all those terms mean and they don't.

The computer industry adopted this naming principal wholeheartedly. That's why in addition to having the term byte (character) and bit (the pieces that make up a character) we also have baud (which means bits per second) and bps (which means bits per second).   *(continued)*

No Baud Dogs (continued)

The only thing you really need to know about bits, bytes, bps, and baud is this: If a modem transfers data at 9,600 baud (bps), then it can send up to 960 characters per second across the phone line. (It normally takes eight bits to make up one character in a computer, but modems add check bits to verify that a character transferred normally; thus ten bits usually make a character in file transfers.) That means the roughly 3,000 characters that make up the average page of plain text in a computer would take a little over three seconds to transfer at 9,600 baud.

That sounds impressive. However, a 1-Mbyte file, the typical file size of today's overweight applications, consists of 1,000,000 bytes or characters. At 9,600 baud that file would take 1,042 seconds (or over 17 minutes) to transfer. And, because a lot of things (such as a blast of static on the phone line) can cause the modem to resend blocks of data or can cause several-second pauses in the middle of a file transfer, your results may differ significantly.

On the surface, the Express modems look reasonably priced. But there's a catch: The Express Modem for the Duo is quite difficult to install. One dealer told us that Duo users could pay upwards of $50 to $100 to get the modem put into their PowerBook because of the time involved. And Apple is adamant that the Duo modem should only be installed by a qualified technician. PowerBook 160 and 180 installation is routine and could be handled by an experienced user, according to Apple.

Compounding those problems is the fact that Apple is using proprietary technology built into Duos, 160s, and 180s to support piggybacking off the CPU. If third parties want to do the same, they'll have to license the technology from Apple, which Apple seems in no big rush to make available to potential competitors. The company will be encouraging third parties to develop software to run on top of the Express, but it only recently began evangelizing developers to construct their own data-pump modems.

Which raises another point, will third parties be able to offer any kind of internal modem for the Duos? At least at this time it seems unlikely, as there's only room for the piggyback design in the Duo case. Until modem components get smaller, there doesn't seem to be enough space for a complete Duo modem. Duo users may have no choice but to buy the Express Modem, at least for a while.

The message here is clear: If you buy a 160 or 180, you'll probably want to opt for a third-party, self-contained modem that doesn't depend completely on your PowerBook's CPU, while Duo users will want to purchase their computer and Express Modem at the same time and hope the dealer will be so overjoyed by the sale that they'll forego the installation charge.

Compression/Correction, what's your function?

Many things can affect the performance of your modem. Once you get past the basic transmission speed of a modem, you run into a "protocol wall" that can baffle the brightest engineer—you've seen it in cryptic notations like V.42, V.42bis, and MNP-5, all of which are communications protocols probably supported by your PowerBook modem.

Here's how it works: A protocol governs the transmission of data between two modems. Some protocols, called modulation protocols, provide only the foundation of the modem conversation, which causes the two devices to scream in the same, weird pitch you hear on the speaker when dialing into another modem. Other protocols guide the encoding of data sent over the telephone line, adding the ability to compress and decompress the signal so that more data can get through faster. And, finally, some protocols control the error correction methods that modems use to double-check data once it's received, to ensure that no bits are missing. Error correction is especially useful when using noisy phone lines that might interfere with the data stream.

At the beginning of each modem call, there is a negotiation between the two modems in which they fall back from their highest functioning protocols to whatever they have in common. When two modems support the same protocol, such as V.42bis or MNP-5, they can talk that language and enhance the call with compression or better error correction. What you want to watch out for are modems that implement a proprietary protocol in order to boost performance and don't also support the standard protocols. This can make a modem almost useless, because it prevents that modem from talking to modems that don't understand their proprietary protocol.

With that said, take a look at the chart below, which outlines the standard protocols.   *(continued)*

Compression/Correction, what's your function? (continued)

Standard Protocols

Name	Description
Bell 103	300-bps modulation protocol
Bell 212A	1,200-bps modulation protocol
V.22	1,200-bps modulation protocol
V.22bis	2,400-bps modulation protocol
V.32	4,800/9,600-bps modulation protocol
V.32bis	14,400-bps modulation protocol
V.42	Error correction protocol
V.42bis	4:1 Data compression protocol (requires V.42 error correction)
MNP-2	Error correction protocol
MNP-3	Error correction protocol
MNP-4	Error correction protocol
MNP-5	2:1 Data compression protocol (requires MNP-4 error correction)
MNP-10	Error correction protocol for cellular telephone connections
V.Fast	19,200-bps modulation protocol

What do you call a rabbit in a sports car? A floppy drive.

PowerBooks have had a stormy relationship with their floppy drives. The first generation 100 eschewed the floppy altogether, requiring that users add an external drive to access the meager removable storage available on diskettes. We knew several folks who, trying to save a little money, passed on the 100's external floppy. They thought they could get away with loading software on the 100 by connecting it to a desktop Mac in SCSI Disk Mode.

There were two problems with that idea. First, you need a special and relatively expensive cable to connect the 100 to another Mac. Second, you'd need to be assured of access to a desktop Mac—for attaching in SCSI Mode or using LocalTalk—any time you want to exchange files while on the open road, never a sure thing. In short, no floppy is no favor.

See the Intentional Tourist note below.

⬇

Now the Duos have forsaken the floppy drive. You'll need to carry a dongle, called a Duo Floppy Adapter, or a dock of some sort if you want to add a floppy drive to a Duo. Ask yourself before you buy: Do I want to put my PowerBook to sleep, connect an adapter and a floppy drive, and wake the computer before I copy a file?

Welcome to My Floppy

Simple and easy to use, the floppy disk is still the number one method for trading files. If you meet someone on the street or at a meeting and want to give them a copy of an important contract, it's unlikely you'll want to create an ad hoc network à la Apple's in-flight network commercials. (In fact, if you were to use LocalTalk on an airplane you might earn the ire of the plane's flight crew, who believe that network connections and cellular telephones create enough electromagnetic interference to give navigational equipment fits. So, the PowerBook may run flawlessly, but you could be escorted from the plane by federal marshals.) It's always easier to pop a floppy into your PowerBook, copy the file, and hand the disk over to your friend.

That's why we suggest that many users will be happier with a built-in floppy drive.

Ports of Call

There was a time when I/O (input/output) ports on a Mac were as standardized as the formula for Coca-Cola (or for John Sculley's sake, Pepsi).

That changed with the introduction of the first PowerBooks, which used shrunken SCSI and floppy ports to connect to external devices. Duos made the picture even more fuzzy because they rely on external bays, called docks, to provide any ports beyond one serial and an RJ-11 modem port.

As a result, knowing your ports will help you figure out what they connect to and what cables you need to acquire to make that connection.

- **Serial Ports**   Two ports are provided on most PowerBooks to allow simultaneous connections to a network and a modem or printer. Apple's 230.4-Kbps (thousand bits per second) LocalTalk networking technology is available on every PowerBook, including the Duos. To connect your PowerBook to a network, you'll need a standard AppleTalk connector or one of the many adapters based on Farallon Computing Corporation's PhoneNet design, which lets you use ordinary telephone wire as network cable. You can add network, modem, or printer connectivity by plugging in the appropriate cables and the selecting the appropriate drivers, files that let your PowerBook identify and use devices connected to a network.

- **Apple Desktop Bus** (ADB)   This is the port used for adding an external keyboard or mouse in a daisy chain. You can also attach other devices to the ADB chain, like an external fax modem that wakes up your PowerBook to receive an incoming fax call.

  In theory you can have up to sixteen devices connected on a single ADB chain, but we'd challenge any Road Warrior to find that many devices that they'd seriously want dangling from their PowerBook.

- **HDI-30 SCSI port**   The Small Computer System Interface (SCSI) port is the standard connector for hard disks, scanners, CD-ROM drives, and other peripherals. PowerBook users can get extra mileage out of their SCSI ports with network interface adapters that give them access to 10-Mbps (million bits per second) Ethernet networks. (Duos can use the Duo Dock to access standard Ethernet NuBus cards). A maximum of six SCSI devices can be attached to a PowerBook, including the internal hard drive, which is also a SCSI device. (Each device must have a unique address from 1-6. The 7 address is reserved for the PowerBook itself; the 0 address is always used by the internal hard drive.) Technically speaking, the Duos actually have two SCSI controllers, one internal and one external. However, System 7 doesn't currently support more than seven SCSI devices.

  The PowerBook 100, 160, 180, and Duo 210 and 230 also support something called SCSI Disk Mode. By connecting a special cable to the HDI-30 port (no, you can't use your normal "special" PowerBook SCSI cable) you can let another Mac use your PowerBook's internal hard drive as an extra storage device. This will cause your PowerBook drive to appear on the other Mac's desktop.

- **HDI-20 port**   This port is specially designed to connect Apple's external 1.44-Mbyte floppy disk drive and only comes on the PowerBook 100, MiniDock, and Duo Floppy Adapter.

- **Modem jack**   PowerBooks support internal modems, which are accessible through an RJ-11 telephone jack on the port panel. (It's the same connector that your telephone probably uses.) In foreign countries, the appropriate modem jack can be added with a special version of the modem card or with the appropriate adapter.

- **Sound-in port**   Users can plug Apple's external microphone into this port to record voice messages (the 160, 180, and Duos come with built-in microphones as well). They can also attach line-outs from a stereo for digitizing prerecorded sounds in mono. Power-Books don't support stereo input or output. (Never connect amplified sound sources to this port; recordings will come out distorted beyond recognition.)

- **Sound-out port**   External speakers, earphones, or a headset can be plugged into this port. Sound will not play on the PowerBook's speaker when anything is plugged into this port.

- **Video-out port**   Available on the 160, 180, Duo Dock, MiniDock, and many third-party docks, the video-out port lets you connect external color or grayscale monitors to your PowerBook (E-Machines' PowerLink Presentor lets you output 8-bit video from your Duo to a television set).

- **Security slot**   This is a hardened point on your PowerBook 160, 180, Duo 210, 230, Duo Dock, MiniDock, and Duo Floppy Adapter where you can attach a third-party security solution for locking your PowerBook down.

Power Play

Your PowerBook lives on a DC diet in an AC/DC world. The AC adapter that comes with the PowerBook is the only one you should use. It converts most power sources to the appropriate voltage and frequency your portable needs, and when combined with plug adapters for international outlets, it will even make that rich foreign current palatable to your PowerBook.

Nickel Cadmium and the NiHy Kid

If the CPU is the brain of your PowerBook, then the battery is its heart. The battery accounts for much of the weight of the laptop, and, in fact, the quality of most batteries is judged by how much current they supply per ounce.

There are three kinds of batteries your PowerBook might use, depending on the model. Although battery technology, capacity, and conservation are gone into at some length later in the *Guide*, here are some quick notes on the differences among types.

Lead Acid

Only the PowerBook 100 uses lead-acid batteries. The advantages of lead acid include a long shelf life (you can store a fully-charged 100 battery for months and still find most of the power in the battery when you go to use it), relatively low cost, and the fact that lead-acid batteries don't suffer from power memory.

Disadvantages include longer charge time and current output that slowly drops off as the battery discharges. Lead acid batteries also contain acid in a liquid state, which could, if the battery case ruptured, leak over your PowerBook's logic board and do irrevocable damage. We've never heard of a 100 battery cracking, though.

Nickel-Cadmium (NiCad)

See the
Digital Nomad
note below.

PowerBook 140s, 145s, 160s, 170s, and 180s use NiCad batteries. Advantages of NiCads include constant current output that drops off rapidly near the end of a discharge cycle as well as higher output for the same weight. Disadvantages include short shelf life (you can store a fully-charged NiCad battery and a month later find that a significant portion of the charge has dissipated) and power memory.

Third-party vendors now offer longer-lived NiCads.

A Battery with a Memory

When a nickel-cadmium battery is only partially discharged and then recharged several times, there is a chance that it will "remember" the power level it was at when partially discharged and won't charge beyond that level.

Although Apple denied for a long time that there was such a thing as power memory in PowerBook NiCad batteries, we've had personal experience with the syndrome.

This problem was first observed in NiCad batteries used with camcorders. Power memory became such a persistent problem with one of our 140 batteries after about six months of regular use, that the battery regularly wouldn't charge past 50-percent capacity. *(continued)*

A Battery with a Memory (continued)

The solution to power memory is to "deep discharge" the battery, purposely removing most of its stored electricity, and then fully recharge it. See Section III, Part 2, for more information on deep discharging.

One bit of good news, NiCad technology is constantly moving forward. Today's NiCads exhibit power memory less often and then to a lesser extent.

Nickel Hydride (NiHy)

These batteries are currently only used by the Duos. The primary NiHy advantage is more power for less weight. Apple rates the NiHy battery as being able to power a Duo from two to four hours. We figure that you could add up to another hour to these minimum figures using some of the power savings techniques outlined in this book.

There really are no disadvantages to using NiHys, as Apple is charging the same price, $69, for both NiCad and NiHy batteries. The only complaint we have about NiHys is that we wish our 180s could use the little power packs!

The Software I've Seen

In every PowerBook box comes software, which you'll want to install or stow away depending on your needs:

System 7

Your PowerBook arrives in this world with an operating system already installed on its hard drive. (For PowerBooks shipped before October 19, 1992, it's System 7.0.1 with a special Tune-Up disk that fixes several known bugs; after that, System 7.1 is supposed to ship with every Apple laptop). You also get a copy of the diskettes to use for reinstallation. Even if you're using an older System 7.0.1-equipped PowerBook, you may want to consider upgrading to System 7.1 to get access to WorldScript extended language support and Apple's EverWatch power management software. Really, there is little outward difference between the nameless power conservation technology in your old PowerBook and EverWatch (besides the trademark), but the EverWatch software that comes with System 7.1 does include some new power conservation options.

Turn to Section II, Part 1, to see tips on customizing your OS.

AppleTalk Remote Access

One of Apple's great portable innovations was the inclusion of client software called AppleTalk Remote Access, or ARA, that lets users dial into a remote Mac, giving the PowerBook access to the files on the remote hard disk (via System 7 file-sharing) and optionally to every service on the remote network. But Apple has always had a leg up on the rest of the personal computer industry when it comes to networking. ARA shipped free with the 100, 140, 145, and 170; Apple no longer bundles the software with PowerBooks, but they'd be glad to sell it to you.

ARA installs on a PowerBook and lets users dial in, using a modem over a phone line, to either a Macintosh without a lot else to do (ARA takes a lot of RAM) or a server device connected to an AppleTalk network (see Section II, Part 3, *A Port for Every Road Warrior*). The PowerBook and the server communicate through the modem, the networked ARA software telling the remote ARA software about everything that's available on the network, such as file servers and printers. In effect, it makes it seem to the PowerBook user that they are attached to the remote network as if they were sitting in that office.

The whole transaction is highly optimized, and involves much less network traffic than connecting directly to LocalTalk, EtherTalk, or Token-Talk. If you have a 9,600-bps or 14.4-Kbps modem at each end on an ARA connection, file-sharing and printing performance across ARA stands up pretty well against plain old LocalTalk.

Fax Software

If you purchase a PowerBook with a built-in modem, you will receive software that lets you send or send and receive faxes from within any application you are using.

The 2,400-bps modem sold with the first 170s, and still available as an option on the 100s, 140s, and 145s, includes a Fax Sender software. We rate the performance of this software as mediocre, though some of the failed faxes we experienced could have been a result of the Apple modem.

The Express Modems ship with send/receive fax software which, at first blush, seems to be a vast improvement over its forebear. However, over Apple's software we still prefer some third-party solutions, such as those that include OCR (Optical Character Recognition) software for translating fax images into text.

```
 File  Edit  Setup  Windows                    7:46:34 PM         ?

   ┌──────── MacWEEK Logon ────────┐
   │                                │
   │ Connect as:  ○ Guest           │
   │              ● Registered User  │
   │                                │
   │     Name : Mitch Ratcliffe     │       ┌──────── Users & Groups ────────┐
   │ Password : ●●●●●●●●             │       │ 6 items    15 MB in disk   24.9 MB available │
   │    Phone : 1-800-555-1234      │       │                                │
   │                                │       │  [ ]    [ ]    [ ]      [ ]     │
   │  ☐ Save my password            │       │ Mitch Ratcliffe Andy Gore Nomad Team  EO Team │
   │  ☒ Remind me of my connection  │       │                                │
   │    every : [ 15 ] minutes      │       │  [ ]    [ ]                     │
   │                    [ Connect ] │       │ <Guest> Stephen Howard          │
   └────────────────────────────────┘       │                                │
                                             └────────────────────────────────┘
```

AppleTalk Remote Access Software

Power Budgets

Before you encounter the demesne of the computer salesperson, make sure you've planned out what you want and how much you're willing to spend on it. Do research, scan the newspaper adds for the best-priced Power-Book, check mailorder listings in the back of *MacWEEK, MacUser,* or *Macworld* for the cheapest add-ons. Don't feel you have to buy everything you need when and where you buy your computer; you should still get the best price if all you walk out the door with is a minimally configured PowerBook.

Most of all, beware the package deal. It may look good, but you have no way of knowing where that larger internal hard drive or "faster" modem came from. By shopping around you can assemble the pieces yourself, save the same money, and be assured of quality components.

Forget about negotiating price on PowerBooks. Most discounters are living with razor-thin margins, so the advertised price is probably as low as they're likely to go. However, that doesn't mean you shouldn't shop around anyway. Just don't be disappointed if all you get for your efforts are sore feet.

And watch out for the "inexpensive" add-ons the salesperson will very likely suggest when you do buy your PowerBook. That box of printer paper or SCSI cable could have as much as a 100-percent mark-up! Shop around for everything or prepare to pay too much.

As to how much to budget, a good rule is take half the cost of your PowerBook and add that to the total to figure what the price of PowerBook and add-ons, such as memory, applications, and peripherals, are going to run. So, a $3,000 PowerBook will probably run you $4,500 by the time you're done revving it up.

Other Places to Look

For more information on RAM, system software, video-out, and storage, and for a cornucopia of data on third-party PowerBook add-ons, please refer to the following sections:

- Section II, *Start Your Engines*
- Section III, *Tips for the Open Road*
- Section IV, *Exploring Cyberspace*
- Section V, *Zoned for Expansion*

PART
2

POWERBOOKS '91-'92,
THE WONDER YEAR

51

Technical Readout: The PowerBook 100

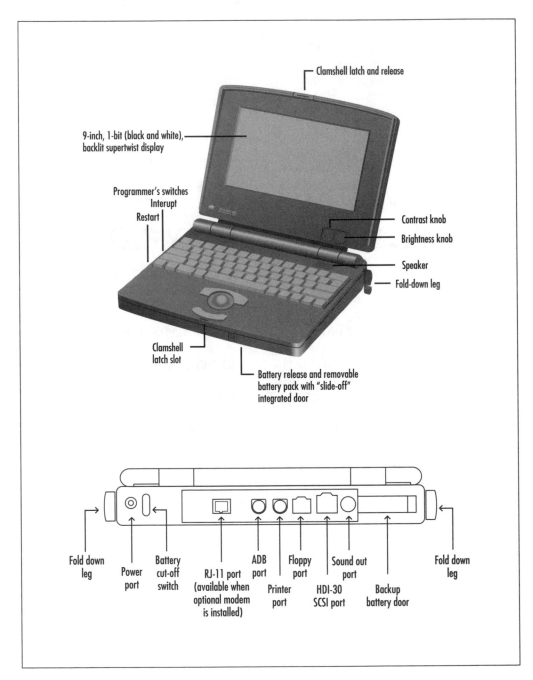

Clamshell latch and release

9-inch, 1-bit (black and white),
backlit supertwist display

Programmer's switches
Interupt
Restart

Contrast knob

Brightness knob

Speaker

Fold-down leg

Clamshell
latch slot

Battery release and removable
battery pack with "slide-off"
integrated door

Fold down
leg

Power
port

Battery
cut-off
switch

RJ-11 port
(available when
optional modem
is installed)

ADB
port

Printer
port

Floppy
port

HDI-30
SCSI port

Sound out
port

Backup
battery door

Fold down
leg

Dimensions	Weight	5.1 lb. (2.3 kg), including battery
	Height	1.8 in. (4.6 cm)
	Width	11 in. (28.0 cm)
	Depth	8.5 in. (21.6 cm)

CPU   16MHz 68HC000

System software   System 6.0.8 and up (Apple recommends you only use System 7.0.1 and up in the 100).

Memory   2-Mbyte or 4-Mbyte pseudostatic RAM, expandable to 8 Mbytes. (In 4-Mbyte configurations 2 Mbytes are soldered to the logic board, and a 2-Mbyte RAM card is installed in the expansion slot.)

Internal storage   One internal 2.5-inch hard disk drive. (Sold by Apple with either a 20-Mbyte or 40-Mbyte hard disk.)

Built-in display   9-inch (229 mm) diagonal, backlit supertwist liquid crystal display. 640 by 400 pixels, 1-bit resolution.

Video-out   Available only through third-party add-on cards. No color output available.

Battery   Sealed lead-acid battery delivers two to three hours of normal usage, up to four hours of typing when the backlighting is turned off. Requires three hours to fully recharge. **Warning:** Draining a lead-acid battery of all electricity can cause damage that renders it unusable. The battery cut-off switch on the back of the 100 stops slow discharging of the battery. Use it when the PowerBook will be stored for a long time.

Ports   One Apple Desktop Bus (ADB) port
One RS-422 serial port (supports LocalTalk)
One HDI-30 SCSI port
One HDI-20 floppy disk drive port
One sound output port (monaural)
One RJ-11 port when modem card is installed

Modem   Internal connector for optional modem card.

Electrical requirements   AC Adapter included, 110 to 220 volts, 50 to 60 Hz.

Known Gotchas

Vanishing Folders

Symptoms You could have sworn that you copied that folder to your PowerBook last night! And where has that "Critical Documents" folder gone? In short, folders intermittently disappear from your desktop.

Diagnosis This affliction is caused by earlier versions of System 7 and is not specific to PowerBooks. However, it can be especially painful in PowerBooks, where you may not have had time to back up files in a missing folder.

Cure Either install System 7.1 or System 7 Tuneup 1.1.1. To get your folder back, do one of the following:

1. Do a Find on the folder name, and the missing folder should reappear. Immediately copy it to a floppy or another volume.
2. Use backup software that can scan the disk to recover the folder.
3. Try rebuilding the desktop by starting up your PowerBook with the Command and Option keys held down.
4. Run Disk First Aid on your DiskTools 7.1 disk to recover lost folders.

Break a Leg

Symptoms One or both flip-down legs break off.

Diagnosis Caused by poor anchoring during manufacture.

Cure Bring it to your dealer or call the Apple S.O.S. line.

Melt in Your Lap, Not in Your Hands

Symptoms Mysteriously, a hole has appeared in the case of your 100.

Diagnosis An affliction of the first 60,000 100s Sony Corp. built for Apple, it affects PowerBook 100s with serial numbers below SQ211xxxxxx and SS216xxxxxx. It is caused by a short where extra lead on the logic board comes in contact with the PowerBook's conductive liner.

Cure Bring it to your dealer, call the PowerBook 100 Safety Helpline (at 800-572-1731), or call the Apple S.O.S. line.

Predicted Reliability

Fair to Good. Considering that Apple has discontinued the 100 in the U.S. and that some of its technology, such as lead-acid batteries, are unique to this model, prospective buyers should be warned that getting this Power-Book serviced may become increasingly difficult over time.

The Orphan PowerBook

Even though it's nearly extinct and only available used, in Europe or through a few clearance outlets, the PowerBook 100 is perfect for the Intentional Tourist who is more concerned with the size, weight, and price of their portable than with niceties like a floppy drive or 68030 processor.

This orphaned, and we feel, unfairly maligned, PowerBook delivers all the power necessary for the traveler who wants to keep an address book, take notes, and occasionally dial into the office or an online service for a message. It's the only notebook from Apple that can run on System 6.0.8, an earlier version of the Mac operating system that uses nearly 400 Kbytes of RAM less than System 7.0.1. The older operating system costs you things like the functionality enabled by Apple events and the improved Finder but frees up the memory needed to run a word processor and an address book simultaneously in 2 Mbytes of RAM. If you choose to run System 6 on your PowerBook, you won't be able to use ARA; it only runs on System 7.

PowerBook 100s suffered from the outset from two drawbacks. The first was poor performance. The 100 was the last Mac to be based on a 68000 processor, the same CPU that powered the original Mac Portable. In fact, the PowerBook 100 is, in terms of functionality and much of its technology, a 17-pound Mac Portable that's been on a serious diet.

If you are planning on crunching numbers on your 100, bring a book to read while it mulls over the calculations. Or, better yet, make the investment in the PowerBook 180 to push the performance envelope.

See the Road Warrior note below.

↓

The other drawback of using a PowerBook 100 is the terrible submarining of the cursor caused by the supertwist screen's slow redraw speed. The combination of the slow screen and processor can really make using a 100 feel like you're computing through molasses.

Submarine Commander

If the raw power and color video-out available on the PowerBook 180 isn't enough to get you Road Warriors to go for broke (or to get you 170 users to trade up), then the little game that comes free with every 100, 140, 145, 160, and Duo should convince you to "Just Say No" to supertwist screens.

We like to call it Submarine Commander.

Because the phosphor technology used in supertwist screens can't re-fresh pixels as fast as active-matrix screens (the speed at which a com-puter can change the color and shade of individual pixels is referred to as the refresh rate), the cursor on supertwist screens sometimes vanishes when moved quickly.

You can easily lose track of the I-beam cursor when you move it, result-ing in frantic mouse-jerking to relocate the prodigal cursor. If you have QuicKeys for Nomads installed, hitting the Control and C keys simul-taneously can shorten the search. See Section II, Part I and Section V for more information on this utility.

The Ascent of PowerBooks

Just as humanity has its ancestor with a tail, the 100 is the *Australopithecus afarensis* of the PowerBook family. Two of this PowerBook's defining traits will live on as recessive genes that will again gain dominance in generations of Apple portables to come.

Be prepared for the return of the 100's external floppy drive, which also hangs like an atrophied tail off the HDI-20 port at the back of the Power-Book Duo MiniDock and Duo Floppy Adapter. If you plan to add an in-ternal cellular modem to your internal floppy-equipped PowerBook, the wireless device will evict the diskette drive and you'll need to regress to an external appendage not unlike the 100's floppy.

See the
Digital Nomad
note below.

Another, more positive PowerBook 100 legacy is the ability to connect to a desktop Macintosh and appear as a hard disk in that machine's Finder. The 100 was the first PowerBook to provide SCSI Disk Mode, but the fea-ture made its return in the new Duos and the PowerBook 160 and 180. SCSI Disk Mode lets you treat your PowerBook as an extension of your desktop Mac, and is particularly useful in a lightweight computer intended for note-taking and information organizing.

Reconcilable Differences

SCSI Disk Mode makes sharing files between computers easier in the 100, 160, 180, and Duo 210 and 230 (the Duos require the addition of a dock with an HDI-30 port to use SCSI Disk Mode).

Before you try to plug your standard HDI-30 SCSI cable into your PowerBook and desktop Mac, you should be warned that you may damage your computers. SCSI Disk Mode requires a special HDI-30 cable with an extra pin that controls communications between the two computers—ask your dealer for a 30-pin SCSI disk adapter cable.

However, it can also be a major pitfall. The PowerBooks don't ship with file reconciliation utilities that keep you from accidentally erasing important data when connected to another Mac.

Imagine that last Friday evening you copied a file from your PowerBook onto your home Macintosh. During the evening you did a little work on the file. On Saturday morning, with only one cup of coffee flowing through your veins, you decide to move a few more files over to your desktop Mac. After docking the two computers, you drag a group of files, including the one you've already been working on, over to the desktop Mac's hard drive. A dialog box appears: "A newer item named 'Kill the Boss' already exists in this location. Are you sure you want to replace it with the one you're moving?" You click *okay* and destroy Friday night's work.

File reconciliation software, like No Hands Software's Synchro, which is included on the PowerBook Roadside Assistance Kit, is essential for PowerBooks that will be connected to another Mac. Synchro lets you control file updates, so that only the most recent version of a file is copied to the target drive.

Technical Readout: The PowerBook 140/145

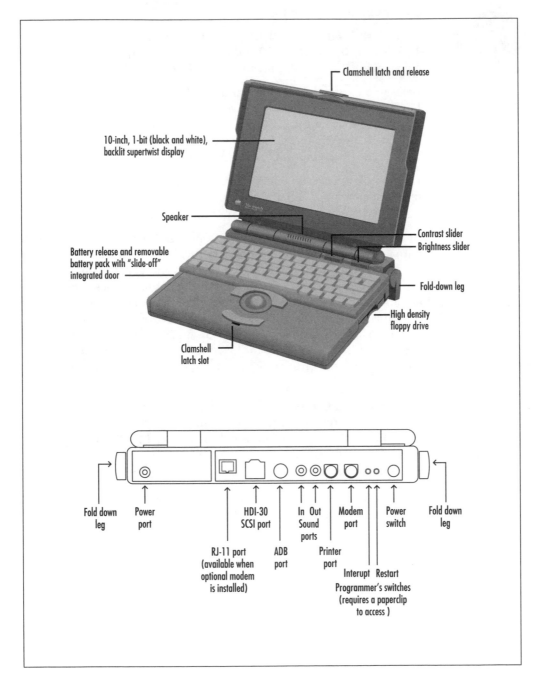

Clamshell latch and release

10-inch, 1-bit (black and white),
backlit supertwist display

Speaker

Contrast slider
Brightness slider

Battery release and removable
battery pack with "slide-off"
integrated door

Fold-down leg

High density
floppy drive

Clamshell
latch slot

Fold down
leg

Power
port

RJ-11 port
(available when
optional modem
is installed)

HDI-30
SCSI port

ADB
port

In Out
Sound
ports

Printer
port

Modem
port

Interupt Restart

Programmer's switches
(requires a paperclip
to access)

Power
switch

Fold down
leg

Dimensions	Weight	6.8 lb. (3.08 kg), including battery
	Height	2.25 in. (5.7 cm)
	Width	11.25 in. (28.6 cm)
	Depth	9.3 in. (23.6 cm)

CPU

140: 16MHz 68030
145: 25MHz 68030

System software

System 7.0.1 and up.

Memory

140: 2-Mbyte or 4-Mbyte pseudostatic RAM, expandable to 8 Mbytes. (In 4-Mbyte configurations 2 Mbytes are soldered to the logic board, and a 2-Mbyte RAM card is installed in the expansion slot.)

145: 4-Mbyte pseudostatic RAM, expandable to 8 Mbytes. (2 Mbytes of RAM are soldered to the logic board with a 2-Mbyte RAM card taking up the expansion slot.)

Internal storage

140: One internal 2.5-inch hard disk drive. (Sold by Apple with either a 20-Mbyte, 40-Mbyte, or 80-Mbyte hard disk.)

145: One internal 2.5-inch hard disk drive. (Sold by Apple with either a 40 Mbyte or 80 Mbyte hard disk.)

Both: Internal 1.44-Mbyte floppy disk drive.

Built-in display

10-inch (254 mm) diagonal, backlit supertwist liquid crystal display. 640 by 400 pixels, 1-bit resolution.

Video-out

Available only through third-party add-on cards.

Battery

Apple NiCad battery delivers 1.5 to three hours of normal usage, up to four hours of typing when the backlighting is turned off. Requires two to three hours to fully recharge.

Ports

One Apple Desktop Bus (ADB) port
Two RS-422 serial ports (printer port supports LocalTalk)
One HDI-30 SCSI port
One microphone port (monaural)
One sound output port (monaural)
One RJ-11 port when modem card is installed

Modem

Internal connector for optional modem card.

Electrical requirements

AC Adapter included, 110 to 220 volts, 50 to 60 Hz.

Known Gotchas

140   Vanishing Folders (see PowerBook 100).

145   No documented problems at this time.

140: Dancing Pixels

Symptoms   Generally an affliction of the lower half of the 140's built-in display, it causes pixels to randomly turn on and off. Because the pixels can "flux" quickly, this disorder creates an illusion that the screen images are bleeding, or dancing, across the screen.

Diagnosis   Squeeze the lower righthand side of the frame that runs around the PowerBook's screen. If the dancing becomes more pronounced or seems to go away completely, your 140 has Dancing Pixel disorder.

Cure   The problem is caused by a faulty ribbon cable. This is a congenital defect of earlier 140s that was supposedly addressed in later units. We experienced this problem with our 140, which was one of the very first Apple produced. It corrected itself before we had a chance to send it back to Apple to have a new cable installed.

Predicted Reliability

140   Fair to Good.

145   Good, based on the 140's record. The 145 is essentially identical to the 140 in most respects, so Apple will have had a chance to resolve minor design problems left over from the 140.

The Ombudsman

The 145, with its 25MHz 68030 processor, was a mid-life replacement for the PowerBook 140. With the exception of the 145's faster clockrate, there is no difference between it and the 140.

The processor upgrade was generally regarded as "fine-tuning." When Apple first released the PowerBooks, they only had theories and user studies to help guess how the portables would be used. Although the company did foresee that the demands placed on PowerBooks by their users would be greater than what had previously been seen with portables, the company underestimated what would be needed to meet those demands. System 7 is a MIPS sponge—the 140's 16MHz 68030 CPU was a bit anemic when it came to processor-intensive applications.

The market failure of the PowerBook 100 presented Apple with a puzzle to solve. Why weren't buyers lining up for its smallest, lightest, and cheapest portable, when heft and price were most commonly cited as the reasons the original Mac Portable sank like a boat anchor? (Not coincidentally, "Boat Anchor" was one of the Portable's more popular nicknames.)

The lack of an internal floppy drive and the sluggish performance (especially running System 7) of the 100's 68000 processor were the two main reasons given for why users were opting for pricier 140s and 170s. Apple had two solutions to address these limitations. The first were the recently introduced PowerBook Duos, which bear a striking resemblance to the 100, but come with much faster 68030 processors and greater expansion capabilities. (However, people involved with the Duo project said that engineering on the tiny portable started well in advance of the 100's market failure and was not in their minds when they designed the dockable Power-Book.)

The other solution was to take the mid-range PowerBook, the 145, and have it hold up the low end of Apple's portable lineup.

Now that it is the entry model of the PowerBook clan, the PowerBook 145 must deliver the kind of power that lets users run their favorite word processing, spreadsheet, or telecommunications applications with reasonable performance, while still carrying a reasonable price tag. With a few additional investments, the 145 can more than carry the load.

Traveling executives, salespeople, and blue collar workers who need to keep in touch with and manipulate data on their office local-area networks will need to add RAM and an internal modem to the 145. Another vital addition, if your company uses an Ethernet network, is an external SCSI adapter that can tap into data moving over the cable at up to 10 Mbps. With these few investments, the 145 will arm you with the tools that will let you work more productively.

The Floating-Point, Supertwist Blues

When it was first introduced, Apple spokespeople claimed the 145 delivered the same performance as the PowerBook 170 and was cheaper only because it shipped with the supertwist screen. We say "phooey." The PowerBook 145 lacks a Floating-Point Unit (FPU), which is standard in the PowerBook 170 and 180.

When running some math-intensive applications, like statistical or engineering programs, you may find yourself aching for the faster math performance available with an FPU. Since there is no socket for an FPU upgrade on the 145 CPU logic board, you'll never be able to add one.

Lastly, before you make the decision to buy a 145, take a good look at the display. Like the 100 and 140 before it, the 145's presentation power is hobbled by its supertwist liquid crystal display. These are made-for-one screens with less than crystal clear image quality. If you'll be using your PowerBook in sales meetings or during a conference, it's next to impossible to show information on the screen to others. Also, because it is a supertwist display, expect to play Submarine Commander with the cursor. It won't be as bad as the 100, but after a few hours of squinting, you may not feel thankful for that small favor.

A video output adapter, which lets you connect your 145 to a larger color or monochrome monitor, could prove indispensable.

Technical Readout: The PowerBook 170

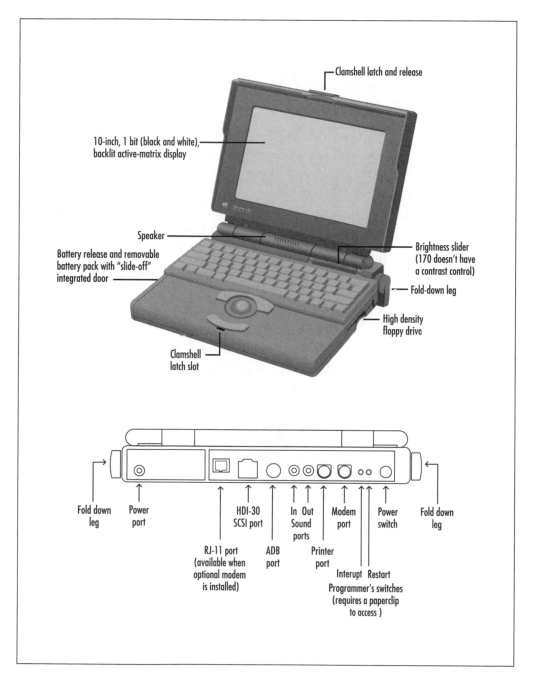

Clamshell latch and release

10-inch, 1 bit (black and white), backlit active-matrix display

Speaker

Battery release and removable battery pack with "slide-off" integrated door

Clamshell latch slot

Brightness slider (170 doesn't have a contrast control)

Fold-down leg

High density floppy drive

Fold down leg

Power port

RJ-11 port (available when optional modem is installed)

HDI-30 SCSI port

ADB port

In Out Sound ports

Printer port

Modem port

Interupt Restart Programmer's switches (requires a paperclip to access)

Power switch

Fold down leg

Dimensions	Weight	6.8 lb. (3.08 kg), including battery
	Height	2.25 in. (5.7 cm)
	Width	11.25 in. (28.6 cm)
	Depth	9.3 in. (23.6 cm)

CPU
25MHz 68030
25MHz 68882 FPU

System software
System 7.0.1 and up

Memory
2-Mbyte or 4-Mbyte pseudostatic RAM, expandable to 8 Mbytes. (In 4-Mbyte configurations 2 Mbytes are soldered to the logic board, and a 2-Mbyte RAM card is installed in the expansion slot.)

Internal storage
One internal 2.5-inch hard disk drive. (Sold by Apple with either a 40-Mbyte or 80-Mbyte hard disk.)

Internal 1.44-Mbyte floppy disk drive.

Built-in display
10-inch (254 mm) diagonal, backlit active-matrix liquid crystal display. 640 by 400 pixels, 1-bit resolution.

Video-out
Available only through third-party add-on cards.

Battery
Apple NiCad battery delivers 1.5 to three hours of normal usage, up to four hours of typing when the backlighting is turned off and processor clockrate is "cranked down" to 16Mhz. Requires two to three hours to fully recharge.

Ports
One Apple Desktop Bus (ADB) port.
Two RS-422 serial ports (printer port supports LocalTalk).
One HDI-30 SCSI port
One microphone port (monaural)
One sound output port (monaural)
One RJ-11 port when modem card is installed

Modem
Internal connector for optional modem card. The Apple internal 2,400-baud data, 9,600-baud send-only fax modem (MNP 4, 5, and V.42 and V.42bis error correction and compression support included) was built into all 170s at first and then later was bundled only with the 4-Mbyte RAM/40-Mbyte hard disk configuration.

Electrical requirements
AC Adapter included, 110 to 220 volts, 50 to 60 Hz.

Known Gotchas:

Vanishing Folders (see PowerBook 100).

Fickle Floppy

Symptoms Your 170 says the floppy diskette you just shoved into its drive is bad, and you're sure it isn't.

Diagnosis Before you call Apple S.O.S., take the diskette in question and try it in another Macintosh (not a 170) with a high-density Apple Super-Drive installed. If it works, then your 170 is probably suffering from Fickle Floppy Syndrome. The cause is improper shielding of the floppy drive from electromagnetic interference from the 170's logic board components.

Cure It's probably an intermittent problem. If you try the floppy a few times, the 170 should eventually recognize it as readable. However, if it persists or you just find it too annoying to live with, you can bring it into your dealer or call Apple for a prescribed shielding refit.

Stuck Pixels

Symptoms A pixel is "stuck" when it is always on (black) or always off (white).

Diagnosis This is a congenital defect that only afflicts the active-matrix screens used on the 170 and 180.

Cure If more than five pixels are stuck (Apple calls these "voided pixels"), or if two or more stuck pixels are within an inch of each other, call (800) SOS-APPL and arrange for your free replacement screen. If your screen doesn't meet these requirements, you can always buy the upgrade.

Predicted Reliability

Good to Excellent. In its first year, this was Apple's top PowerBook. It has proven to be a most reliable model, the least you'd expect considering the price tag.

VigorBook

You can't buy the 170 anymore. But while its anemic sibling, the 100, went down in disgrace, the 170 retired a champion, backordered right up to the day it was put out to pasture.

Delivering speed, an FPU math chip, and a sharp, backlit, active matrix liquid crystal display—and capable of running any desktop application with output to video through third-party attachments—its robust performance will keep the 170 appearing young for several years.

With performance greater than a Macintosh IIci, the 170 is a laptop computer that can serve not only as a portable office, it can handle the day-to-day duties of your current workstation with aplomb. Buyers recognized the need for power on the road, not just on the desktop, and flocked to the 170 in droves. For months after it first shipped, this high-end model was nearly impossible to get. Like the Mazda Miata, which at the height of its popularity was fabled to sell for up to $5000 over the manufacturer's suggested retail price, the 170 often cost buyers Apple's list, a price so rarely paid for other Mac products that it was thought extinct among computer resellers.

Versatility can be a problem, however. While the 170 is a match for many desktop computers in performance, internal hard disk space and RAM come at a premium. The 170 is "memory-scrawny" with a top end of 8 Mbytes. In comparison, a IIci can handle up to 128 Mbytes. The IIci can also use internal hard drives in excess of 230 Mbytes and has three NuBus expansion slots—abilities missing from the 170.

Focusing this PowerBook on delivering full productivity requires a thoughtful approach to add-on hardware and software. Think first about what it is you want do with this laptop, then make your purchases. If you try to piece together a system as disparate inspirations strike, you'll end up spending a lot of money unnecessarily.

For example, if you make business presentations while on the road, then make investments in a 6-Mbyte RAM upgrade, an 80-Mbyte hard disk, and a SCSI video adapter that allows you to connect the 170 to an external color or monochrome monitor.

If you are an engineer or an accountant who likes to work on CAD files or corporate balance sheets while flying from meeting to meeting, your essential purchases will include more RAM, a larger hard disk, and lots of extra batteries. You may also want to opt for an internal combination RAM/color video-out card. We've observed markedly better screen refresh rates and overall video performance from internal cards than what's available from SCSI-based video solutions.

Say you're the workaholic type who just can't let a project rest until it's finished, the 170 is ideal for processor- and communications-intensive tasks, wherever your work takes you. Put your expansion dollars into a SCSI Ethernet adapter and an internal 14,400-baud cellular modem and install the AppleTalk Remote Access software that shipped with the PowerBooks, so you can trade information with collaborators as you move through the day—at home over breakfast, from your office desktop, or on the train home in the evening. Adding an 80- or 120-Mbyte internal hard drive or carrying an external 400 Mbyte drive, will give you the storage you need to accommodate all the productivity and analysis applications and data files you want to take away.

Mediocre Modem

See the
Road Warrior
note below.

The only really disappointing feature of some 170 configurations is the internal 2,400-baud data/9,600-baud fax-send modem Apple included. As we mentioned in the PowerBook overview, it is an unreliable and testy little bugger. We know many 170 users who have had a transmission fail in the middle of a communications session. The bug, which involves Apple's use of a nonstandard alternative to the Hayes modem escape sequence, won't ruin your data, but it does cost valuable time. We recommend you avoid 170s with Apple's 2,400-baud modem installed.

If you're one of the cursed souls who has this modem, perhaps this explains all those inexplicable problems you've had communicating. However, we do have a simple solution to your modem troubles. Go down to your dealer and have them remove the Apple modem. When this is done, get the modem board, take it outdoors (this works best on a sunny day), and examine it carefully for one minute.

Apparent Trap

Another nasty surprise with Apple's 2,400-baud PowerBook modem is a tendency to grab the RJ-11 phone jack and not give it back.

This happens because the top of the RJ-11 port on some of Apple's modem cards is too close to the top bezel on the modem port opening in the back of the PowerBook. The little plastic tab that locks and releases the phone jack sometimes gets jammed between the modem card and the PowerBook bezel.

The first thing to remember when this happens is: Don't yank the cable, you'll just snap off the tab. Instead, push the jack in and use a pencil or other long, tapered tool to hold the top of the phone jack tab down. Then, gently pull the plug out.

For an even easier and more permanent solution, refer to the end of the "Mediocre Modem".

Then, drop it on the pavement and stomp on it with uninhibited glee until it is an unrecognizable pile of plastic and silicon fragments.

Reenter the store and purchase one of the several third-party internal PowerBook modems (from PSI or Global Village's, for example) that feature higher data transfer rates, fax send *and* receive, and better software.

POWERBOOKS '92-'93, THE NEXT GENERATION

Zero Defect

If it is rare for a sequel to a successful film to make it as big as its predecessor, imagine how much harder it is for technological lightning to strike twice in the same place. The second generation of PowerBooks, which were introduced on October 19, 1992, are evidence that commitment to a "user-centric" view of development can produce one hit product after another.

As we noted in the Manifesto, the business of computing is moving off the desktop and into the closets and briefcases of business users everywhere. Apple's dilemma when trying to come up with a second round of PowerBooks was this: how to continue expanding its lead in mobile computing while addressing the needs of users who no longer work in four-wall offices.

It isn't enough just to make Macintoshes small enough to fit in a bag. If the first generation of PowerBooks was about bringing Mac functionality to a mobile package, then the challenge of the second generation was to scale down enough capabilities to make the escape from the desktop complete. Mobile users shouldn't need to switch to another computer to do their work—all the comforts of their desktop systems should be available wherever they are. That includes file, mail, and network services, as well as system expansion, color video display, and processing power.

Another issue that Apple needed to address, if it was to make the liberation of users from the office complete, was how systems managers will control, service, and protect their company's widely-dispersed computing resources. In other words, Apple has taken on the twofold challenge of selling on both sides of the wire. If it is to hold onto its mobile business, it must supply solutions that work well—consistently, flexibly, and with as little hassle as possible—for both the company and its digital nomads.

With all this in mind, Apple had two choices when designing its new portables: build more powerful PowerBooks or build more flexible Power-Books.

Apple decided to do both.

Pushing the Envelope

In some ways the PowerBooks' runaway success took Apple by surprise, especially the decidedly high-end appeal of the PowerBook 170, which was its bestseller. The company quickly recovered from this initial miscalculation and began to focus its design efforts on building more capable Power-Books.

The main advantage of focusing the portable line toward higher-end functionality was that Apple could charge a premium for premium Power-Books. In the last couple of years, Apple has seen its gross margin, the money it makes from Macintosh sales, steadily decline as competition forced it to cut prices. Now, as though the profit cavalry had charged over the hill just in time to save the day, the company found a way, through higher margin PowerBook sales, to recoup some of the margin it was losing on cheaper desktop systems.

And with RISC-based mobile competitors waiting in the wings, it was critical to push PowerBook performance as far as it could go.

There are only two problems with a business strategy focused on high-end portables. First, if you build a lot of capability into your portables, us-ers will have less and less reason to buy your desktop systems. The Duos seem especially tuned to this possibility, and we feel that most Duo buyers will opt not to use a desktop Mac at all. The other danger is that you will price your product line out of the reach of a whole class of users. People with budgets under $2,000 may buy Windows or DOS notebooks instead, which can be had for considerably less money than a PowerBook. Unfortu-nately, these users will probably find the new PowerBooks priced out of reach.

The company needs its next generation of PowerBooks to be an even bigger hit than its first models; at stake is its vitality and perhaps its sur-vival. As we mentioned earlier, Apple sold roughly 420,000 PowerBooks in its first year. Now it reportedly is projecting total sales of over 500,000 for the second PowerBook year. These are conservative numbers, especially considering that a good percentage of PowerBook sales will come at the ex-pense of desktop systems.

But if Apple is to be successful leading the way into the mobile society, then these are numbers it needs to make, at least.

Measuring Up to User Expectations

The second-generation PowerBooks offer considerably more choices for the digital nomad. Most of these portables are replacements for a desktop computer, so it's easy to imagine how you can begin to shape a new work-style with the 160, 180, and the Duos. Also, the new PowerBooks' ability to display sixteen shades of gray in their built-in displays makes working with imaging software, like Adobe Photoshop, while on the road more than an idle fancy.

Here are some general observations about the new product line:

- **PowerBook 180** is a great computer. One of the authors, Mitch Ratcliffe, gave up his desktop Macintosh for a 170 last year. But the transition has been rough on occasion, because there wasn't enough room on the 170 motherboard for adequate RAM expansion and the available hard drives had fallen short of his storage needs. The 180 solves all those problems. And, the option to attach an external color monitor without having to purchase a third-party video solution combines with faster performance to make Mitch much happier.

- **PowerBook 160**   While its 25MHz 68030 CPU and 16-grayscale screen provide performance that is a far sight better than the 100, 140, and 145, it still doesn't make going completely portable an option. The supertwist screen retains some of the muddier eddies that plagued this computer's predecessors. Users may want for an FPU and the 180's active-matrix screen when doing complex spreadsheets, desktop publishing, and many day-to-day tasks.

  In most other respects the 160, which can attach to your desktop Mac in a number of ways, including across the network or in SCSI Disk Mode, is a good balance of price and power.

- **Duo 210**   If, for any reason, you can't use the 180 to replace your desktop computer, you may want to consider going for a less expensive mobile solution. For example, Mobile Commuters might find the Duo 210 with MiniDocks at home and at the office a nice, lightweight option.

- **Duo 230**   Even without an FPU, this is a formidable system. For people who have spent many hours with a PowerBook bag slung over their shoulders, the 4-pound Duo is a real temptation. But, oh, the 180's active-matrix screen is such a pleasure to read! After spending many hours reading off of a 140, developing chronic eyestrain caused by blurry, faded supertwist displays, the active-matrix screen is how we spell relief.

See the
Digital Nomad
note below.

Burstin' PowerBook Bags!

While we're on the subject, evaluating how much weight you're willing to lug around takes more than hefting a 180 a couple of times. You've got a lot of other items to figure into total weight. The result of stuffing all your "needful things" into a bag with your PowerBook could mean doubling the effective weight of your portable.Remember, the majority of the time you spend moving your mobile computer, it will be hanging on your shoulder in a bag.   *(continued)*

Burstin' PowerBook Bags! (continued)

You've got to add the weight of extra batteries, the power supply, any special documentation, plus the weight of the bag itself. There's also the additional bulk of all the paper you normally carry around with you, files and such, unless you plan on carrying two bags everywhere.

One alternative is to get an add-on strap, such as the one offered by Premier Technology of San Francisco, that attaches to the flip-up legs on your PowerBook. This way you can carry just your PowerBook when you don't need to lug along the entire contents of your bag. A definite shortcoming of the PowerBook design is its lack of a strap or handle. But sometimes you have to give up a little convenience for style.

Talking Security

Certain features are common to all PowerBooks. For example, all come with a speaker and an external microphone. But Apple's new PowerBooks also come with an integrated microphone.

With the built-in microphone and the addition of an internal modem with voice capability, like those available from Applied Engineering of Dallas, Texas, you can turn your 160 or 180 into an integrated computer/telephone. Of course, if you use your PowerBook as a telephone in public, you may want to watch what you say (if you can hear it, so can the people around you). The pygmy modems needed to fit inside the Duos don't currently offer voice capability, just one of many little compromises Duo users must make in order to get a four-pound PowerBook.

See the Digital Nomad note below.

Worth noting is another minor modification to the 160 and 180 PowerBook and Duo Dock, MiniDock and Floppy Adapter cases, the addition of a security slot. This gives you a place to hook up a lock-down device like those available from Kensington Microware Limited. An investment in a security solution of some sort might not be a bad idea if you use your PowerBook in an office setting where many people might have access to it.

Theft By Mail

One of the very first PowerBooks bought by *MacWEEK* did a disappearing act on its way back to our lab from Apple Service. Apparently the perpetrator recognized the "Apple Service" label and identified the box contents as valuable. Something to consider before sending your PowerBook through the mail to be fixed...

Technical Readout: The PowerBook 160

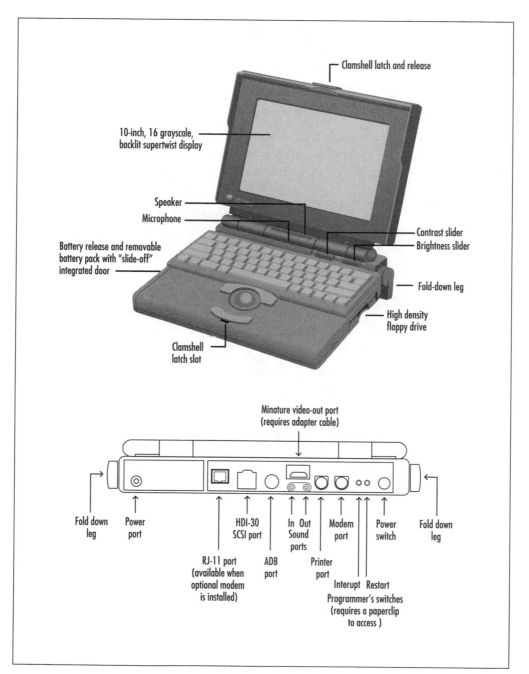

Clamshell latch and release

10-inch, 16 grayscale, backlit supertwist display

Speaker

Microphone

Contrast slider

Brightness slider

Battery release and removable battery pack with "slide-off" integrated door

Fold-down leg

High density floppy drive

Clamshell latch slot

Minature video-out port (requires adapter cable)

Fold down leg

Power port

HDI-30 SCSI port

In Out Sound ports

Modem port

Power switch

Fold down leg

RJ-11 port (available when optional modem is installed)

ADB port

Printer port

Interupt Restart Programmer's switches (requires a paperclip to access)

Dimensions	Weight	6.8 lb. (3.1 kg), including battery
	Height	2.25 in. (5.7 cm)
	Width	11.25 in. (28.6 cm)
	Depth	9.3 in. (23.6 cm)

CPU 25MHz 68030

System software System 7.1 and up.

Memory 4-Mbyte pseudostatic RAM, expandable to 14 Mbytes.

Internal storage One internal 2.5-inch hard disk drive. (Sold by Apple with a 40-, 80- or 120-Mbyte hard disk.)

Internal 1.44-Mbyte floppy disk drive.

Built-in display 10-inch (254 mm) diagonal, backlit supertwist liquid crystal display. 640 by 400 pixels, 4-bit resolution.

Video-out Built-in support for 8-bit color on up to 16-inch monitors (512-Kbyte VRAM, not expandable). Also works with some VGA and SVGA monitors.

Battery Apple NiCad battery delivers 2.5 to three hours of normal usage, up to four hours of typing when the backlighting is turned off and processor clock rate is "cranked-down" to 16Mhz. Requires two to three hours to fully recharge.

Extra security One security slot for use with third-party locking solutions.

Ports One Apple Desktop Bus (ADB) port

Two RS-422 serial ports (printer port supports LocalTalk)

One HDI-30 SCSI port

One video-out port (8-bit color). Users should note that this connector is not the standard (DB-15) Apple video port and requires a special cable to work most monitors. The cable is included with the PowerBook.

One microphone port (monaural)

One sound output port (monaural)

One RJ-11 port when modem card is installed

Modem Internal connector for optional modem card.

Electrical requirements AC Adapter included, 110 to 220 volts, 50 to 60 Hz.

Known Gotchas

No documented problems at this time.

Predicted Reliability

Good. Although the 160 uses some new display technology, it is still based on the tried-and-true 140/145 PowerBook design and should prove to be above average in reliability.

A Shady Character

It may look suspiciously familiar, but besides sharing the same "all-in-one" design (what Apple calls the 140/145/160/170/180 case), the PowerBook 160 has more going for it under its plastic skin than the 140 it resembles.

First, it's fast. At 25 MHz, its '030 CPU can nearly match the performance of a 170. The only thing it lacks is an FPU, which may give pause to Road Warriors or Mobile Commuters looking to displace their desktop systems. Among next-generation PowerBooks, 25 MHz is only average performance. Where this shady operator really drops its Clark Kent facade is when a user lifts up the hood and takes a peek inside.

See the Digital Nomad note below.

The first thing you'll notice is the faster supertwist screen. The 120Hz, 16-grayscale supertwist technology utilized in the 160 goes some distance toward alleviating the submarining cursors and motion-blurring that plagued the 140. Those fourteen extra shades of gray add a lot of on-screen distinction to this PowerBook, making it a must-have for users who want to see graphics of greater detail (such as the aesthetic appeal of icons with some depth). It is also especially nice when playing QuickTime movies; dithering to sixteen shades produces much better results than dithering to black and white. However, QuickTime motion blur on a supertwist screen is still enough to make us seasick.

The 160 does sport a larger, and therefore more readable, screen than the Duo 210; it also includes a built-in floppy, and its performance is equivalent. It comes with video out for 8-bit color on up to a 16-inch monitor, making it perfect for the Mobile Commuter who isn't prepared (or authorized by her company) to sink the bucks into a 180. You will have to lug around an extra two pounds for those conveniences, something the Intentional Tourist may want to consider before buying a 160 over the Duo 210. (If you factor in carrying a Duo MiniDock, to gain access to the standard port array and video-out, the 160 is only 1.35 pounds heavier than the Duo and MiniDock combo.)

When evaluating whether you want to purchase the 160 or a Duo, you may want to try connecting and disconnecting all the cables you'll be using on the back of the 160. It can become tedious attaching and detaching a modem, network, SCSI, and monitor cable several times a day. This is a big advantage of the Duo's single 152-pin rear connector: one shove and all the connections are taken care of for you.

Finally, Road Warriors on a budget might find the 160 acceptable. Its performance falls just a little short of the 170, while adding video-out and a grayscale display at a reasonable cost. However, we believe few Road Warriors will ever be truly satisfied with anything less than a 180, so you may have cause to call in those childhood debts or to be extra nice to the boss.

Just a Dithering Idiot

Dithering is the process by which an image containing a lot of data is "scaled-down" so that a display not capable of showing all that data won't have to shut out the image completely.

For example, let's say you have a 24-bit (millions of colors) scanned image on your hard disk but your PowerBook has only an 8-bit (256 colors) display on its external monitor. The computer averages the colors in each pixel to the closest color available. The result is a good representation of the image that may suffer from jaggy transitions from one color to another but still gets the point across.

Most QuickTime movies captured from video are stored in 16-bit (32,000 colors) format, which gives them good fidelity without over-taxing the CPU with a lot of extraneous color data. When you play a 16-bit color QuickTime movie on your 16-grayscale PowerBook screen, QuickTime will not only remove all the color, it will dither the image to match the screen's 4-bit capabilities. The result will probably not look great, but will be a damn sight better than the bare-bones black and white of a 1-bit display.

Technical Readout: The PowerBook 180

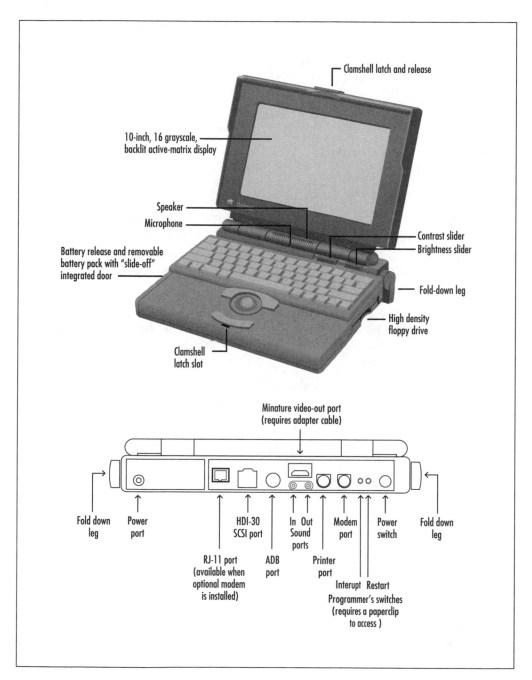

Clamshell latch and release

10-inch, 16 grayscale, backlit active-matrix display

Speaker

Microphone

Contrast slider

Brightness slider

Battery release and removable battery pack with "slide-off" integrated door

Fold-down leg

High density floppy drive

Clamshell latch slot

Minature video-out port (requires adapter cable)

Fold down leg

Power port

HDI-30 SCSI port

In Out Sound ports

Modem port

Power switch

Fold down leg

RJ-11 port (available when optional modem is installed)

ADB port

Printer port

Interupt Restart Programmer's switches (requires a paperclip to access)

Dimensions	Weight	6.8 lb. (3.1 kg), including battery
	Height	2.25 in. (5.7 cm)
	Width	11.25 in. (28.6 cm)
	Depth	9.3 in. (23.6 cm)

CPU

33MHz 68030
33MHz 68882 FPU

System software

System 7.1 and up.

Memory

4-Mbyte pseudostatic RAM, expandable to 14 Mbytes.

Internal storage

One internal 2.5-inch hard disk drive. (Sold by Apple with either an 80- or 120-Mbyte hard disk.)

Internal 1.44-Mbyte floppy disk drive.

Built-in display

10-inch (254 mm) diagonal, backlit supertwist liquid crystal display. 640 by 400 pixels, 4-bit resolution.

Video-out

Built-in support for 8-bit color on up to 16-inch monitors (512-Kbyte VRAM, not expandable). Also works with some VGA and SVGA monitors.

Battery

Apple NiCad battery delivers 2.5 to three hours of normal usage, up to four hours of typing when the backlighting is turned off and processor clock rate is "cranked-down" to 16Mhz. Requires two to three hours to fully recharge.

Extra security

One security slot for use with third-party locking solutions.

Ports

One Apple Desktop Bus (ADB) port

Two RS-422 serial ports (printer port supports LocalTalk)

One HDI-30 SCSI port

One video-out port (8-bit color). Users should note that this connector is not the standard (DB-15) Apple video port and requires a special cable to work most monitors. The cable is included with the PowerBook.

One microphone port (monaural)

One sound output port (monaural)

One RJ-11 port when modem card is installed

Modem

Internal connector for optional modem card.

Electrical requirements

AC Adapter included, 110 to 220 volts, 50 to 60 Hz.

Known Gotchas

Stuck pixels (see PowerBook 170 in Part Two of this Section).

Predicted Reliability

Good. Although the 180 uses some new display technology, it is still based on the sucessful 170 PowerBook design and should prove above average in reliability. The question of battery life in the 33Mhz 180 remains unclear.

The PowerBook to Be Your Best

Every prestige product line should have its Secretariat, its Contach, its ultimate performer, its best of breed. The 170 led the way in speed and functionality for the first round of PowerBooks. It is only fitting that its successor, the 180, should not only be worthy of its lineage but surpasses its progenitor in every way possible.

With the quality of the built-in screen, the color video output, and the speed of the processor, the 180 is the first Mac laptop that can be used for serious professional desktop publishing. Imagine being able to fold up your electronic offset system and stuff it in your briefcase at the end of the day so you can go home, be with the family, and still get your project completed on time.

We should admit up front that both authors have already replaced their older PowerBooks with the 180. As loyal PowerBook fans, we couldn't resist this 33MHz screamer. The charms of its active-matrix grayscale screen, the only PowerBook to come with this sparkling display, are probably what finally won both of us away from the Duo 230. You have to see this screen to believe it; the blacks are really black, and the gray-green cast of the 170's active-matrix is gone, replaced by cool blue tones. It's also brighter than the 170 screen and has improved light diffusion, giving it smoother images from screen edge to screen edge.

Combined with the extra punch available from its built-in 33MHz math coprocessor, the convenience of its 120-Mbyte internal hard drive and internal floppy makes carrying the 180's extra two pounds worth it. Of course, the premium price of Apple's top-of-the-line PowerBook may not appear to be "worth it" for many buyers.

Unless you really feel the need for NuBus slots, we doubt you'll ever miss your desktop Mac once you trade it in on a 180. With standard 8-bit color video-out we doubt you'll miss your color card, unless you won't be satisfied with less than 24-bit color—in which case a Duo 230 and a Duo

Dock might offer a better alternative (although we have a sneaking suspicion that some industrious third party will figure out a way to add 24-bit color to 180s). Ethernet connectivity might be another reason to hold off on replacing your desktop system, although there are third-party SCSI-based Ethernet solutions that will work fine on a PowerBook 180.

Then there is the 180's performance. It absolutely flies running everything from Microsoft Word to Claris CAD. Even that notorious MIPs hog, System 7, seems comfortable running on a 180. For Road Warriors, that extra speed will come in handy, especially once you expand memory to the 180's 14-Mbyte capacity and you start running ARA, a spreadsheet, a relational database, and Photoshop *all in memory, all at the same time.* Ah, bliss!

A Powerful Question

When we first heard about the PowerBook 180 we said, "there goes the battery budget!" The 170 already had problems making it three hours on a single battery, what with supporting an active-matrix screen and a 25MHz processor.

So, we figured that with video-out, the 16-grayscale active-matrix display, and the 33MHz CPU, we'd just about be able to boot up the 180 before we'd get the first "battery low" warning.

But, according to Apple, both the 160 and 180 use improved power conservation methods to hold the line on battery fatigue. Even so, we expect that if you drive an external monitor while running on batteries, you'll hit the battery's red line (well, at least the gray line) a lot quicker than three hours. As for the rest of it, we suggest you suspend your judgment until you've gotten about halfway through your first PowerBook battery's useful life, say about 200 charges, before proclaiming that there is little or no difference in battery life between a 140 and a 180.

Technical Readout: The PowerBook Duo 210/230

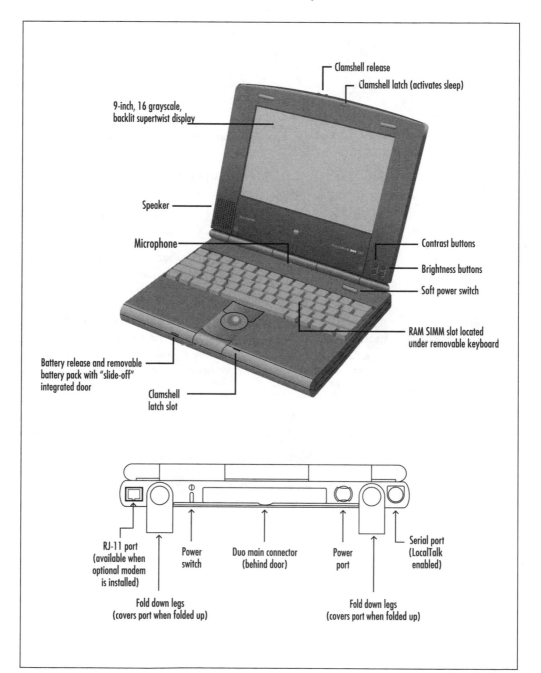

Clamshell release

Clamshell latch (activates sleep)

9-inch, 16 grayscale, backlit supertwist display

Speaker

Microphone

Contrast buttons

Brightness buttons

Soft power switch

RAM SIMM slot located under removable keyboard

Battery release and removable battery pack with "slide-off" integrated door

Clamshell latch slot

RJ-11 port (available when optional modem is installed)

Power switch

Duo main connector (behind door)

Power port

Serial port (LocalTalk enabled)

Fold down legs (covers port when folded up)

Fold down legs (covers port when folded up)

Dimensions	Weight	4.2 lb (1.9 kg), including battery
	Height	1.4 in. (3.6 cm)
	Width	10.9 in. (27.7 cm)
	Depth	8.5 in. (21.6 cm)

CPU

210: 25MHz 68030

230: 33MHz 68030

System software   System 7.1 and up.

Memory   4-Mbyte high-density dynamic RAM, expandable to 24 Mbytes.

Internal storage   *210:* One internal 2.5-inch hard disk drive. (Sold by Apple with an 80-Mbyte hard disk.)

230: One internal 2.5-inch hard disk drive. (Sold by Apple with either an 80- or 120-Mbyte hard disk.)

Built-in display   9-inch (229 mm) diagonal, backlit supertwist liquid crystal display. 640 by 400 pixels, 4-bit resolution.

Video-out   Available through Apple or third-party docks.

Battery   Apple NiHy battery delivers two to four hours of normal usage, up to five hours of typing when the backlighting is turned off and processor clock rate is "cranked-down" to 16Mhz. Requires two to three hours to fully recharge.

Ports   One RS-422 serial port (supports LocalTalk)

One 152-pin, 32-bit main expansion connector for interfacing with Apple or third-party docks.

One RJ-11 port when modem card is installed

Modem   Internal connector for optional modem card.

Electrical requirements   AC Adapter included, 85 to 270 volts, 47 to 63 Hz.

Known Gotchas

No documented problems at this time.

Predicted Reliability

Fair to good. The Duos are a completely new design for Apple and utilize a number of exotic components that can be found nowhere else in the Mac product line. For this reason, and because Apple has a history of having minor problems when it first employs new technologies, buyers should be warned that they could be doubling as Duo quality assurance testers if they are among the first to buy these tiny PowerBooks.

MacLite Up Your Life

What's thinner than an Economics textbook, faster than a Mac IIci, and able to slip inside an expansion dock with a single push? It's a notebook, it's a deskbook, it's a Duo!

See the Digital Nomad note below.

Apple claims that the Duo 210 and 230 give users the best of both desktop and mobile worlds. But, like a lot things that try to be both a dessert topping and a floorwax, the Duos may not fill either the desktop or mobile bill well enough to suit some users.

The Duo is a marvel of miniaturization and clever engineering. It's 35 percent lighter than a 180; it's almost an inch slimmer in every dimension (height, width, and depth); and it sports either a 33MHz (Duo 230) or 25MHz (Duo 210) CPU. The Duo CPU can support up to 24 Mbytes of RAM, ten more than a 180 or 160. Under its plastic skin is a magnesium subframe that gives it a sturdy feel and also helps dissipate the heat generated by all the technology that's crammed into its tiny chassis.

See the Intentional Tourist note below.

The Duos also offer the longest battery life of the PowerBook clan, with the latest in lightweight mobile power sources, a nickel hydride battery. In combination with Apple's EverWatch Battery Saver technology, NiHy batteries give the Duo an impressive runtime of over four hours off a single charge (more if you exercise other power-saving techniques). To go with its unique batteries is a unique AC adapter that is easier to adapt to foreign power sources than the supply that comes with the 160/180.

Don't worry, be happy.

Apple has always been a bit overly obsessed with secrecy. Protecting the various skunkworks and clandestine labs the Cupertino company has scattered around the world from nosy individuals (like this *Guide*'s authors) is the part-time preoccupation of many of its most loyal adherents. After all, Mac products start their lives on a piece of drafting vellum many years before they burst full-grown upon the world. In fact, the industrial design (the look and feel) of most Apple products is finished a year before the product ships—which gives engineers the boundaries within which they need to make the Mac magic happen. So, you must protect those trade secrets from competitors' prying eyes during the years it takes to bring a new design to market.

However, we do think Apple, at times, gets just a bit silly about the whole process. For example, take code names. We can understand giving a nifty new PowerBook project a convenient alias, just so you don't have to refer to the machine as "it." We can even understand giving the logic board inside the computer a code name. In the case of the Duo, the tiny logic board was code-named Metropolis, an appropriate handle for a board with such a dense population of silicon.

But code names for design philosophies? For instance, the "Best of Both Worlds" Duo slogan is more than somewhat clichéd marketing jazz, it's also what the Duo design code name, BOB W, stands for.

As Berke Breathed, author of the irreverent and inspired *Bloom County* comic strip, once noted, "It's never too late to have a happy childhood."

See the Mobile Commuter note below.

More subtle features that distinguish the Duo from other PowerBooks include an LED indicator that lights up on the Caps Lock key when it is engaged (a feature sorely missing from other PowerBook models), push-button adjustable contrast and brightness controls, and a power switch mounted on the top of the keyboard, inside the clamshell. The Duo also automatically goes to sleep whenever the clamshell is closed, a feature that some users may find inconvenient.

Getting a Charge out of Duos

Intentional Tourists and other long-haul PowerBook users will be happy to note that, along with better batteries, the Duo has a power supply they can really get a charge out of.

Instead of the hang-off-the-wall power box that comes with most PowerBooks, the Duo's adapter sits at the end of a six-foot-long cable and has a standard Mac II-compatible power cord port that plugs easily into an outlet. (It also has two pop-up arms which form a convenient place to wrap the adapter cable.) The Duo adapter ships with two power cord options, a short plug, which hangs the power supply off the outlet like the 160/180 AC adapter, and a long power cord.

The long cord is required when using the optional two-battery recharger that docks to the side of the Duo power supply. (Apple just loves docking!) We recommend that Duo users buy the dual recharger; it makes a convenient place to charge spare NiHy batteries, so you're always assured that your spares are fully powered.

International travelers will be especially pleased about the Duo power supply's power cord port. All they have to do to power up their PowerBook when traveling abroad is locate the nearest desktop Mac and borrow the power cable from the back of the computer. The Duo's charger will accept the cord, which will already come equipped with the correct plug for that country.

One sour note about the Duo power supply. Unlike all other PowerBooks, the Duo requires the use of a three-prong plug. Of course, you can get around this fairly easily with a common household plug adapter; but it's just one more thing you have to remember to put in your bag before you hit the road.

Clam on, Clam off

There's a good reason why your Duo goes to sleep every time you close it. If it didn't, and you accidentally inserted a running Duo into a Duo Dock, it would crash the PowerBook, wiping everything out of memory (including your RAM disk). *(continued)*

Clam on, Clam off (continued)

We can only think of one scenario where the Duo's auto-sleep might prove inconvenient: when you want to move from one location to another, and you don't want to waste time or battery power sleeping and then waking up the Duo. We wouldn't recommend walking around the house with an open clamshell (I've fallen and my PowerBook can't start up), so you'll just have put up with putting your Duo to sleep while you move.

As far as we've been able to determine there are only two ways to have a Duo running when its clamshell is closed. First, a closed Duo will run once it's installed inside your Duo Dock. You can also close the clamshell when the Duo is installed in a MiniDock without putting it to sleep.

The other way is to start up the Duo and then immediately close the clamshell, before the PowerBook has a chance to finish the startup sequence. However, we don't advocate using this auto-sleep workaround; we can't think of a situation where it would have any measurable benefit for Duo usage, and, as mentioned earlier, it could lead to unfortunate docking accidents.

See the Digital Nomad note below.

⬇

The Duos, the 160s, and the 180s all come with System 7.1 installed on the drive, including the PowerBook control panel that supports settings for overall battery conservation, the SCSI address your PowerBook uses when in SCSI Disk Mode, and the ability to automatically wake up at a predetermined date and time.

Some differences between the Duos and other PowerBooks that might not be so appealing include the smaller supertwist screen; a tiny, 19mm-diameter trackball (the 140/145/160/180 trackball is 30 mm in diameter); and a shrunken keyboard that could cramp less nimble fingers. Although the Duo's supertwist screen is rated by Apple as having a 120Hz refresh rate, twice the speed of the 140/145 display's 60 Hz, the Duo display seemed to run a little slower than the 140/145 supertwist screen. This could be the effect of redrawing the moving cursor in four bits, something the 1-bit 140/145 screen doesn't need to contend with.

Oddly, the 160's screen didn't seem to exhibit as much of a delay, although it too is a 120Hz, 16-grayscale supertwist display. Which only suggests that the "lag" we observed could be subjective (a nice way of saying a figment of our imaginations).

As for the trackball, which Apple ridiculously claims is designed to be rolled for over 50 miles before failure, it is the input device's smaller size that we found cumbersome. The trackball is mounted on ruby bearings, which give it a smooth roll and crisp, precise reactions. But when using the PowerBook in the "fast type" position (fingers on keys, thumb on trackball) we were, well, all thumbs. The trackball's recessed positon made us feel like we were reaching for the plug at the bottom of a small sink. However, someone not accustomed to the larger PowerBook trackball may not have the adjustment problems we experienced.

A Universal Power

The PowerBook control panel that adds the new battery conservation slide bar, which lets you adjust your PowerBook to trade application performance for longer battery life, will work with any PowerBook running System 7.0.1 or 7.1. When installed on a 170 or 145, users receive all the basic settings described here, including battery conservation, sleep when plugged in, processor cycling (which shuts your CPU down when you aren't using the computer), and processor speed controls. PowerBook 140 and 100 users won't be able to take advantage of automatic processor speed step-down, as their CPUs don't support a slower mode.

For Lack of a Port

The biggest difference between the Duo and other PowerBooks is what isn't there: most of the ports. Instead, Apple has placed on the back of the Duo a door that flips up to reveal a 152-pin, 32-bit data bus. (The door must be opened manually for docking; the Duo Dock will eject a Duo if it is inserted with a closed door.) This connector hooks the Duo into its dock, where the familiar Mac I/O ports and a lot of its capabilities actually reside. It's as if Apple took a chainsaw and cut the PowerBook 180 logic board in half, leaving the SCSI ports, serial ports, video-out, ADB, FPU, and floppy drive lying on the ground. The only way to reconnect this divided computer is to slide it into a Duo Dock or connect it to a MiniDock (or third-party dock). This Janus division could prove to be a serious annoyance for Road Warriors and Intentional Tourists alike.

Apple supplies three docking solutions for the Duos, the Duo Dock, MiniDock, and Floppy Adapter. In brief, the Duo Dock is a complete mini desktop Mac housing that provides NuBus slots, ports, video-out, and an optional hard drive; the MiniDock is a shelf-like device that the Duo sits in and that supplies ports and video. The Floppy Adapter is a small snap-on dongle that has an HDI-20 port for an external floppy drive, a single ADB port, and a security slot that, when in use, makes it impossible to remove the adapter from the Duo.

See the
Road Warrior
note below.

⬇

E-Machines also offers two docking solutions: the PowerLink DeskNet, physically identical to the MiniDock except that it also includes a built-in Ethernet transceiver; and the PowerLink Presentor, a dongle slightly larger than a Duo Floppy Adapter, which adds an HDI-20 port, stereo jack, power connector, and an 8-bit video-out port. Unlike the MiniDock, the Presentor doesn't block either of the Duo's rear ports when connected while adding the ability to use a TV set as an external display.

The Duo/dock combination makes the new PowerBooks best suited for Mobile Commuters, who generally use their PowerBooks only at home and in the office. The reduced weight of the Duo will make the trip back and forth that much less of a hassle, and the docks will make up for anything the Duo lacks (an ideal arrangement would be to have a Duo Dock at the office and a PowerLink Presentor at home).

If you will be on the move all day long, packing and unpacking a Duo, a MiniDock (or Floppy Adapter for those times you just need to quickly plug in a diskette), a floppy drive, and the power adapter may be cause for headaches. More annoying still is the fact that you'll have to shut down a Duo to switch docks.

As to the difference between a Duo 210 and 230, it's only a matter of processor clock rate; the 230 uses a 33MHz '030 while the 210 uses a 25MHz CPU. In all other respects they are identical. Overall, we'd recommend the 210 to Intentional Tourists who care only about weight and are willing to live with the inconvenience of a two-step dongle to connect to a floppy. Otherwise, we recommend the 230 for that extra hit of speed.

Designs for Better Living

After looking through this section, the reader may think that the authors are down on Duos. Nothing could be further from the truth.

Our problem with the Duos extends from Apple's effort to sell the portable as being all things to all people. For the reasons we've listed above it just doesn't quite make it as the omnibus PowerBook.

The Duo itself is a wonder of engineering. It proves that Apple still has what it takes to integrate hardware and software into a gestalt unmatched in the computer industry.

To appreciate this you just have to pick up a Duo. It doesn't feel like a subnotebook (what the PC world calls portables of the Duo's size and weight). It feels substantial, solid; its rubber bumpers give it a smooth, durable texture; its subtle curves give it a tactile interface that invites the user to handle the machine without fear for its fragile components.

Even the fluid motion of the Duo's clamshell as it opens and closes gives the user a sense of security. A lot of the credit for this solid feel has to go to the Duo's magnesium underwear; it is the only PowerBook that doesn't rely on a plastic shell for a large part of its structural integrity.

We think the Duo has a lot of potential. In the future we can see many good things coming in this small package, as Apple adds features like flashRAM slots, active-matrix screens, and perhaps more ports on the case. And the current Duo design, despite its shortcomings, will prove to be the ultimate PowerBook for people who are willing to make a few concessions.

After Careful Consideration

We can't stress this point strongly enough—Road Warriors should carefully evaluate the Duo before purchasing it. While it has some powerful capabilities, including the ability to support more RAM than a 180, dealing with docks and giving up ready access to ports and a floppy could prove more than you're willing to live with.

If you stayed away from the 100 in part because of the external floppy, keep in mind that with the Duo you now have two attachments, the Floppy Adapter *and* the floppy drive, that you must add before you can use a floppy diskette. You may also find prohibitive the expense of having a dock everywhere you regularly use your PowerBook. And if you're thinking about carrying both the MiniDock and floppy drive along with you when you travel remember this: The weight of the Duo and both dock and floppy drive will almost equal the weight of a 180.

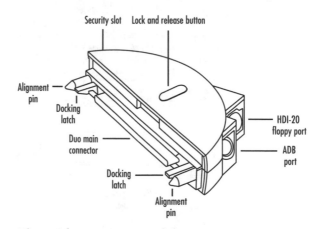

The Duo Floppy Adapter: two steps to diskettes

Technical Readout: The Duo Dock

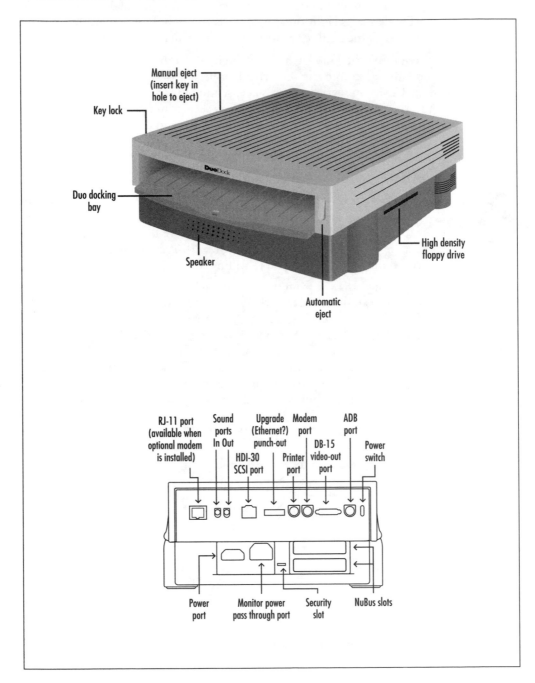

Manual eject
(insert key in
hole to eject)

Key lock

Duo docking
bay

Speaker

Automatic
eject

High density
floppy drive

RJ-11 port
(available when
optional modem
is installed)

Sound
ports
In Out

Upgrade
(Ethernet?)
punch-out

Modem
port

ADB
port

HDI-30
SCSI port

Printer
port

DB-15
video-out
port

Power
switch

Power
port

Monitor power
pass through port

Security
slot

NuBus slots

Dimensions	Weight	13.1 lb. (5.9 kg)
	Height	4.75 in. (12.1 cm)
	Width	12.25 in. (31.1 cm)
	Depth	16.25 in. (41.2 cm)

CPU
None
Socket for plug-in 68882 math coprocessor.

System software
System 7.1 and up.

Memory
None

Internal storage
One optional, internal 3.5-inch hard disk drive.
Internal 1.44-Mbyte floppy disk drive.

Video-out
Built-in support for 8-bit color on up to 16-inch monitors with 512-Kbyte VRAM. With the addition of a 512-Kbyte VRAM expansion SIMM (Single Inline Memory Module), up to 16-bit color can be displayed on a 16-inch monitor (see chart below). Also works with some VGA and SVGA monitors.

Slots
Two 15-watt standard NuBus slots.

Extra security
One security slot for use with third-party locking solutions.

A key switch locks and unlocks the Dock (see chart below).

Ports
One Apple Desktop Bus (ADB) port

Two RS-422 serial ports (printer port supports LocalTalk)

One HDI-30 SCSI port

One video-out port (8-bit or 16-bit color with expansion)

One microphone port (monaural)

One sound output port (monaural)

One RJ-11 pass-through port for Duo modem card when installed

Modem
The combination of an RJ-11 adapter card and the Duo's main connector hooks the Duo Dock to the optional, internal modem in the Duo. The Duo Dock's adapter card could be replaced with an alternate card for foreign phone plug types.

Electrical requirements
AC power only, 85 to 270 volts, 47 to 63 Hz.

Known Gotchas

No documented problems at this time.

Predicted Reliability

Good. Although the Duo Dock is a completely new design and concept for Apple, it is a fairly simple device compared to the Duo itself. The odds are that if anything goes wrong, it'll be the result of problems with the Duo and not the dock. The automatic Duo docking mechanism is rated for 5,000 insertions, or about ten years' worth of five-day work weeks.

Any Port in a Dock

What looks like an overgrown floppy drive, works like a front-loading VCR, and can turn a practically portless portable into a full-functioning desktop computer?

The Duo Dock uses a motorized system, called PowerLatch, to reel in the PowerBook Duo and give it access to the Dock's ports, floppy, optional hard drive, and an external monitor. (Half the fun of owning a Duo is inserting it into the Dock and watching it get sucked in. The other half is ejecting it and watching the Dock spit the Duo out.) All your networking cables, monitor cables, and other connections stay put; you don't have to wrestle with a handful of plugs every time you want to set up your portable.

The Duo supports intelligent docking, with the ability to remember all the network and printer connections you use when connected to your Dock. When you insert the Duo into the Dock, you're automatically connected to the server you had set up when you left the previous day; the Duo also sets up the monitor according to how you had it configured and will even restore virtual memory that relies on the Dock's optional internal disk drive. This is especially clever when you consider that the Duo has a Local-Talk-enabled serial port and could, in the interim, have been connected to network facilities elsewhere.

See the
Road Warrior
note below.

➡

What makes the Dock (which is useless until a Duo is inserted) special is that it gives Apple's tiniest portable access to two standard NuBus slots, the desktop Mac's main route to the expanded capabilities which no other PowerBook can utilize. These NuBus slots will let you access Ethernet cards, 24-bit accelerated video cards, and other NuBus expansion boards, which hang like silicon bats from under the Duo Dock's logic board.

Any Duo Dock owner will want to immediately invest in an FPU to plug into the Dock's math coprocessor socket. Road Warriors especially may want to buy an internal hard drive; we'd recommend investing in a large-capacity drive, available from any number of third-party vendors.

Apple would also tell you that the Duo Dock gives you access to a full-sized keyboard and mouse. While this is true, it also suggests that Power-Books, other than a Duo in a Duo Dock, can't use an external keyboard. They can, and the Duos can't unless they're docked—so you need a dock to level the playing field (the Dock's lower lip does leave a nice cranny in which you can nest an external keyboard).

The Dock will be a must-have for Duo-toting Mobile Commuters and Road Warriors. The convenience of having a VRAM-equipped, NuBus-expanded, and storage-loaded Duo Dock on your office desktop and at home is one of the best things about Duo ownership. Buying a $3,000 Duo and *two* $1,500 Docks is the ideal Duo scenario—tempting isn't it? Well, at least it sounds good to Apple sales types.

Reserved for Future Expansion?

Something interesting you'll notice on the back panel of your Duo Dock is a small rectangular plastic bezel. This plastic punch-out, not co-incidentally, is exactly the same shape as the Apple Ethernet connector on the Quadra 700, 900, and 950.

Not that we're starting any rumors, but we think it's highly unlikely Apple would have put space for an Ethernet connection on the back panel of the Duo Dock unless they were planning on using it on some future, Ethernet-savvy incarnation of the docking station. So, if you're a Duo owner dying for a Duo Dock with Ethernet, try getting by with a MiniDock and wait to see what happens. In the interim, your Mini-Dock can gain Ethernet connectivity with inexpensive SCSI adapters from Dayna Communications, Inc. or Asanté Technologies, Inc.

This could be considered caving into the FUD factor, but we thought we'd mention it anyway.

Mixing It Up in Duo Country

The Duo Dock introduces a whole new mix of possible conditions when Duos are inserted, docked, or ejected. The additional ability to lock up your Duo in its Dock with a key, can make for a confusing array of configurations. The following chart explains some of the results you get when locking and docking your Duo:

Action	*Duo Dock* Condition	*Duo* Condition and Result
Insert Duo	Dock unlocked.	*On:* Duo crashes and power shuts off.
		Asleep: Duo can be awakened from external keyboard; Dock will shutdown Duo or will eject Duo if shutdown isn't possible.
		Off: Normal. Use external keyboard to start up Duo.
Insert Duo	Dock locked.	*On, Asleep, or Off:* It is not possible to insert the Duo when Dock is locked.
Run Duo	Dock locked or unlocked.	*On:* Normal.
		Asleep: It is not possible to put a Duo to sleep when it is in a Duo Dock. *Off:* Not applicable.
Eject Duo (auto)	Dock unlocked.	*On:* Uses software shutdown to eject Duo automatically.
		Asleep: Can be ejected if the Duo was just inserted.
		Off: Press eject button to eject.
Eject Duo (manual**)	Dock unlocked.	*On:* Duo crashes and power shuts off.
		Asleep: Can be ejected if Duo was just inserted.
		Off: Normal.
Eject Duo (auto or manual)	Dock is locked.	*On, Asleep or Off:* Manual Eject is disabled when Dock is locked.

*   It is nearly impossible to insert a running Duo into the Dock because of the Duo's clamshell-sleep function. You must close the Duo to dock it, and doing so puts the Duo to sleep.

** You eject a Duo from the dock manually by inserting the key from the Duo lock into the slot on the left side, under the cowl. When the dock is locked, the eject hole is covered, disabling the eject function.

What you've got is what you'll see.

In addition to being able to use color NuBus video cards, the Duo Dock gives a Duo user access to 8-bit color video-out, as if they were using a 160 or 180.

One thing a Dock user can do that no other PowerBook owner can is add an additional 512 Kbyte VRAM card to the Dock's 512 Kbytes of built-in VRAM, increasing the color depth it can display on an external monitor.

The following chart shows you how much color on what size monitor that extra VRAM can buy:

Monitor Type	Dock with 512-Kbyte VRAM	Dock with 1-Mbyte VRAM
12-inch color	up to 8-bit color	up to 16-bit color
13- or 14-inch color	up to 8-bit color	up to 16-bit color
15-inch black and white	up to 4-bit grayscale	up to 8-bit grayscale
16- or 17-inch color	up to 8-bit color	up to 16-bit color
VGA	up to 8-bit color	up to 16-bit color
SVGA	up to 8-bit color	up to 16-bit color

Technical Readout: Duo MiniDock

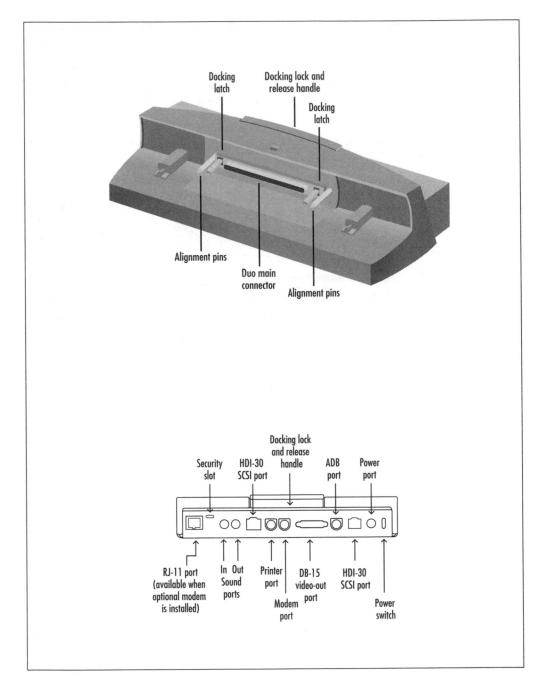

Dimensions	Weight	1.24 lb. (.56 kg)
	Height	2.1 in. (5.3 cm)
	Width	10.6 in. (26.9 cm)
	Depth	3.2 in. (8.1 cm)

CPU — None

System software — System 7.1 and up.

Memory — None

Internal storage — None

Video-out — Built-in support for 8-bit color on up to 16-inch monitors (512-Kbyte VRAM, not expandable). Also works with some VGA and SVGA monitors.

Battery — Draws power off of Duo battery when docked and not plugged into Duo AC power adapter.

Extra security — One security slot for use with third-party locking solutions.

Ports —
One Apple Desktop Bus (ADB) port

Two RS-422 serial ports (printer port supports LocalTalk)

One HDI-30 SCSI port

One HDI-20 floppy port

One video-out port (8-bit color)

One microphone port (monaural)

One sound output port (monaural)

One RJ-11 port when modem card is installed

Modem — The combination of an RJ-11 "pass-through" port and the Duo's main connector hooks the Duo Dock to the optional, internal modem in the Duo.

Electrical requirements — Uses Duo AC power adapter or Duo battery when docked, 85 to 270 volts, 47 to 63 Hz.

Known Gotchas

No documented problems at this time.

Predicted Reliability

Good. Although the MiniDock is a completely new design and concept for Apple, it is a fairly simple device compared to the Duo itself. The odds are that if anything goes wrong, it'll be the result of problems with the Duo and not the Dock. The manual MiniDock docking mechanism is rated for 5,000 insertions, or about ten years' worth of five-day work weeks.

A Shelf for Your PowerBook

Sometimes a Duo Dock is overkill, either because of its weight, size, or price tag. Mobile Commuters especially may question the value of having full-sized Duo stations at home and at the office. And Intentional Tourists won't fancy the idea of lugging along the boxy Duo Dock on a trip just to access a floppy drive or get color video-out.

For those users, Apple offers the Duo MiniDock, a collection of ports lined up on the back of a desktop bar. Although the snap-on MiniDock can run off of the Duo's battery as well as AC power, most users will probably find it a little too bulky to carry around with them on anything but long trips, where access to the MiniDock's array of ports is critical. Besides, it defeats the purpose of using Apple's lightest portable to carry an extra one-and-a-quarter-pound port dongle around with you all the time. If what you need on a trip is to attach a floppy drive (remember, the Duo comes with a serial port and modem port only), then the Duo Floppy Adapter might make more sense.

Because the Duo "sits" on a small shelf that protrudes from the front of the MiniDock, once the Duo is seated users won't be able to flip down the PowerBook's adjustable legs to access the RJ-11 or serial ports hidden behind them. Instead, those ports are supplied on the back of the MiniDock.

One nice feature of the MiniDock is that, unlike its full-sized sibling, a connected Duo can have its clamshell open or closed. With the clamshell open, you can use both the Duo's nine-inch screen and an external monitor at the same time, as though they were one large screen. Or you can have the Duo's screen mirror the images displayed by the MiniDock on the external monitor just like the 160 and 180. This is especially useful if you're using your Duo for presentations. The Duo with MiniDock attached can sit in front of you on the podium while the Dock's video-out sends the appropriate color image to the projector.

It's also possible to work on an external monitor with the Duo screen backlighting turned off. Although we haven't tested it, we assume that the power saved by having the Duo's backlighting turned off will at least partly make up for the power being expended to drive the MiniDock's VRAM. This way you could run a 16-inch color monitor, which will require its own power source anyway, while running the Duo on batteries—without significantly shortening the Duo's battery life. You can also close a Duo clamshell while docked without it going to sleep, even if a monitor isn't attached to the MiniDock—although we can't imagine why you'd want to. Also, don't forget that you'll need an external keyboard and mouse to get anything done with a closed Duo.

Don't disconnect the Duo from the MiniDock while the Duo is asleep or running, as this can cause the system to crash. Users can plug ADB devices, such as keyboards and floppy drives into the MiniDock while the Duo is asleep; the devices will work normally when the Duo wakes up. Devices added to the SCSI chain while the Duo sleeps won't be recognized until the computer is restarted.

The Power of Presentor

Another thing you may what to consider before buying a MiniDock is E-Machines' PowerLink Presentor. It offers the same video-out capabilities as the MiniDock, plus the ability to display output on a TV in 8-bit, convoluted (flicker-free) color. It also has a stereo output jack, HDI-20 floppy drive port, and an ADB port, and leaves the Duo's serial and RJ-11 ports accessible when connected. It weighs less than a pound.

About the only things you're giving up with Presentor is the HDI-30 SCSI connector and the MiniDock's second serial port. In return for those compromises you save about $90 over the MiniDock.

E-Machines also offers the PowerLink DeskNet, practically an identical twin of the MiniDock but with a built-in Ethernet transceiver, for which you'll pay a $100 premium.

Technical Readout: PowerBooks of the Tomorrow

This photo, courtesy of Tonic, a Palo Alto, California-based industrial design firm, shows many of the conceptual prototypes that led up to the first PowerBook. Tonic was founded by Gavin Ivester, an five-year veteran of Apple's Industrial Design group and one of the lead ID engineers on the PowerBook and PowerBook Duo projects.

FutureBook

Predicting the future can be a dangerous thing for your reputation. However, we can hardly consider this section a complete guide to the Power-Books of 1993 if we don't at least touch on some of the new tricks we think Apple will teach its PowerBooks over the next year. Just keep in mind that these predictions are coming to you from sometime in October, 1992 and without official Apple sanction.

More, More, More

A few predictions are easy. PowerBooks will get lighter, mostly through the aid of things like PCMCIA (Personal Computer Memory Card International Association) slots, which will allow the company to forego the additional weight of built-in hard drives. Instead, users will be able to install additional storage as credit card-size PCMCIA cards.

Another easy prediction is the addition of an active-matrix screen to the Duo 230, once active-matrix technology advances to where it's possible to build a screen thin enough for a Duo case.

Apple has openly stated that it will add a color PowerBook to the line-up, as soon as availability and price of color LCD screens improves. We expect to see a color PowerBook by summer, if not sooner. There are already some nice, but expensive color display upgrades available for your PowerBook from third parties like Newer Technology. If you can't wait for Apple to deliver a color portable, you should look into these displays.

Other, more mundane things we expect to see on PowerBooks include longer-lived batteries and reduced power demand in the PowerBooks themselves. We also expect to see Apple proliferate nickel hydride or other improved battery technology throughout the PowerBook family, as soon as possible.

Predictions of a more far-out flavor include PowerBooks that can use pens as optional input devices. Apple has publicly demonstrated Mac-based handwriting and gesture recognition. We're sure that once a Macintosh pen extension is available, PowerBook users won't have to wait long before enjoying the benefits of inputting notes directly into their portables.

Calling all PowerBooks.

Further out on the technology-prediction limb is wireless networking on PowerBooks. While adding Ethernet to both the Duo Dock and Mini-Dock in the next year qualifies as a definite "no-brainer" (after all, if E-Machines can do it, so can Apple), we think the possibilities of cellular and other wireless connections are much more exciting. Apple has petitioned the U.S. Government to set aside certain radio frequencies for use by computers. We feel it's highly unlikely the company would go to the trouble of dealing with the Washington bureaucracy unless they had something special in mind for those radio waves.

Cellular solutions for PowerBooks are on their way from farsighted third-party developers. Multi-port ARA servers are already shipping from Cayman Systems Incorporated and Shiva Corporation. We fully expect to see Apple join the game with competing products in both these areas, once the intrepid third parties have pioneered and developed ARA servers and the cellular marketplace. (You can always tell the pioneers in the Mac market by the rainbow-colored arrows in their backs.)

PocketMac

As to seeing Macs smaller than a subnotebook, a pocket-sized Mac would be a direct competitor for another Apple mobile computing device, Newton. Also, we're not sure the Mac interface would scale well to a 3-inch screen. While we're not saying you won't ever see a Mac you can fit in your jacket pocket, we feel pretty confident you won't see such a device in 1993.

SECTION II

START YOUR ENGINES

_____

I'm a System Folder junky. I admit that freely.

My first Mac, a Plus that had as many miles on it as my grandfather's Buick, is where my addiction started. It introduced me to the dark world of graphic interfacing. I should have known something that simple, that gave such pleasure when I used it, would come at a price. I know better now. I shouldn't have strayed from the pure discipline of the command line. But back then, well, I was a rebel. I was prime for the downward spiral into the sordid world that the Mac's bright, shining visual metaphor hid.

I started on System 5. A gentle high, not particularly dangerous, but it would lead to greater risks. First it was a mild case of upgrade fever. I rushed out to get the latest Apple had to offer, System 6 and 6.0.1 and 6.0.5, and so on. But, soon, I'd discovered the subtle magic of INIT files— the kids today call them extensions—which added functions from the useful to the stupid. I should have known when I spent hours parsing out sentences into their phonetic equivalent for the Talking Moose (I'd type in Moose phrases that I'd use to proposition my wife when she came into my office late at night), I was hooked.

My downward spiral into system dependency accelerated. And it was starting to cost me—time, money, and nearly my sanity. Apple is clever. It gets you started cheap—$1,000 for a Classic II. But as it takes more MIPs to get the same kick, the cost for your high also rises. As I moved up the ladder of addiction from the Plus to the SE/30 and a IIsi, my system folders grew with me. At its height, the System 7 System Folder on my IIsi, the mainstay of my *MacWEEK* office, was an 8-Mbyte monster. Things got so bad I started fantasizing about knocking over a bank so I could pay for the really heavy stuff: Quadras. Yes, Quadras, and not just one, but two, three, six, a dozen—and all of them with 100 Mbytes of memory! I could build my own network. And not just any network, but an Ethernet-based network!

I had extensions that gave me a hierarchical Apple menu, a collaborative scheduler that linked my personal calendar to those of the entire editorial staff, and control panels that regulated the colors on the screen like a well-made faucet—not too much color in exchange for more available RAM —as well as the crazed screen backgrounds I liked to compose. Not to mention more than 50 different preferences files and a score of fonts.

Then came the fateful day when I got my PowerBook 170. I had just returned from a trip with a loaner 170 under my arm and noted that a new intern had no desktop Mac. It was my opportunity to exercise the new corporate policy that said employees could have one computer, desktop Mac or PowerBook. I copied the few essential applications I needed to survive onto the 170's hard disk and hauled the IIsi over to the new kid's desk. Then I told the system administrator that I had given my computer away and needed to keep the 170. A couple of meetings later and a few forms later, I finagled my PowerBook.

There was a catch. With the limited hard disk and RAM capacity in the 170 (a system administrator's revenge for finaglers: he never doled out a RAM or hard disk upgrade), I needed to slash the fat from my System Folder.

Now, I live with a puny 5-Mbyte System Folder, and I stretch that to get all my memory's worth out of it! Withdrawal was a nightmare. There were times, late at night working on a story, when I'd imagine I heard the friendly, funky voice of the Moose saying "We've got to stop meeting like this!" Only to realize it was just another DT-induced hallucination.

I've repented my RAM and storage-hogging ways. But like all recovering system abusers, I'll never be cured. There's always temptation waiting around every corner and in every new, nifty utility that comes out. So, be warned, my friends. Be careful and conservative about what you add to your PowerBook. Remember, every extension takes up RAM and drive storage. Every font and control panel does as well. Plan your system and keep it under control, or before long you may find yourself without enough memory to run TeachText or store a ten-page report. Don't follow the path I chose.

Your bundle of joy is home! After extricating your PowerBook from its cardboard and plastic wrapping, cradling it in your arms for the first time, and filling out the registration card, you anxiously plug it in. The hard drive whirls to life and a dialog box appears: *Welcome to Macintosh.*

Now what? It's just a machine, and a pretty dumb one—Macs rely on application software to teach them most of their skills. A PowerBook can act as a calculator, a typewriter, a telephone, a network interface, an analytical assistant—you have only to add the appropriate software. But when you click on the hard drive icon, all you'll find is one application called TeachText. In fact, all you see besides TeachText is a 4.2-Mbyte System Folder and something called Read Me! (See Figure 1.)

As a budding digital nomad, you have miles to go before you sleep comfortably in the knowledge that this PowerBook is up to the task.

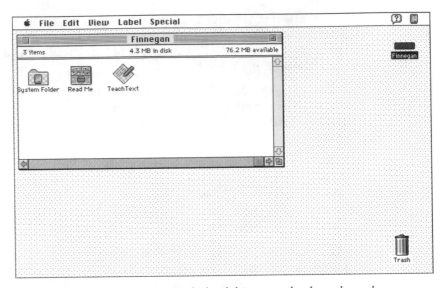

Figure 1.   Tabula Rasa—only the hard drive name has been changed.

PART

1

LAYING THE FOUNDATION OF YOUR MOBILE HABITAT

ToolBending

The Industrial and Pre-Industrial Age tools we know so well, like the hammer and sickle, came out of their packaging ready to work. You didn't need a book full of instructions on how to operate a hammer! When you pick up a sickle, its purpose is clear and the method intuitive, you just swing it. But the critics who scream about how difficult it is to use a computer are really missing the point: Adaptability is the hallmark of truly powerful tools. They can perform so many different tasks that, from the beginning, you must tailor an information device's capabilities to the jobs you need to do. Your PowerBook is like a telescope. Focus it on a single planet, and a world of information comes into view. But try to take in the whole universe, and everything becomes a blur.

Sun Tzu, the ancient Chinese warrior-philosopher and author of *The Art of War*, suggests that a successful campaign starts by studying the conditions in the field and then bringing only what you need to deal with those conditions. "User strategies" is the catchphrase of the modern Road Warrior, referring to the plans that let you deal with the limitations of your personal computer in the field, without having to drag along your entire office. For example, the first-generation PowerBooks can be somewhat stifling, because they don't support enough RAM to run multiple applications and mobile necessities like RAM disks. Users of these earlier systems must carefully balance their need to run a day planner, notetaker, and contact manager simultaneously against the need for battery savings (via a RAM disk) and their budgetary limits.

With the advent of the 160, 180, and Duos, there's plenty of RAM available in the shipping models (although there's still the nasty monetary pain, of purchasing the extra RAM). But the folks who buy into the second generation still need to keep a handle on power consumption, since these new machines can gulp down battery reserves faster than their older siblings.

Your strategy should be based on what you want to do with your Power-Book, its physical limits—such as the RAM budget and available storage—and the requirements of the software you need to accomplish your goals. Only then can you sculpt your operating system and stored applications to meet those needs.

Take a moment to review the digital nomad user taxonomy in the Manifesto before reading the next section, where we discuss how to shape System 7.0.1 and System 7.1 to particular tasks. Compare the work you need to do with the workstyle descriptions to decide which of the recommended RAM and operating system configurations, located at the end of this chapter you want to follow.

Remember, there are no hard and fast rules. The PowerBook would be a miserable tool if it didn't allow for an expression of individuality.

Jumping back into the tool metaphor with both feet (no one can murder a metaphor like your humble authors): It's just like buying a hammer. After all, you don't buy a hammer when the job calls for a screwdriver. A PowerBook can be a hammer or a screwdriver, it merely depends on how you configure it.

No PowerBook is an island.

Even if you can afford to buy the best tools, you've got to have a place to hang them (we especially like shopping in the "He-Men with Small Brains Who Think $50 is a Good Price for a Hammer, Especially If It's Got a Red Rubber Handle" section in Sears). With PowerBooks, the challenge is molding the corporate infrastructure to support your roaming users, whether they be Road Warriors, Mobile Commuters, or Intentional Tourists. Network connections, security, and applications should be selected to facilitate easy connections without compromising the security of critical data. At the same time, the software products that PowerBook users rely on can't act like only half-applications when they are on the road.

The second part in this section, *Setting Sail on the Network Clipper*, is an extended discussion of System 7 file-sharing. Mobile Commuters and Road Warriors especially will want to study this section and then spend some time deciding how to configure their PowerBooks for the office. Using your PowerBook in SCSI Disk Mode—attaching it to a desktop Macintosh and treating it like an external hard disk—does give you very fast access to your files, but that dismisses the possibilities born of connecting two full-functioning computers.

File-sharing is built into the operating system, but the PowerBook utilizes special programs stored in the Apple menu, control panels, and Extensions folders of your System Folder to control access to files stored on your hard disk. For clarity's sake, we will deal with the lot of them in the next chapter. Based on our experience, most readers will want to use file-sharing in their day-to-day work, and the "Digital Nomad System Rundowns" suggestions at the end of this chapter reflect that assumption. All the file-sharing extensions and control panels taken together only account for about 325 Kbytes of disk storage and require about 214 Kbytes of RAM to operate when you have a few clients logged onto your PowerBook. Your RAM budget will climb as you share data with more of your coworkers. So, unless you're absolutely sure you don't want access to this capability, at the

See the
Road Warrior
note below.

↓

very minimum we'd recommend you store the files in a special folder outside your System Folder where they won't load into memory but will still be on your hard disk should you need them.

Beware, you'll want to refer to both this chapter and the next when paring down your own system!

If your base of operations is a home office, you also can make a few special preparations to facilitate your new portable computer. It could involve adding a simple network connection to your home computer, or if you'll want to dial home to grab important files, you can stretch Apple's file-sharing capabilities across thousands of miles of telephone cable.

After you've finished configuring your PowerBook for optimal performance using the concepts laid out in this chapter, turn to the third chapter in this section, *A Port for Every Road Warrior*, to learn the secrets of the perfect office for a mobile computer user.

Careful with that ax, Eugene!

Okay, we know you Road Warriors just aren't going to be able to resist the temptation and will probably hack around with your system the first chance you get. So, as long as you're going to be swapping extensions as often as you swap floppies, here are a couple of suggestions for safe system manipulation. Regardless of the method you choose, these changes won't take effect until you restart the PowerBook.

First, decide if you can spare the disk space for all your extensions, control panels, fonts, and Apple menu items. (Your operating system refers to Apple menu items as desk accessories (DAs), a holdover from pre-System 7 days when programs had to be in a special format to be installed in the Apple menu). In the era of System 7, you can drop just about anything into the Apple Menu Items Folder, so that you can launch an application, document, or desk accessory by selecting its name in the Apple menu. All the files you'll need shouldn't require much more than a couple of megabytes of disk storage, which you should be able to spare, especially if you've purchased one of the newer PowerBooks with 80- or 120-Mbyte drives. If you absolutely can't spare the space, follow the instructions below; but instead of putting the files in folders on your desktop, put them on floppy diskettes. To restore the files you want, just insert the floppy. To remove the files, put them in the trash can and choose *Empty Trash* from the Finder's Special menu.

(continued)

Careful with that ax, Eugene! (continued)

Whether you have storage to spare or not, no PowerBook user has RAM to waste. So, to free up some memory, you'll probably want to yank out extensions you're not using.

There are two ways to do this. One, you can create a series of folders on your desktop where you store all the files necessary for each function you're removing. For instance, you can make a file-sharing folder where you store the files needed to make the networking connection fly. Having a special folder for each function makes it much easier to restore those files later. Simply open the folder, do a Select All (choose *Select All* from the Edit menu), and drag the files to your System Folder. You'll be rewarded with a dialog box asking permission to put the files where they belong. If the selection contained different kinds of files (control panels and extensions, for example), a second message will display when you click *OK* in the first dialog box (see Figure 2) and tell you what System 7 put where.

Of course, if you don't want the hassle of having to locate and remove all those files every time you want to take them out of memory, you can use a utility like Startup Manager, which comes with Now Software's Now Utilities. You can use this control panel to selectively turn on or turn off control panels and extensions without having to change their location.

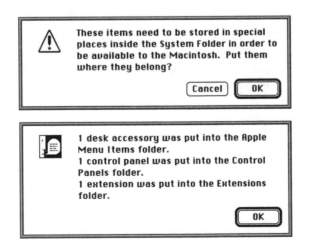

Figure 2. **Restoring Files**   *First your Mac will ask permission to move your System Folder files to their appropriate places, and then it will tell you what it did with them.*

New Beginnings: Tuning Up Your PowerBook

It may seem logical that the first step in configuring a PowerBook is to load on all your favorite programs. Wrong.

There's a lot of optimizing you can do that will:

- Save you 1.6 Mbytes or more of storage space on your hard disk
- Scoop out about 400 Kbytes' worth of extra RAM for your applications
- Improve the overall performance of your PowerBook.

Perhaps you've been using your PowerBook for some time, and there are a dozen or more applications and hundreds of documents stored on your hard drive. If you didn't start with these optimization strategies, now may be a good time to back up your hard drive and start over.

A Tale of Two Systems

Apple's Macintosh operating system has matured over many years, honed in version after version, into the premier environment for personal productivity. The latest upgrade, System 7.1, is the first "world-ready" operating system from Apple, which means the underlying code is able to support "double-byte" character sets needed for many foreign languages. The long and the short of world-readiness comes down to this: You can load more than one language in your PowerBook and toggle back and forth between them at will. The screen characteristics stay the same, but menus and dialog boxes switch automatically.

The price of flexibility when world-ready modules are loaded is System 7.1's extra-large RAM footprint, which swallows about 200 Kbytes more memory than System 7.0.1.

Apple released two upgrades, or "Tuners" (which fixed the disappearing folders problem described on page 54, before rolling out System 7.1. It also reversed itself on a longstanding tradition of not requiring users to pay for the Mac OS. Unlike earlier versions, System 7.1 cannot be copied and distributed freely by either Apple dealers or Macintosh user groups. So, for the first time you have very limited rights to use the system diskettes that accompany your PowerBook. For instance, you are not supposed to install System 7.1 on your desktop Macs without first paying for the right to do so.

This should not concern you as an individual user, because recently enacted Federal legislation that felonized software piracy applies only to persons who make ten copies of software, with a total retail value of $2,500 or more. But, if you are a network administrator or user group member who wants to distribute System 7.1 to your coworkers or cohorts, be warned.

Depending upon whether your PowerBook was manufactured before or after October 19, 1992, you'll get System 7.0.1 with the Tune-Up installed, or you'll receive System 7.1.

Step One—Erase *everything*

If you receive your PowerBook with System 7.0.1 or System 7.1 installed, you can restore up to six percent of your drive's total storage capacity that was lost when the hard drive was formatted at the factory. Use the Apple HD SC Setup utility, which is on the Disk Tools diskette included with your system software. Be careful—if you've already been using your PowerBook for a while, back up your drive before continuing, because this process will erase all the files on the disk!

See the
Digital Nomad
note below.

Follow these step-by-step instructions:

1. Reboot (restart) your PowerBook with the Disk Tools floppy in the PowerBook's diskette drive.

2. Launch Apple HD SC Setup, select your hard disk, and click the Partition button. A second window with a scrollable menu will appear. Select the Custom button.

3. You'll see a rectangular window divided into three parts: an area called Mac Driver, a large white area labeled with your hard drive's name that shows how much space you currently have to store files in, and a small gray area at the bottom of the rectangle (see Figure 3). That gray area is what you want to reclaim.

   Select the area labeled with your hard drive's name and click the Remove button. When you receive a warning that the data in the partition will be destroyed (you have backed up your disk, haven't you?), click *OK.*

4. Now, most of the rectangle will be gray. Point the cursor just beneath the Mac Driver area and click, dragging downward to the bottom of the rectangle. When you reach the bottom, let go of the mouse button; a new dialog box will appear. Select *Macintosh Volume* and click *OK.* The original rectangle reappears without that lost gray space at the bottom (see Figure 4).

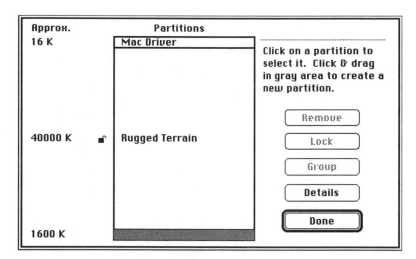

Figure 3. The Macintosh Partition and Driver in Apple HD SC Setup

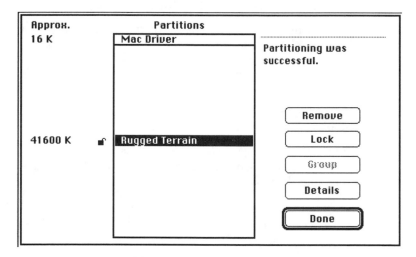

Figure 4. A successful partition adds 1.6 Mbytes of storage to a 40-Mbyte hard drive.

Now, instead of 38.3 Mbytes of disk space, there is 39.9 Mbytes' worth of storage—enough extra acreage to homestead a small farm on the electronic frontier.

5. Click *Done.* In the last dialog, click *Quit.*

More Space, More Waste

With the new PowerBooks come larger drives and more formatted disk space left inaccessible for no apparent reason. The production prototypes Apple supplied us for testing, a 180 and a Duo 230, had 80-Mbyte and 120-Mbyte hard drives, respectively. We checked both of these drives with the Apple HD SC Setup utility and found a whopping 8.4 Mbytes of unused drive space on the largest drive!

Here's the disk space that digital nomads can recover using the procedure outlined above (these leftovers will vary from disk to disk — they do on desktop Macs, anyway):

Drive Capacity	Wasted Space
40 Mbytes	1.6 Mbytes
80 Mbytes	3.9 Mbytes
120 Mbytes	8.4 Mbytes

Amazing, isn't it? We have yet to get an credible explanation from Apple as to why they do this.

The Starting Lineup

Now that the storage reclamation work is done, it's time to begin construction of your electronic homestead. Every computer needs an operating system, and that's where you'll start.

System software is the foundation for everything your PowerBook will do; it's made up of dozens of files that handle different tasks, like displaying fonts, playing sounds, printing a document, and looking out over a network to let you select file servers and printers. These files are organized by their function inside folders within the System Folder (see below for detailed descriptions of your system's resources). There are some minor differences in the way System 7.0.1 and 7.1 are organized, but you can expect to find that your System Folder fills between 3.1 and 3.6 Mbytes of space on the hard disk.

You don't need all the files that arrive installed on a PowerBook for every task, and some you won't need at all. By carving away deadbeat files it is possible to cut the amount of RAM the operating system requires by one-third or more.

Below, we'll go over the list in more detail to help identify the files you can trash and the basics of how to use the ones you'll want to keep. But to start, refer to Figure 5 below to see what you get with preinstalled systems and the size of each file by system version. These are, by the way, the true sizes of the files, and they may appear differently on different-sized hard disks. For instance, the Alarm Clock takes up 20 Kbytes on a 300-Mbyte disk.

Figure 5. Your Crowded System Folder

	System 7.0.1	System 7.1
Apple Menu Items Folder		
Alarm Clock	11 Kbytes	17 Kbytes
Battery	14 Kbytes	14 Kbytes
Calculator	7 Kbytes	7 Kbytes
Chooser	22 Kbytes	29 Kbytes
Control Panels alias	1 Kbyte	1 Kbyte
Key Caps	12 Kbytes	12 Kbytes
Note Pad	9 Kbytes	9 Kbytes
Puzzle	14 Kbytes	14 Kbytes
Scrapbook	10 Kbytes	10 Kbytes
Control Panels Folder		
Color	11 Kbytes	12 Kbytes
Date and Time	N/A	35 Kbytes
Easy Access	12 Kbytes	12 Kbytes
File-Sharing Monitor	4 Kbytes	4 Kbytes
General Controls	16 Kbytes	22 Kbytes
Keyboard	8 Kbytes	8 Kbytes
Labels	3 Kbytes	3 Kbytes
Map	28 Kbytes	28 Kbytes
Memory	38 Kbytes	39 Kbytes
Monitors	40 Kbytes	40 Kbytes
Mouse	8 Kbytes	9 Kbytes

(continued)

(continued)	System 7.0.1	System 7.1
Control Panels Folder (continued)		
Network	13 Kbytes	13 Kbytes
Numbers	N/A	16 Kbytes
Portable	27 Kbytes	N/A
PowerBook	N/A	63 Kbytes
PowerBook Display	N/A	34 Kbytes
Sharing Setup	4 Kbytes	4 Kbytes
Sound	17 Kbytes	17 Kbytes
Startup Disk	5 Kbytes	5 Kbytes
Users and Groups	4 Kbytes	4 Kbytes
Views	3 Kbytes	3 Kbytes
Extensions Folder		
AppleShare	72 Kbytes	75 Kbytes
AppleTalk ImageWriter	51 Kbytes	51 Kbytes
Caps Lock	5 Kbytes	5 Kbytes
DAL	84 Kbytes	N/A
EtherTalk Phase 2	10 Kbytes	10 Kbytes
File-Sharing Extension	167 Kbytes	170 Kbytes
Finder Help	36 Kbytes	36 Kbytes
ImageWriter	46 Kbytes	46 Kbytes
LaserWriter	219 Kbytes	219 Kbytes
LQ AppleTalkImage	73 Kbytes	73 Kbytes
LQ ImageWriter	65 Kbytes	65 Kbytes
Network Extension	92 Kbytes	96 Kbytes
Personal LaserWriter SC	72 Kbytes	72 Kbytes
Personal LaserWriter LS	92 Kbytes	92 Kbytes
Print Monitor	58 Kbytes	63 Kbytes
StyleWriter	74 Kbytes	74 Kbytes
QuickTime	N/A	442 Kbytes

(continued)

(continued)	System 7.0.1	System 7.1
Fonts Folder		
	N/A	1,231 Kbytes (includes font files)
System Folder		
Finder	355 Kbytes	369 Kbytes
*Scrapbook	29 Kbytes	29 Kbytes
*System Suitcase	1,677 Kbytes	**1,062 Kbytes
Preferences Folder		
DAL Preferences	14 Kbytes	N/A
Finder Preferences	1 Kbytes	2 Kbytes
Users and Groups Data File	8 Kbytes	9 Kbytes
Totals	**3,641 Kbytes**	**4,775 Kbytes**

N/A means the file in questions doesn't come standard with that version of System 7.

* These numbers reflect the data stored on our test system. Your results may vary with these files and folders, as they can contain different data on different systems. For example, you may have different fonts in your Fonts folder or different graphics in your Scrapbook than we had in ours.

** The reason the System Suitcase got smaller with System 7.1 is that the fonts, which were stored in this file in System 7.0.1, are stored in the Fonts folder in System 7.1.

Apple Menu Items

System 7 lets you place a battery of applications and documents at the ready under the Apple icon in the top lefthand corner of the Finder. The applications you use most often can be placed within easy reach when you drag the file or an alias of the file into the Apple menu items folder in the System Folder. While the System Folder swells, it doesn't increase the amount of RAM required to run the operating system.

The question is, do you need all the files Apple puts in Apple Menu Items Folder? The answer is no.

The basic set, which is installed with Systems 7.0.1 and 7.1, is described below.

Alarm Clock

It does just what it sounds like it does—wakes you up at a preset time. You can easily replace this with the much more useful SuperClock! (see "Digital AAA" below).

Battery

This gives you an eight-level indicator showing how much power you have remaining in your battery. It also includes a "mail-flag" that extends the dialog box to display a sleep button. It can be used on 170s to decrease the processor's clockrate to 16 MHz. Battery can also be replaced by Super-Clock! on most PowerBooks (see "Digital AAA" below).

The Battery DA will remember where you leave it on the screen. We recommend positioning it with the mail flag up (sleep button hidden) at the bottom of your screen next to the trash, where it'll be visible but tucked safely out of the way. It will appear in that location every time you call it up, until you move it to a new location (see Figure 14).

Figure 6. The Battery Display

Calculator

The Calculator offers simple addition, subtraction, multiplication, and division. As an alternative, we would suggest you take a look at freeware programs like Calculator +, Number Crunch, and Calculator II, all of which can be found online. You might also check out MMCalc from MicroMath Scientific Software of Salt Lake City, a scientific calculator for the engineer in you. Otherwise, you could probably live without a calculator; the PowerBook's keyboard makes a lousy calculator keypad substitute anyway.

Chooser

The Chooser is the Apple interface to network services (see Section II, Part 2, *Setting Sail on the Network Clipper*).

Control Panels Alias

Aliases are software pointers to files and folders stored elsewhere on your hard disk. By installing an alias for the Control Panel folder in the Apple menu folder, Apple avoided crowding all the control panels into the Apple menu folder.

Key Caps

This utility lets users find the key combinations for symbols such as ™ and diacritical marks like the é used in French.

Note Pad

This is an electronic scratchpad. This program can be replaced by a number of more useful shareware and freeware programs or by Spiral (see "Digital AAA" below).

Puzzle

This game has graced the Apple menu since the first 128K Mac rolled out the door. You can make your own puzzles by pasting in images from the clipboard. Puzzle is fun, for a few minutes, but otherwise it can be disposed of at no expense to your productivity.

Scrapbook

This utility lets users store often-used text and graphics, like letterheads, which can be copied or cut from the Scrapbook and then pasted into documents.

Some users may also want to scrap the Scrapbook. It's a good place to store graphics, like templates for your faxes. However, the authors' experience has been that there's really no need to keep Scrapbook around, if you've got fax coversheets and letterhead installed elsewhere on the hard drive.

Digital AAA—Roadside Assistance Kit PowerBook Tuners

Replace Alarm Clock and Battery with SuperClock!

SuperClock! is a freeware control panel, authored by Steve Christensen and included on the Roadside Assistance Kit accompanying this book. It adds a digital 12- or 24-hour clock, an alarm clock, and a battery charge indicator to the menu bar (it displays in all applications and in the Finder). It can also show when the PowerBook is plugged in. By holding down Control ("ctrl" on the PowerBook keyboard) and clicking on the battery icon in the menu bar from within any program, you can put your Power-Book to sleep with this useful utility.

Power Saver, the option that let users toggle the 170 CPU between its full 25MHz clock speed and a power-parsimonious 16MHz rate, is incorporated into the Battery DA in System 7.0.1. With the release of System 7.1, the Power Saver control has been pulled into the new PowerBook control panel, which integrates a broad selection of settings that, with a single slider, lets users trade power savings for performance.

The Battery DA as it survives in System 7.1 has very little to do—it's more like Floyd the barber on the Andy Griffith Show—just sitting out front like a relic of days gone by. You might want to keep it around for old times sake, but, *if you are using System 7.1,* the authors suggest you dump Battery and substitute SuperClock! You'll probably find, as we did, that the indicator icon that appears in the menu bar is more convenient than opening the Battery DA. It displays the battery level as a diminishing portion of the icon, as well as showing when your battery is charging. It doesn't have as many gradations as Battery does, so if having a finer readout is important to you, you may want to keep Battery around. (There's also a QuicKey sequence, included with QuicKeys for Nomads on the Roadside disk, that will open Battery any time you need it.)

A commercial alternative to the Battery DA is available in the Connectix PowerBook Utilities (look for it by the name CPU) from Connectix Corp. Like SuperClock!, it adds a battery charge monitor to the menu bar, but it also displays the percentage of a full charge remaining in the battery.

Scratch that Note Pad.

TechWorks' Spiral note-taking application provides a lot more space for notes than Apple's Note Pad, and it's a great battery saver because it hardly ever uses the hard disk. A special version of Spiral, that only lets you open the Spiral documentation file and the Nomad Notes file, comes on the Roadside disk. Digital nomads can easily replace Apple's pipsqueak Note

Pad DA with this robust application by putting the Nomad Notes file into the Apple Menu Items Folder. Or, if you want to locate the Notes file elsewhere, you can create an alias of the file to store in the Apple Menu Items Folder.

Spiral does take a lot more disk space and RAM than Note Pad. But, frankly, the Note Pad DA is so underpowered it's hardly worth bothering with. Of course, it only takes up 9 Kbytes, so losing it will save more space in the Apple menu than on your drive.

A Not-so-Secret Agent

The Roadside kit also comes with a time-locked demo of an excellent calendar and day planner program called AgentDA. The demo is fully functional but will only run for 90-days from the day you first install and start it up.

AgentDA will let you schedule and take notes about an unlimited number of appointments. The program's easy-to-configure interface can display from one to seven days in a week and up to five weeks at a time. Buttons on the program's window make changing the view of your appointments as easy as pointing and clicking.

AgentDA can also alert you to upcoming appointments. The program doesn't need to be running for it to send out the appointment-pending message.

We recommend keeping AgentDA in the Apple Menu Items Folder for quick access. You can set your personal calendar as the default whenever you start up the program.

Let your pointer do the walking.

Another application that comes with the *Guide* is Dynodex 2.0.7. This electronic Rolodex lets you store names, numbers, addresses, and notes for all your contacts. You can sort and search by any field in a record and can add frequent selections (like the list of all the good restaurants in town) to a menu.

Dynodex is really fast, able flip through a 1,000 records in a matter of seconds, and it almost never needs to access the hard drive except to save a record. That's because it loads the entire file into RAM. Even so, version 2.0.7 is very memory-frugal and can easily hold 750 records in a megabyte of memory.

You'll probably want to keep an alias of your primary contact database in the Apple Menu Items Folder for quick access, leaving the main file in a more convenient location for reconciliation. Seeing as you'll probably be making changes to this file often, keeping the most current version of your database straight with older versions will be critical.

Synchro-nicity

As we said, making sure that the version of a file you're using is the most current incarnation of that file can become a logistical nightmare. Intentional Tourists and Mobile Commuters especially need to guarantee that a data file they've got on their portable is as up to date as a file by the same name left behind on their office Mac.

There are two ways to keep file versions straight. There's the old-fashioned method where you, the human, try to remember which copy of a file on what drive you updated last. Once you've figured that out, you get to copy the file to all the other places you keep it, overwriting older versions of the document.

A much better way is to use Synchro, a file reconciliation program that comes on your Roadside disk. Synchro, which was written by No Hands Software of Palo Alto, California, will automatically reconcile two versions of a file any time the folders they are in are available. For example, if you use file-sharing to connect your PowerBook to your desktop Mac, all you need to do is start Synchro and it will automatically update all folder pairs you've previously set up for reconciliation.

Because Synchro lets users match folder pairs by simply dragging them to the program's icon in the Finder, it's a good idea to put Synchro on the desktop under your PowerBook's internal drive icon. We recommend creating a Synchro alias to place in the Apple Menu Items Folder so you can easily call up the program whenever you want to reconcile files. Synchro does take up about 400 Kbytes of RAM, so you probably don't want the program running in memory until you need it.

See Section V, Part 1, *The Roadside Assistance Guide*, for more information on SuperClock!, Spiral, AgentDA, Dynodex, and Synchro. For more information on file reconciliation, see Section III, Part 3, *The Difference Engine*.

Control Panels

Like the dashboard in a superbly engineered sports car, the controls of a PowerBook are within easy reach. Just click on the Apple icon at the upper left of your PowerBook's screen and select the Control Panels folder. If you use Now Software's NowMenus, you can get at control panels directly from the Apple menu without having to go to the Control Panels folder first.

Apple includes many control panels that are vital to PowerBook users. However, there are several others installed with the Mac OS that are unnecessary to portable operation and can be disposed of with ease.

Color

Color is a misnomer for this control panel, since it doesn't give you control over the number of colors displayed on your Mac. Rather, it allows you to set the color of highlighted text and the borders of active windows in the Finder.

Unless you have video-out capabilities, you can toss Color on Day One. If you add an external monitor later, and want to add color to your windows, pop the Tidbits diskette included with your system software into your PowerBook and drag the Color control panel back into your System Folder.

Even if you do have an external monitor attached to your PowerBook, unless you're absolutely rabid about customizing the look of every aspect of your Mac, we'd say you should lose this one.

Date & Time

This is a System 7.1-specific panel that controls the format of dates as presented by applications running on top of different language modules. If you're a monoglot with no particular interest in using Continental date conventions, you can erase Date & Time.

General Controls

It looks like this in System 7.1:

When you want to adjust the environment in your car, you reach for the dashboard, but with a Mac you click General Controls (see Figure 7). Tired of a 12-hour clock and hankering for military time? General Controls lets you make the switch by clicking a radio button—just as simple as turning on the air conditioning. Here's where you can set the time or date, speed up the blinking of the Insertion Point cursor, or change the desktop pattern from gray to black, white, or polka-dot. System 7.1 does come with some new patterns that look particularly nice on the 180's 16-grayscale screen. The combination of the 180's cobalt blue active-matrix and certain patterns makes for a desktop that look like it was forged from pure platinum.

Every digital nomad should keep this control panel.

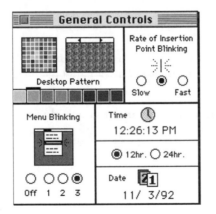

Figure 7. ***General Controls*** *The PowerBook Dashboard*

Easy Access

This is a control panel that, unless you are disabled and need special key and mouse commands to control your PowerBook, you'll want to drag into the trash.

However, keyboard freaks may want to hang onto Easy Access. It does let you manipulate menus from the keyboard, which slashes your mousing time.

Keyboard

System 7.1 lets you use Keyboard to deal with different language modules, if you choose to run more than one character set on your PowerBook. This is the mechanism that lets you switch the input from the keyboard when you change language modules. The WorldScript extensions also add a menu to the menu bar, between the Help and Application menus, that lets you toggle between languages.

System 7.0.1 users with a hankering for fast key repeats (we can't think why you might need a thousand *k*s inserted in a document, unless you compose deconstructionist poetry for fun), might want to keep this control panel. But if you use one language and don't want fast key repeats, Keyboard can go out with your spring cleaning.

Labels

Some people need a reminder that indicates the importance of a particular file. The labeling utility in the Finder lets you change the color of a file according to its importance, a capability that requires the video-out available in third-party adapters and second-generation PowerBooks. If you don't have a color screen, Labels can be pretty lame.

Labels can be of use on a black-and-white screen. The Mac's Find File function (accessible through the Command+F key combination in the Finder) can search by labels. Or, you can configure your Finder windows to display files with a text-based label. But, this is an organizational philosophy that defies our understanding—if the authors came across a file marked "Essential" six months after the subject went cold, we think we'd be confused or embarrassed, not more organized. We say Labels should go out with the trash.

Map

A cool tool, if you need to know the longitude, latitude, and time zone of cities around the world. Perhaps Map will be a necessity when PowerBook users attach Global Positioning Service transceivers to their computers, but until then, this control panel is a candidate for the trash.

Mouse

If you can't keep up with your cursor, with the Mouse control panel you can adjust how quickly the cursor moves when you roll the trackball. Happy with how fast the cursor moves? Then you'll be safe trashing Mouse. The system will simply remember the last Mouse settings you selected.

Numbers

Here's another System 7.1 control panel that prepares your applications to conform to the local language. Numbers could be very useful if you switch currencies while building spreadsheets. But there's a limitation: output is converted to, say, French francs, when you change numbers; switch it back to U.S. dollars, and those francs are transformed into the same number of greenbacks as you had francs. Believe us, your PowerBook isn't clever enough to convert currencies to reflect their relative values.

Sound

See the Road Warrior note below.

PowerBooks ship with several voices that can act as a beep sound, including the simple beep, a droplet, and the infamous "wild eep" preferred by discerning nomads everywhere (it really gets people's attention in the airport lounge). The Sound control panel lets you choose which voice will speak for your PowerBook and, in those CPUs with a built-in microphone (the 160, 180, and Duos), you can record new sounds. Speaker volume is also controlled here. If you can settle for the simple beep sound, this control panel can go, too

---

Awstala Veesta, Baby!

Another thing we're sure the "tweakers" among our readers won't be able to resist playing with is beep sounds. Beep sounds must be loaded into memory for your PowerBook to access them. Using a shareware program like SoundMaster, you can attach beeps to a number of different system events (like having Ah-node S. say "I'll be back" whenever you shut down your computer). This can be entertaining, for short periods of time. But after a while the beeps really can become a waste of space, because sounds consume a lot of RAM.   *(continued)*

Awstala Veesta, Baby! (continued)

One of the authors thought it would be cute to give his PowerBook a Valley Girl voice. Andy particularly enjoyed people's expressions when his 140 would cry out, with that plaintiff and familiar accent, "Like, beep, okay?" in public places.

While this may sound clever (certainly Andy thought it was), long beep sounds are not always a great idea. Certain programs use the Mac's beep as an alarm by playing it over and over again. One such program hit the panic button on the author's 140, and treating him to several minutes of "Like-Like-Like-Like-Like-Like" while he tried to figure out how to shut the damn thing up. It sounded like a deranged Max Headroom had taken possession of his PowerBook.

Our advice is, save a couple of hundred kilobytes of RAM and forego the cute sound effects.

 Startup Disk

Macs with multiple hard disks can benefit from having Startup Disk, which lets you choose which disk you will use as your boot volume. This is really useful when you need to run two versions of system software, though it's unlikely that most PowerBook users, whose computers digest only System 7.0.1 and 7.1 (except for users with System 6-capable PowerBook 100s), will have call for a second system.

One exception might be that if you need to use different languages, you may want to install a second copy of System 7.1, with the second language on an external hard disk, and switch between the two copies as needed.

Or, you could just trash this one. Your PowerBook will just boot from the internal disk thereafter.

Views

Here's another control panel we recommend that you keep. Views lets you choose the font, icon size, and arrangement of file information in the Finder. This can be especially useful if you have trouble seeing filenames on a supertwist display, because you can crank up the font size to improve your view.

Memory

A Quick Walk Down Memory Lane

This can be the most useful and most dangerous control panel that comes with your PowerBook. Memory lets you do four things: set the disk cache; set up virtual memory; activate 32-bit addressing (on 68030-equipped PowerBooks only); and create a RAM disk.

```
┌─────────────────────────────────────────────────┐
│ ▢               Memory                            │
├─────────────────────────────────────────────────┤
│  ▨      Disk Cache      Cache Size    [512K]  ⬆  │
│         Always On                             ⬇  │
│  ─────────────────────────────────────────────  │
│                        Select Hard Disk:         │
│         Virtual Memory   ⌷ Bob W 230        ▼    │
│  ◉      ○ On            Available on disk : 30M   │
│         ◉ Off        Available built-in memory : 7M │
│  ─────────────────────────────────────────────  │
│         32-Bit Addressing                        │
│  [32]   ◉ On                                     │
│         ○ Off              ▸                      │
│  ─────────────────────────────────────────────  │
│                     Percent of available memory  │
│                       to use for a RAM disk:     │
│  ▨      RAM Disk    ├──────█──────────┤          │
│         ◉ On        0%     50%      100%         │
│         ○ Off       RAM Disk Size    [4800K]     │
│  ─────────────────────────────────────────────  │
│                    ( Use Defaults )              │
│  v7.1                                            │
└─────────────────────────────────────────────────┘
```

Figure 8. Memory Dialog Box

Disk Cache   Lets you set aside a portion of your PowerBook's RAM as a "buffer" between the hard disk drive and application memory. This allows applications that frequently access the hard drive to retrieve data to run faster. It can also cut down on battery consumption, because instead of spinning up the hard drive to get the code it needs, the program can sometimes find it in the cache.

You can allocate up to 4 Mbytes of RAM to a disk cache. Our tests with large caches (over 2 Mbytes) shows that they don't seem to speed things up much more than smaller caches. We seem to hit the best space-versus-performance ratio at about 512 Kbytes.

If you have enough memory (8 Mbytes or better) to build a RAM disk, we'd recommend going with a small cache (128 Kbytes), donating the memory you save to your RAM disk. If memory is tighter, disk cache is a more memory-frugal method for boosting performance while reducing battery consumption than a RAM disk. And finally, if memory is really tight (4 Mbytes with two or more applications running simultaneously), set disk cache to the minimum of 32 Kbytes to regain RAM for your programs.

Virtual Memory   Is bad for PowerBooks. It's so bad that even your Mac will warn you against using it (try turning *Virtual Memory* on in the Memory control panel and see what we mean). The reason it's so bad is that it uses space on your hard disk drive to expand RAM memory. First, hard drives make poor substitutes for RAM chips; they slow things down so badly that you'll think you're watching reruns of the *Six Million Dollar Man*. Second, your hard drive will have to constantly spin to keep up with the demands of your PowerBook's processor. The CPU is used to having RAM on demand and doesn't take kindly to memory that sleeps on the job.

32-Bit Addressing   Allows your computer to access more than 8 Mbytes of RAM installed on its logic board. Up until the 160, 180, and the Duos, 32-bit addressing really wasn't an issue for PowerBooks because you couldn't have more than 8 Mbytes of RAM chips in your computer anyway. But now with a potential for up to 24 Mbytes of RAM, you must switch to 32-bit mode to access that extra memory.

This brings us to the issue of "clean" applications. In short, your programs are either 24- or 32-bit clean. If they are the former, they probably won't work on a computer running in 32-bit mode; you'll get lots of crashes with type-1 error bomb messages when you try to run the program. If they are the latter, they will run.

Most applications you can buy today are 32-bit clean. Apple has been after developers for years to only program 32-bit clean code, but when System 7 came out in 1991, users began to scream that programs didn't work properly in 32-bit mode. That really lit a fire under programmers, which is why today almost all shipping software works fine in 32-bit mode.

Up until System 7 shipped, it was impossible to access more than 8 Mbytes of RAM without special third-party add-on software. Of course, in those days there were no PowerBooks, so there was no great need for large RAM disks. How things have changed in just two short years.

RAM Disk   Is possibly the most useful program Apple includes with your PowerBook. It's the only thing that can reduce power consumption while increasing the performance of your computer.

A RAM disk is a portion of RAM memory that's set aside and used like a disk drive. It creates a volume on your desktop that looks like a floppy disk icon but has a memory chip blazoned across it. If you double-click on the RAM disk icon, it'll open just like any other window in the Finder. You can copy files to and from it, and if you double-click an icon in the disk's window, it'll open the document or start the program, just like your regular disk.

So, why give up valuable memory if all it does is give you more storage space? Because a RAM disk is based on chips and not spinning platters like a hard drive. As a result, RAM disks run a lot faster than drives and use less power as well. If you were to create a RAM disk big enough to hold your System Folder, all your applications, and documents, you could run your PowerBook without ever spinning the hard drive, extending battery life by as much as 50 percent.

To set up a RAM disk, just move the slider until the amount of memory you want to allocate displays in the little window labeled "RAM Disk Size." You can never allocate more RAM than is free when the Memory control panel is running, so be sure to quit all applications before configuring your disk (or run all the programs you'll want to have in memory simultaneously, so you can't build a RAM disk that precludes any of those programs from booting). You'll need to restart your PowerBook before the RAM disk will show up. Luckily, you don't need to restart to get rid of a RAM disk that's taking up too much memory. Just call up the Memory control panel and switch the RAM disk off.

Once you've created a RAM disk, it'll show up every time you start your computer. Unfortunately, Apple didn't think to add the ability to automatically back up a RAM disk to the hard drive when the computer shuts down. When you do shut down and then start up again later, your RAM disk will be wiped clean of all your files. However, Connectix's Maxima extension can add RAM disk backups that preserve data when you shut down. Restarting your computer or putting it to sleep won't clean out the RAM disk.

For more on RAM disk and memory strategies see "Adding RAMjets" in Section III, Part 2, *The Conservation of Energy*.

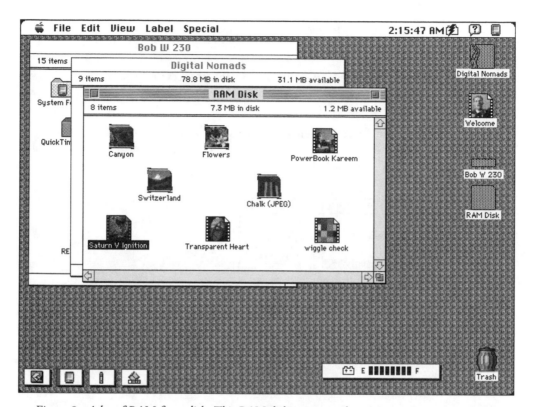

Figure 9. A lot of RAM for a disk. This RAM disk was created on a Duo 230 with 12 Mbytes of RAM. It was docked in a Duo Dock when the screen shot was taken. RAM disks are especially useful for files that load from the disk at regular intervals, like QuickTime movies.

Monitors

With the new PowerBooks came new capabilities, chief among them the ability to use an external color monitor and to display grayscale images on the PowerBook's built-in screen.

Selecting what bit depth (the amount of gray or color the PowerBook displays) and whether the images displayed are in color or black and white is accomplished through the Monitors control panel. You can also position monitors on a "Virtual Desktop" where one display's screen real estate is added to another's. With the new PowerBooks' multiple monitor feature, this ability to configure two screens' relationship to each other or even to determine which screen is dominant (meaning that it includes the menu bar), can come in handy (see Figure 10).

Monitors also lets you select each screen on your virtual desktop and set the bit depth for that display independently from the other screen's settings. For example, you might want to set an external color monitor to 4-bit grayscale instead of 8-bit color, so that images don't suddenly "colorize" when they cross the boundary between your PowerBook screen and external display.

Just remember, when you disconnect your PowerBook from the display, any icons you had sitting on the external monitor's screen will get piled onto your portable's display.

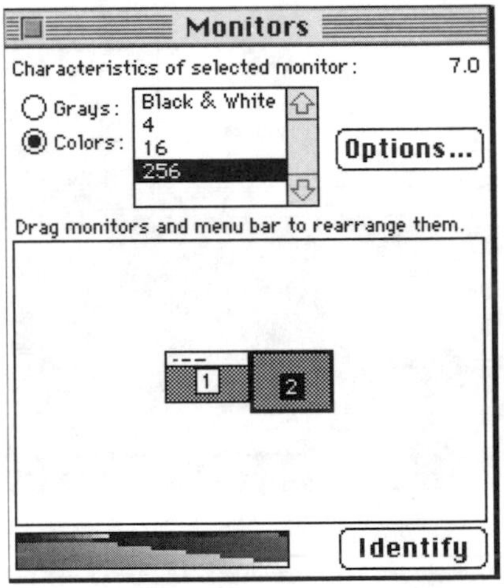

Figure 10. Setting Up Your Virtual Desktop

PowerBook Display

To complement Monitors, Apple ships a special control panel just for the PowerBook's internal display—it's a definite "keeper." PowerBook Display, which comes with all System 7.1-equipped Mac portables, does two things. First, it allows users to switch on Video Mirroring, which causes the image on an attached external monitor to mimic the PowerBook's internal display. Video Mirroring is only available when an external monitor is connected.

See the
Road Warrior
note below.

Screen shots taken while Video Mirroring is on will default to the highest bit depth available. So, if you have 8-bit color set for your external monitor, any screen shots you take will come out with 256 colors. (Screen shots are digital photographs your Mac takes of the current desktop whenever you hit the Command, Shift and 3 keys simultaneously. You'll find your pictures stored in PICT files in the internal drive's main window.)

The second thing PowerBook Display does is allow users to set their portable's backlighting to turn off after a predetermined length of "idle" time, from one to five minutes. For screen dimming purposes, your PowerBook is idle when you aren't interacting with it—moving the mouse, clicking, dragging, or typing. The moment you do any of these things, backlighting will snap back on. Screen dimming also applies to external monitors. If you have an external display attached to your PowerBook and screen dimming kicks in, your external screen will black out as well.

Although earlier PowerBook models don't support Apple's Video Mirroring, they all have backlit screens. If you install System 7.1 on your PowerBook 100, 140, 145, or 170, you'll be able to take advantage of the screen dimming feature of the PowerBook Display control panel. Because backlighting can be responsible for as much as 50 percent of your PowerBook's battery drain, having it switch off during idle periods can extend battery life enormously.

Here's a little tip: If the idea of upgrading your PowerBook to System 7.1 sends shivers down your spine, you can run PowerBook Display on System 7.0.1 (we've done it and haven't run into any problems). However you should keep in mind that copying the control panel from a System 7.1-equipped PowerBook does technically constitute software piracy now that Apple no longer allows system software to copied and distributed freely. Of course, as long as you don't get caught...(nudge, nudge, wink, wink!)

Hold Up Those Cue Cards!

As we mentioned earlier in the *Guide*, Video Mirroring will prove especially useful for presentations. One of the authors used to outline his presentations in Microsoft Word and then bring his PowerBook up to the podium so he could read along with the Director presentation playing out behind him.

The PowerBook can make a wonderful TelePrompTer (yes, it's really spelled this way). But using hand signals to get the person sitting in front of a desktop Mac to advance your presentation slides isn't only inconvenient, it looks stupid too.

(continued)

Hold Up Those Cue Cards! (continued)

With Video Mirroring and a PowerBook 160, 180, or Duo (in dock), you can be the ringmaster of your circus, controlling the slides' advance from your laptop's screen. Even if you don't want to use Video Mirroring (maybe there are notes in your outline you'd rather the audience didn't see), you can still display your outline on the PowerBook screen and run the presentation on the external monitor (in this case, a video projector).

Another advantage of taking along a complete presentation system is that some multimedia programs, most notably Macromedia's Macro-Mind Director, are extremely persnickety about the systems they run on. Change the processor speed or even the amount of file fragmentation (files are rarely stored on a single contiguous section of disk; usually they are broken up into pieces and spread around the hard drive platter), and suddenly your carefully sculpted presentation will start misbehaving. This is why it's always a good idea to plan for a couple of hours of "debugging" if you're going to be running your presentation on a strange system. But bring along your PowerBook and you can avoid this kind of presentation trauma.

Portable/PowerBook: EverWatch keeps going and going and going...

We recommend that all PowerBook users (except those with 100s) upgrade to System 7.1. (PowerBook 100s won't get as much utility out of the PowerBook features of System 7.1 and therefore don't need to waste the drive and RAM space to run this larger version of the system.) There are some tradeoffs involved because the new system requires approximately 200 Kbytes more RAM than 7.0.1, but the big win is the EverWatch battery conservation capabilities that come in the new PowerBook control panel.

System 7.0.1 includes the Portable control panel with two sliders that let users set the length of time before the system and hard disk go to sleep, a checkbox that prevents the PowerBook from going to sleep when using AC power, two "radio" buttons that set the default modem port, and a checkbox that allows the PowerBook to wake up when a call comes in on the modem line, useful for receiving faxes while you're out (see Figure 11).

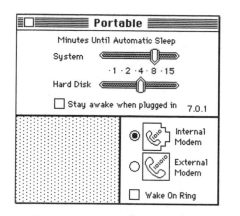

Figure 11. System 7.0.1's Portable Control Panel

System 7.1's PowerBook control panel gives you more control over power usage, mostly as a result of the clear relationship between power savings and performance degradation. A simplified conservation slider control allows you to trade performance for increased battery life (see Figure 12). What you're actually adjusting incorporates the system and hard disk sleep functions of the old Portable control panel, as well as new CPU controls that let the processor sleep through most of its clock cycles when you are not working at the keyboard.

Like PowerBook Display, System 7.1's PowerBook control panel will work just fine under System 7.0.1. Features not applicable to that particular model (like stepping down processor speed on a 140) won't be accessible. Just remember that inconvenient software piracy cloud hanging over your head.

For Duo, 160, and 180 users, there are added features, including the ability to set the SCSI address your PowerBook will use when connected to a desktop computer in SCSI Disk Mode and an automatic wake-up control, which is useful when running scripted events. For instance, you may need to get a late Japanese stock quote at the same time you have a breakfast appointment. Just set your PowerBook to wake when the Nikkei closes, leave it in your hotel room, and head out to eat. At the appropriate time, your PowerBook will power up and your telecommunications software can automatically log on to DowVision to grab the data.

One advantage of owning a PowerBook 100 is that it is the only first-year model that included a timed wake-up capability. But, for that matter, so did the old Mac Portable.

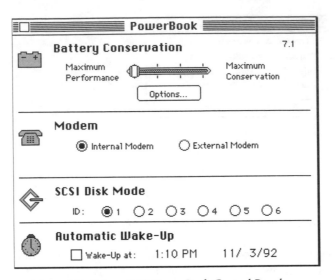

Figure 12. System 7.1's PowerBook Control Panel

The second layer of the PowerBook control panel, which you reach by clicking the Option button in the first dialog box, lets you get under the Battery Conservation hood to fine-tune the functions (see Figure 13). You'll find the checkbox that prevents your computer from sleeping when it's plugged in and processor speed controls that let you turn down to 16 MHz those power-hungry 25MHz and 33MHz CPUs that dominate the second generation. This was part of the Battery desk accessory in pre-7.1 days and worked only on 170s. If you have a pre-October 19, 1992 issue PowerBook 145, you will most definitely want to upgrade to System 7.1 as soon as possible; the PowerBook control panel is the only way you can crank down your CPU's performance from 25 MHz to 16 MHz.

If you preferred the one-click convenience of 7.0.1's Battery Saver, you may not like drilling down through the PowerBook control panel in order to change the processor speed. But there's another benefit that can motivate you to upgrade to EverWatch: processor cycling.

A 68030 processor can get a lot of rest in a few milliseconds. Processor cycling shuts down the CPU when it determines that only a little CPU power is needed to support whatever the PowerBook is doing. You can save a fair amount of power, because the processor can get by on one-tenth the power it normally does when it grabs these electronic catnaps. This capability is incorporated in the Battery Conservation slider control—you can increase how often the processor naps by moving the indicator toward

See the Road Warrior note below.

⬇

Maximum Conservation. You can also override this function by turning processor cycling off in the second PowerBook Control Panel dialog box (see Figure 13). If there is a noticeable lag in the performance of some of your applications, you might want to try switching processor cycling off to see if that helps.

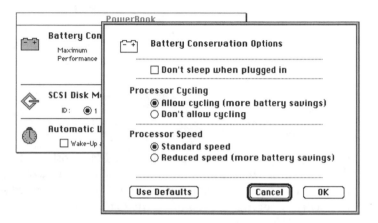

Figure 13. Under the PowerBook Control Panel Hood

Now I lay me down to sleep...

An offshoot of obsessive tinkering is the desire to have direct control over every aspect of your PowerBook's life. That's why many Road Warriors will probably be disappointed by Apple's "no-brainer" approach to the PowerBook control panel's single battery conservation slider. The advantage of this approach for most people is that they no longer have to tinker with getting just the right balance of time before the hard drive sleeps and overall power savings. But for control freaks half the fun is experimenting, discovering the secret formula for the best battery/functionality mixture.

Unfortunately for the tinkerers, if you've bought a 160, 180, or Duo, you're out of luck. We tried out the Portable control panel on the new PowerBooks, but they ignored the old control panel's instructions.

The best we can offer you is the chart below, which translates the new slider's settings into system and hard drive sleep times: *(continued)*

Now I lay me down to sleep... (continued)

PowerBook control panel settings	Maximum Performance			Maximum Conservation
Minutes before System sleep:	15	8	4	1
Minutes before hard drive sleep:	15	4	2	0.5

Digital AAA—Roadside Assistance Kit PowerBook Tuners

Life in the Automated Finder

One big complaint still levied against the Macintosh operating system is the amount of time users' hands are off the keyboard, trying to steer the mouse around the Finder. System 7 went a long way toward solving those problems by adding all sorts of smarts that allow navigation through the Finder with just a few keystrokes.

To significantly enhance and extend these key combinations, CE Software Inc. of West Des Moines, Iowa, offers QuicKeys[2], which links macro sequences and programs to keystrokes. For instance, you might create a QuicKey that automatically starts AppleTalk Remote Access, dials the correct connection, and then logs you onto your company's server. Those little timesavers can add up.

CE created a special version of QuicKeys[2], called QuicKeys for Nomads, especially for owners of this *Guide*. QuicKeys for Nomads is on the Roadside Assistance Kit disk that came with this book and includes key sequences for running System 7, navigating the Finder, and controlling your PowerBook. The PowerBook keys are:

- **Control+Option+B, Battery**   Opens the Battery DA.
- **Control+C, ShowCursor**   Actually it does more than show the cursor—the key sequence causes it to explode, which is especially helpful for supertwist screens where the cursor can disappear in the murk.
- **Control+Option+S, Shutdown**   Powers down your computer.
- **Control+S, Sleep**   Puts the PowerBook to sleep.
- **Control+D, Spin Down**   Puts the hard disk to sleep, a great way to save power when the hard drive spins up and you don't want it to.

- **Control+B, TogBL**   Turns off backlighting to save power, letting you work while the screen is dark. Repeating the TogBL key sequence turns backlighting on.

The installer included with Runtime QuicKeys[2] installs a control panel of the same name and an extension called CE Toolbox. While you'll be trading some memory for these macros, we think it's a worthwhile exchange (see Appendix Two, *The Roadside Assistance Guide*, for more information on QuicKeys for Nomads).

Extensions Folder

Adding new tricks to your operating system's repertoire is as easy as dragging a file into the Extensions folder. Extensions are chunks of code that latch onto your OS to deliver new capabilities. That might include the ability to see an AppleShare server in the Chooser, which is provided by Apple with Systems 7.0.1 and 7.1, or it may stretch into the realm of hierarchical Apple menus and support a battery of hot keys that launch convenient macros.

If you can do without a particular extension, you can recover some memory for use by your applications.

Caps Lock

This file doesn't actually turn on the caps lock key, it just gives you a visual cue (the arrow that appears in righthand side of the menu bar) when you've set the caps lock key. We think the indicator is too small and that it's not even slightly intuitive to glance at the upper righthand corner of the screen to see if the caps lock key is indeed locked. And it's worthless when you are taking notes with the PowerBook's backlighting turned down, creating the potential for an all-caps surprise when you turn backlighting back up.

This is another area where Duo users have an advantage over owners of other PowerBook models—the Duo has a little red LED that lights up when caps lock is engaged. Still not as good as a two-position key, but better than no keyboard indicator at all.

For the rest of Apple's laptops, Caps Lock Notify, a 3-Kbyte freeware extension available from many online services, does a better job at keeping you attuned to capitalization. It sounds an alarm tone and brings up a small dialog box to tell you that the caps lock key has been pressed.

Once you download and install Caps Lock Notify, trash Caps Lock.

DAL

Apple's battle to be taken seriously by corporate information systems managers was waged deep inside the Macintosh operating system. DAL, or Data Access Language, is one of the relics of that great struggle.

DAL is a software mechanism that converts database requests from Mac applications into a sort of universal language that can be sent on a network to database servers. A DAL "back end," which runs on SQL (pronounced "sequel") database servers, is also necessary to catch your PowerBook's DAL requests and translate them, this time into the SQL language that's running on the server. The communication process is reversed when data is returned from the server to your PowerBook, delivering to your desktop the answer to the question you asked.

You probably know if you need DAL. If you don't know, ask your company support engineer or IS (Information Systems) manager. If the answer is no, or you don't work for a company with a SQL server, trash this sucker tout de suite. System 7.1 users won't need to make the DAL-delete decision, as the extension was excised from the new system. It is now available separately from Apple and third-party database developers.

Finder Help

Unless you are just starting out on a Macintosh, toss this extension into the trash. Even after you trash this, your PowerBook will let you use Balloon Help, which is activated by pulling down the menu from the balloon in the menu bar, to search pop-up cartoon balloons for hints about Finder commands and menus.

Print Drivers

Your PowerBook uses special software, called *print drivers*, to prepare files for printing and to control each type of printer. The chances are pretty slim you'll need every printer driver your PowerBook comes with, so you can get rid of those drivers you think you won't need.

Road Warriors and Intentional Tourists should be warned that they're likely to encounter a passle of printer types in your travels, some of which you'll want to interface with. Of course, the one printer you need access to will be the one you won't have a driver for. However, if the printer in question is already connected to a Mac, just dip into that Mac's Extensions folder and find the driver you seek.

Generally, it's a safe strategy to save memory and drive storage space by trashing all but the printers you know you'll be using. As long as you keep a backup copy of your drivers (they're already on the System disks that come with your PowerBook), you can always restore them later.

Choose the drivers you'll need and trash the rest.

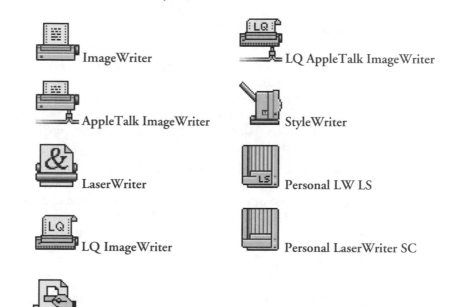

ImageWriter   LQ AppleTalk ImageWriter

AppleTalk ImageWriter   StyleWriter

LaserWriter   Personal LW LS

LQ ImageWriter   Personal LaserWriter SC

PrintMonitor

PowerBooks can print a document in the background using the PrintMonitor, a small application that lives in your PowerBook's Extensions folder. Usually that means printing to an Apple or third-party laser printer or a StyleWriter, other printers do not necessarily support Mac print spooling.

Keep PrintMonitor, even if you seldom or never print to a networked LaserWriter, because you'll appreciate having your PowerBook freed up to other things on those rare occasions you are connected to the appropriate output device.

System 7 Tuner

Remember the vanishing folders problem we told you about back in Section I? This extension eliminates the disappearances, plus fixes several other bugs in System 7.0.1. It's a must-have file if you have not upgraded to the latest OS.

The Tuner, however, does not make files reappear after they are gone. Run the Disk First Aid application on the Disk Tools disk that ships with System 7.1 to snatch those missing folders back from the void or follow the directions outlined in Section I, page 54.

QuickTime: You should be in pictures!

QuickTime is the most magical of the extensions your System 7.1 Power-Book comes equipped with. System 7.0.1 users can get the QuickTime extension by purchasing Apple's QuickTime Starter Kit, which also comes with lots of nifty example movies and QuickTime utilities, or they can get it from many online information services or users groups. QuickTime-enabled programs like Adobe Premier 2.0 generally include the Quick-Time extension as well.

The nuances of QuickTime usage, from recording and editing your own movies to selecting and configuring your digital video system, goes beyond the scope of the *Nomad's Guide* (look for the upcoming Random House book, *Mastering the World of QuickTime* by Jerry Borrell and the editors of *MacWorld*, which covers the topic in detail). Instead, we've listed some PowerBook-specific QuickTime tips below.

What a hog!

QuickTime synchronizes moving images with sound at the speed a particular computer can process. QuickTime will only run on a 68030 Power-Book, so it looks like you 100 users are left out in the cold on this one, too.

Because the fastest PowerBook can just maintain speeds of around fifteen frames per second (fps), half the speed of an analog movie playing at your local cinema, you can pretty much depend on QuickTime movies to eat up every MIP your portable can supply and then some.

QuickTime is also a storage hog. Even though it compresses movie files, a 30-second piece of video playing in a window only of 160 by 120 pixels can still take up 2 Mbytes of disk storage. Just remember, for every frame in a movie, QuickTime needs to store a single, usually color, picture. Multiply than by 10 fps (a reasonable frame rate for a 25MHz PowerBook to maintain) over 30 seconds, and you've got 300 little color pictures, plus a 30-second sound track, stored on your hard disk.

Keep QuickTime's hoggish ways in mind if you decide to use your PowerBook as a digital video player. We advise keeping all your Quick-Time stuff on an external drive, so you're not wasting valuable space on your PowerBook's internal hard disk. You can always carry the drive with you when you need access to your QuickTime library.

QuickTime is much easier on RAM than it is on disk storage. You need only 4 Mbytes of memory installed in your PowerBook to run QuickTime, a requirement almost every Mac laptop can comply with.

MooV Violations

Here are some things *not* to do when running QuickTime on a Power-Book. First, you probably don't want to bother with QuickTime if you're using a 140, 145, or 170, unless you've got a third-party color video-out card. The fidelity of movies played on a 1-bit PowerBook screen is so poor that it's hardly worth the bother, disk space, or RAM. If you own one of these PowerBook models, just toss the extension out.

If you have one of the grayscale-capable PowerBooks, avoid running QuickTime movies from the hard drive. Instead, set up a RAM disk and play your movies from there. This way, not only will your QuickTime movie run faster, it won't keep your hard drive spinning.

QuickTime plays movies by loading them, frame by frame, from the hard disk. This means your hard drive must constantly spin while Quick-Time movies are playing (unless you're using a RAM disk). Also, the combination of the slow supertwist screens on the PowerBook 160 and the Duos and QuickTime's need to access the portable's platters causes excessive cut-out when playing most 10-fps or better movies. (*Cut-out* means the QuickTime soundtrack plays with gaps and/or the movie seems to jump frames and isn't properly synchronized with the audio.)

The RAM disk can address this problem nicely, speeding QuickTime frame access so much that it almost makes up for the PowerBook's slow display. QuickTime cut-out is less of a problem with the 180 because of its active-matrix screen.

Over the Rainbow

The best way to play QuickTime movies from your PowerBook is to use an external color display. Not only will you see the movie in glorious, life-like color (okay, 256 colors doesn't quite qualify as Technicolor, but it's better than 16 grayscales), you'll also eliminate cut-out. Because QuickTime video is optimized to record and play back movies as 16-bit (thousands of colors) images, most PowerBooks' video-out still won't do your movies justice. A Duo in a Duo Dock with a 13-inch color monitor attached and with 1 Mbyte of VRAM can display QuickTime in full bloom. You can get very good video output by installing a third-party video card in a Duo-Dock, as well.

QuickTime, the Sequel

Those of you out there who received QuickTime with your PowerBook probably got version 1.5. The main enhancements in 1.5 are the ability to record video that can play in larger windows (up to 320 by 240 pixels), better playback performance on slower Macs, and the ability to use the Apple Compact Video codec (*codec* stands for compressor/decompresser). It's always been possible to record movies at any size, but the problem has been whether the Mac could play it back with better performance on slower Macs. The Compact Video codec delivers better quality video in larger windows with smaller files than the codec that comes with Quick-Time 1.0. (The 1.0 codec was code-named Road Pizza. Not that it's important, we just thought you'd like to know.) It can also play movies from a fast CD-ROM drive without cut-out on most Macs, a neat trick considering how slow CD-ROM drives are (buy a "dual-speed" CD-ROM drive that delivers at least 150-Kbps throughput).

Fonts Folder and the System Suitcase

There was a time when the Macintosh System was so impenetrable that an application, called Font/DA Mover, was needed to pry it open before users could install fonts and sounds. System 7 simplified the installation of fonts and sounds, making it possible to drag them into the System Suitcase. System 7.1 took ease of installation a step further by breaking out fonts from the System altogether.

Your fonts and sounds take up a lot of space. The System Suitcase in version 7.0.1 can take up a whopping 1,893 Kbytes or more, depending on what you've got living in there. That's a minimum for pre-installed versions of the system! The combined size of 7.1's suitcase and Fonts folder can take up a good deal more space. We think you can chop out many of the font files in the System Suitcase or Fonts folder without sacrificing good-looking printed output. if you're using System 7.0.1, remove the fonts we discuss from the System Suitcase. If 7.1's your game, the Fonts folder is where you'll want to do your trimming (see Figure 14).

The beta version of System 7.1 we used to do this testing included 198 Kbytes of fonts that were inexplicably installed in both the System Suitcase and Fonts folder; this may not be the case with the shipping version of 7.1.

Font Suitcase

The system's obesity results in part from the redundancy of installed fonts; there are two of everything inside of many font suitcases (just double-click one and you'll see for yourself). You'll find bitmapped versions of fonts, characters that are drawn pixel-by-pixel for each type size and that produce "jaggy" printed output, right alongside the TrueType versions of the same fonts. TrueType fonts are produced using a mathematical description, or outline, of the character. Using a TrueType or PostScript outline you can increase or decrease the point size of a font as much as you like; the mathematical coordinates provide smooth-edged screen images and even smoother printed output as they scale the type to the resolution of the output device. By contrast, when you increase the point size of a bitmapped font, the characters just get more jaggy.

Therein lies the decision you have to make about your fonts. TrueType fonts are larger than bitmapped files, although if you were to try to load bitmapped files for all the possible point sizes that an outline can produce, collectively they would take many times the storage of the outline. (Actually, you couldn't load all the bitmaps an outline can produce. A single outline can recreate a nearly infinite number of point sizes.)

Add the bulk of outlines to the fact that you also need a separate outline for each type style (bold, italic, etc.) of each font and what you end up with is a very fat Fonts folder.

There is a benefit to bitmapped fonts, however: they are tweaked to look especially good in common sizes. For instance, the 12-point bitmapped Courier font actually looks a lot better on screen than the TrueType version of the same font.

How do you tell bitmaps from outlines? Bitmapped fonts appear with a single *A* on the icon and always include a number (the bitmap's point size) in the font name. TrueType font icons have three *A*s and do not include a font size indicator, since they scale to whatever size you want.

If you use a LaserWriter to do business writing, you could dump the TrueType fonts out of your System Folder. The built-in PostScript fonts in a laser printer will take your bitmapped fonts and make them look great on the page. Composition can be a little dicey without TrueType, which lets you see the type on your PowerBook just as it will appear on a LaserWriter page; bitmapped fonts have a tendency to scale out of proportion, making the page layout job difficult, at best. However, if you usually print to an ImageWriter or another dot-matrix printer, TrueType delivers pretty good output, smoothing the jaggies on the page.

We suggest that you take a while to make this decision and definitely check the quality of the print before implementing this part of the Power-Book reduction plan. There is also an opportunity to compromise on fonts, mixing TrueType and bitmapped fonts. For instance, you could toss the TrueType versions of fonts you seldom use, only keeping one bit-mapped version handy, while holding on to the outlines you use regularly.

Another strategy would be to keep only a few different sizes of a bit-mapped font. If you never use 24-point type, why keep it around?

Figure 14, below, shows the breakdown on font sizes that come with your System. However you cut it, as you can see, you can save a lot of storage space and preserve RAM by eliminating outline fonts.

Figure 14. All Them Fonts

	TrueType	*Bitmaps (all available sizes)*
Chicago	44 Kbytes[*]	N/A
Courier	58 Kbytes	39 Kbytes
Courier (bold)	56 Kbytes	N/A
Geneva	54 Kbytes	31 Kbytes
Helvetica	60 Kbytes	72 Kbytes
Helvetica (bold)	58 Kbytes	N/A
Monaco	49 Kbytes	3 Kbytes
MT Extra (A symbol font)	7 Kbytes	15 Kbytes
New York	58 Kbytes	32 Kbytes
Palatino	72 Kbytes	46 Kbytes
Palatino (bold)	68 Kbytes	N/A
Palatino (bold, italic)	72 Kbytes	N/A
Palatino (italic)	71 Kbytes	N/A
Symbol	41 Kbytes	35 Kbytes
Times	67 Kbytes	53 Kbytes
Times (bold)	65 Kbytes	N/A
Times (bold, italic)	67 Kbytes	N/A
Times (italic)	68 Kbytes	N/A

[*] The Chicago font is built into the PowerBook ROM, because it's used in the Finder and menus. You can trash the Chicago font in your system and still use Chicago in your documents.

The Sound and the Furious Sosumi

The System Suitcase is the receptacle of all sounds in System 7. If you trashed the Sound control panel, you can also toss the sounds you find here. We're kind of fond of the eclectic sounds collected by Apple, so we keep them around. Before System 7, you had to visit Osaka to hear a sosumi!

System 7.1's Flexible Tongue

As we said above, the latest Mac operating system is "world-ready;" it lets you drop language modules into the system, restart, and start typing in a new character set. When you change languages, you'll be changing keyboard layouts, too. Be sure you drop the new keyboard layout file into your System Suitcase, or else your input will look like gibberish to your multilingual PowerBook.

The System 6 keyboard layout panel installed with System 7.1 can be trashed for the whole 2 Kbytes that'll save you.

Preference folder

Your applications keep their records of the settings you prefer in this folder. Leave it in peace.

Startup Items Folder

Shutting down your PowerBook undoes a lot of the arranging and tailoring you do while you're working. Perhaps you find yourself working with the same three applications most of the time, but you get tired of launching them after every PowerBook restart or shutdown. Put aliases of those programs in the Startup Items folder. Now, every time you start anew, those applications will open automatically.

It can also be helpful to drop a key document, like a tickler file you like to have open at all times, into the Startup Items folder.

Be sure not to get carried away, though, because you can consume all your RAM if you launch too many applications at startup.

Digital AAA—Roadside Assistance Kit PowerBook Tuners

Included on the Roadside Assistance Kit disk is another application that you'll want to install whether you're an Intentional Tourist, Mobile Commuter, or Road Warrior.

Applicon

System 7 forsook the venerable MultiFinder interface, which let users toggle between applications by clicking on the application icon at the upper right corner of the System 6 screen. Users who want to switch between running applications without pulling down the Mac menu at the far right of the menu bar will flip over Applicon, a freeware program created by Rick Holzgrafe.

We suggest you install this small application in your Startup Items folder, so it launches when you begin your day. It creates a tile for each application you have open and displays them in whatever location on the screen you specify. You can place tiles anywhere on the screen and have a choice of tile styles and sizes. You must configure a "hot corner" that brings the Applicon tiles to the front. When you need to switch to another program, just roll the cursor into the appropriate screen corner and click the appropriate tile when Applicon appears in the foreground.

Taking in the Lay of the Land

Once you're done customizing your System, you'll probably want to start decorating your new habitat with programs, files, and various other window dressings.

While there is no perfect PowerBook layout, experience has taught us that decorating styles should run more toward Minimalist than Victorian. For example, set your PowerBook drive window to fill most of the desktop space, except for a band of open desktop at the bottom and on the right side. This space is reserved for Applicon's tiles, the trash can, and your drive, floppy, and server icons. The space under the main drive window also makes a convenient place to stow your most critical and often-used files, like your contacts database and Notes file (see Figure 15).

Put folders in the drive's window and organize your folders by usage or file type. For instance, a single folder for all your applications makes a convenient repository. You almost always start a program by double-clicking a document that was created in that application, so the location of the program itself is only important on those rare occasions when you want to start a new file. (You can still start up the program by double-clicking one of its documents and then selecting *New* from the File menu.)

It probably makes the most sense to organize and store your documents by project. You can create one folder for work and one for personal files and further divide those folders up with folders for each project. It's a good idea to keep the folder containing documents for your current project in the main drive's window so you don't have to go digging for it. Don't make the mistake of organizing documents by the program they were created in; you'll go nuts trying to track down all the related files for a project. Also, don't nest folders (a folder inside another folder is a "nested" folder) too many layers deep. It's a real pain to have to open four folders to find one file.

For miscellaneous files, like games or extra control panels, create folders for each kind of file (like "Fun Stuff" and "Extra Panels").

Arrange folders around the inside of the main drive's window, so that the folders you access the most are closest to the edge of the window. This makes getting at important files easier when another window is open on top of the main window (just move the offending window to one side). Also, group folders by type: program folders in one group, data file folders in another.

Whatever layout you decide to set up for yourself, make sure it's flexible enough to grow. Remember, PowerBooks have a limited amount of screen real estate—use it wisely. Even if you have an external monitor, you probably don't want to rely on it being there for your desktop to stay in order. Otherwise, just use common sense. If you wouldn't immediately think to look in a certain folder for a file, you probably should find another place for that file.

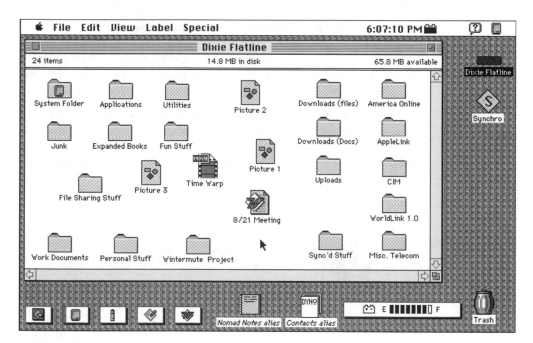

Figure 15. A Good Layout

Digital Nomad System Rundowns

See the
Digital Nomad
note below.

Now that we have discussed the building blocks of your mobile habitat, here are the foundations we suggest you construct, depending on the user category you fall into. Please feel free to depart from these guidelines; the PowerBook you make is the PowerBook you have to live with!

What's all this then?

You may notice several files, tucked away in various corners of your System Folder, that we haven't told you what to do with. There's one of three possible explanations for these files.

One, yours isn't a virgin PowerBook, and the files you encountered were put there by third-party programs previously installed. We can't possibly hope to cover all the files that might be installed in this manner, so if you're looking to clean house and want to lose some of these files, try putting them in a folder outside your System Folder first. Restart and see if the absence of the files in question adversely effects your PowerBook (be sure to try all your applications as well, just in case the files are needed by them).

The second explanation is that you've encountered one of a cornucopia of exotic files that Apple includes to support things like the CommToolbox and TokenTalk. Some of these items are covered later in the *Guide*. If you can't find a reference to the file in question, refer to the first explanation above and follow the recommended testing procedures.

If the first two explanations don't seem to cover your mysterious file, then this one should: We blew it. Somehow, despite long, sleepless nights wandering the trackless wastes of Apple's labyrinthine system software, we missed something. The testing procedure suggested above should still cover anything we missed.

The Intentional Tourist

As the grand traveller, you need a lean system to deliver the maximum in performance within a narrow RAM and storage budget. Since you probably don't use a network connection, we suggest you excise the file-sharing control panels and extensions.

We also suggest that you stick with bitmapped fonts, since you probably transfer your files to a desktop Macintosh before printing documents. Keep storage-hungry TrueType fonts in that fat desktop machine!

Figure 16. *Intentional Tourist's System Folder*

	System 7.0.1	System 7.1
Apple Menu Items Folder		
AgentDA	200 Kbytes	200 Kbytes
Calculator	7 Kbytes	7 Kbytes
Chooser	22 Kbytes	29 Kbytes
Control Panels alias	1 Kbytes	1 Kbytes
Dynodex alias	1 Kbytes	1 Kbytes
Key Caps	12 Kbytes	12 Kbytes
Nomad Notes alias	1 Kbytes	1 Kbytes
Synchro alias	1 Kbytes	1 Kbytes
Control Panels folder		
General Controls	16 Kbytes	22 Kbytes
Memory	38 Kbytes	39 Kbytes
Portable	27 Kbytes	N/A
PowerBook	N/A	63 Kbytes
PowerBook Display	N/A	34 Kbytes
Sound	17 Kbytes	17 Kbytes
SuperClock!	16 Kbytes	16 Kbytes
Views	3 Kbytes	3 Kbytes
QuicKeys[2] RunTime	204 Kbytes	204 Kbytes
Extensions folder		
CE Toolbox	65 Kbytes	65 Kbytes
ImageWriter[*]	46 Kbytes	46 Kbytes
LaserWriter[*]	219 Kbytes	219 Kbytes
Print Monitor	58 Kbytes	63 Kbytes
The Alarm (AgentDA)	35 Kbytes	35 Kbytes
The Alarm Data (AgentDA)	5 Kbytes	5 Kbytes
Fonts folder	N/A	121 Kbytes[**]

(continued)

Intentional Tourist's System Folder (continued)

	System 7.0.1	System 7.1
Startup Items folder		
Applicon	84 Kbytes	84 Kbytes
System Folder		
Finder	355 Kbytes	369 Kbytes
System Suitcase	773 Kbytes**	862 Kbytes
Totals	**2,210 Kbytes**	**2,523 Kbytes**

N/A means the file in question doesn't come standard with that version of System 7.

* ImageWriter and LaserWriter are offered as examples.

** Only bitmapped fonts between 12 and 18 points in size were included in this sample configuration.

Note: QuicKeys for Nomads adds a 55-Kbyte folder to the Preferences folder.

The Mobile Commuter

You haul your PowerBook back and forth between home and office and out to hotels on business trips. This requires a flexible system that can meet the demands of changing environments. Sometimes, the Mobile Commuter's PowerBook is a notepad, and during critical projects it can be a file server for an entire workgroup. It's also a conduit to the world while the Commuter is on the road, providing remote access to the office's local area network and dial-up connectivity to the Internet.

As a Mobile Commuter, you most likely use a PowerBook 145, 160, 170, or Duo 210. There are some things worth paying for in this world, but not the 180—the extra speed and better screen on the 180 would be like French food on your budgetary palette—too rich!

Print quality is important to you, but only in certain documents, so your keep the TrueType versions of Palatino and Courier in your system with the bitmapped versions of other fonts. You love your beep sounds, so you kept those too. You have a letter-quality StyleWriter at home, and at work you rely on the company's LaserWriter IIg.

Figure 17. Mobile Commuter's System Folder

	System 7.0.1	System 7.1
Apple Menu Items Folder		
AgentDA	200 Kbytes	200 Kbytes
Calculator	7 Kbytes	7 Kbytes
Chooser	22 Kbytes	29 Kbytes
Control Panels alias	2 Kbytes	2 Kbytes
Dynodex alias	2 Kbytes	2 Kbytes
Key Caps	12 Kbytes	12 Kbytes
Nomad Notes alias	2 Kbytes	2 Kbytes
Synchro alias	2 Kbytes	2 Kbytes
Control Panels folder		
File-Sharing Monitor	4 Kbytes	4 Kbytes
General Controls	16 Kbytes	22 Kbytes
Memory	38 Kbytes	39 Kbytes
Monitors	40 Kbytes	40 Kbytes
Network	13 Kbytes	13 Kbytes
Portable	27 Kbytes	N/A
PowerBook	N/A	63 Kbytes
PowerBook Display	N/A	34 Kbytes
Sound	17 Kbytes	17 Kbytes
SuperClock!	16 Kbytes	16 Kbytes
Views	3 Kbytes	3 Kbytes
QuicKeys^2 RunTime	204 Kbytes	204 Kbytes
Extensions folder		
AppleTalk Remote Access	70 Kbytes	70 Kbytes
AppleShare	72 Kbytes	75 Kbytes
CE Toolbox	65 Kbytes	65 Kbytes
File-Sharing Extension	167 Kbytes	170 Kbytes
LaserWriter*	219 Kbytes	219 Kbytes
Network Extension	92 Kbytes	96 Kbytes
Print Monitor	58 Kbytes	63 Kbytes

(continued)

Mobile Commuter's System Folder (continued)

	System 7.0.1	System 7.1
Extensions folder (continued)		
Remote Access Aliases[***]	32 Kbytes	32 Kbytes
Remote Only[***]	4 Kbytes	4 Kbytes
Serial Port Arbitrator[***]	7 Kbytes	7 Kbytes
The Alarm (AgentDA)	35 Kbytes	35 Kbytes
The Alarm Data (AgentDA)	5 Kbytes	5 Kbytes
Fonts folder	N/A	459 Kbytes[**]
Startup Items folder		
Applicon	84 Kbytes	84 Kbytes
System Folder		
Finder	355 Kbytes	369 Kbytes
System Suitcase	887 Kbytes[**]	1,062 Kbytes
Totals	**2,775 Kbytes**	**3,522 Kbytes**

N/A means the file in question doesn't come standard with that version of System 7.

[*]   LaserWriter is offered as an example.

[**]   Courier and Palatino TrueType outline fonts, plus bitmapped versions of other fonts between 12 and 18 points in size were included in the system.

[***]   These files were added by AppleTalk Remote Access.

Note: QuicKeys for Nomads adds a 55-Kbyte folder to the Preferences folder.

The Road Warrior

Perfection is all. Versatility is critical. Your PowerBook is an extension of yourself.

Between the constant meetings and trips out of town, you occasionally get to sit down at what people in your office think of as your desk. During those rare reprieves, you plug a road-weary 170, 180, or Duo 230 into the office Ethernet network to search the corporate accounts payable database.

When travelling, you're the center ring attraction at meetings, and your PowerBook is your best and only prop.

AppleTalk Remote Access is like having a hand that stretches back to your desk, and you use it liberally—so much that you have to carry an extra hard drive with you to store all the files you download on an average week-long tour of the company's district offices. While in Europe, you have to compose spreadsheets in French and German, so you praise the heavens for System 7.1's world-ready capabilities.

No time for funny sounds, you've *x*'d out everything but the simple beep.

You demand only the best print output, since your PowerBook is the only computer you ever use; it doesn't even occur to you to leave desktop publishing to the sods with desktop Macs. The problem is, during a given month, you use four or five different kinds of printers, so your system is full of print drivers.

Good thing you've got your RAM slot and drive bay maxed out.

Special Note   You'll notice that The Road Warrior's Extensions folder includes EtherTalk Phase 2 extensions not covered in this section. Not to worry, those files are discussed in Part Two of this section, *Setting Sail on the Network Clipper.*

Figure 18. The Road Warrior's System Folder

	System 7.0.1	System 7.1
Apple Menu Items Folder		
AgentDA	200 Kbytes	200 Kbytes
Calculator	7 Kbytes	7 Kbytes
Chooser	22 Kbytes	29 Kbytes
Control Panels alias	2 Kbytes	2 Kbytes
Dynodex alias	2 Kbytes	2 Kbytes
Key Caps	12 Kbytes	12 Kbytes
Nomad Notes alias	2 Kbytes	2 Kbytes
Synchro alias	2 Kbytes	2 Kbytes

(continued)

The Road Warrior's System Folder (continued)

	System 7.0.1	System 7.1
Control Panels folder		
File-Sharing Monitor	4 Kbytes	4 Kbytes
General Controls	16 Kbytes	22 Kbytes
Memory	38 Kbytes	39 Kbytes
Monitors	40 Kbytes	40 Kbytes
Network	13 Kbytes	13 Kbytes
Portable	27 Kbytes	N/A
PowerBook	N/A	63 Kbytes
PowerBook Display	N/A	34 Kbytes
Sharing Setup	4 Kbytes	4 Kbytes
SuperClock!	16 Kbytes	16 Kbytes
Users and Groups	4 Kbytes	4 Kbytes
Views	3 Kbytes	3 Kbytes
Quickeys[2] RunTime	204 Kbytes	204 Kbytes
Extensions folder		
AppleTalk Remote Access	70 Kbytes	70 Kbytes
AppleShare	72 Kbytes	75 Kbytes
CE Toolbox	65 Kbytes	65 Kbytes
EtherTalk Phase 2	16 Kbytes	16 Kbytes
EtherTalk Prep	N/A	30 Kbytes
File-Sharing Extension	167 Kbytes	170 Kbytes
LaserWriter[*]	219 Kbytes	219 Kbytes
Network Extension	92 Kbytes	96 Kbytes
Personal LaserWriter SC	72 Kbytes	72 Kbytes
Personal LaserWriter LS	92 Kbytes	92 Kbytes
Print Monitor	58 Kbytes	63 Kbytes
Remote Access Aliases[***]	32 Kbytes	32 Kbytes
Remote Only[***]	4 Kbytes	4 Kbytes
Serial Port Arbitrator[***]	7 Kbytes	7 Kbytes
StyleWriter[*]	80 Kbytes	110 Kbytes

(continued)

The Road Warrior's System Folder (continued)

	System 7.0.1	System 7.1
Extensions folder (continued)		
The Alarm (AgentDA)	35 Kbytes	35 Kbytes
The Alarm Data (AgentDA)	5 Kbytes	5 Kbytes
Fonts folder	N/A	971 Kbytes**
Startup Items folder		
Applicon	84 Kbytes	84 Kbytes
System Folder		
Finder	355 Kbytes	369 Kbytes
System Suitcase	1,322 Kbytes**	887 Kbytes
Totals	**3,465 Kbytes**	**4,174 Kbytes**

N/A means the file in question doesn't come standard with that version of System 7.

*   LaserWriter, StyleWriter, Personal LaserWriter SC and Personal LaserWriter LS are offered as examples.

**   TrueType fonts only

*** These files were added by AppleTalk Remote Access.

Note: QuicKeys for Nomads adds a 55-Kbyte folder to the Preferences folder.

PART

2

SETTING SAIL ON THE
NETWORK CLIPPER

An Upstanding Network Citizen

Before the Macintosh came along, computer networking meant spending hundreds of hours and thousands of dollars buying and installing special hardware and software. Today's PC networks are still as complex as the cross-laced colors on a Jackson Pollack canvas, while Apple's computers can be networked simply, with only a telephone cable, a connector, and a couple of mouse clicks.

PowerBooks propelled Apple's networking prowess to a higher level. Its sheer lack of bulk makes connecting a PowerBook to a network a fabulously easy task. Moving a desktop Mac can be a production—lugging the monitor, keyboard, and chassis to a new location, trawling for the Local-Talk cable, getting the monitor connected to the CPU, getting the CPU hooked to some juice. But with PowerBooks, once you've anchored the network and power cable to the desktop, all it takes is pulling your seven-pound system from its bag and plugging it in. With a Duo it's even simpler—just lift up the back door and lock into a MiniDock or better yet, slide it into the Duo Dock.

It's just as well that jacking your PowerBook into the net is simple, because you'll be changing those network connections frequently. Think about how seldom you move your Mac—it's like a cornerstone, an electronic brick that's been mortared to your desktop. The PowerBook is lithe, sturdy, and able to fly with you from meeting to meeting, city to city, a veritable computerized pterodactyl that can nest on any narrow ledge of network connectivity.

Flexibility can be a curse, because it requires that you know what you want to do and understand how to do it in a variety of environments. It also requires you come to each network prepared with the right software and hardware. You'll need only two things for PowerBook networking: a clear space on a desk and the right kind of adapter to connect the laptop to the network cable in question. Your operating system already includes file-sharing software that lets you log onto and use an AppleShare file server. A few adjustments to the operating system will let your PowerBook speak in many connectivity tongues, let other people on a network access information stored on its hard disk, and even screen the files that networked users will be able to see.

At Your Server

AppleShare is a file server. It's not a full-blown network operating system like Novell Inc.'s NetWare or Banyan Systems Inc.'s VINES, which govern everything that happens on a network from the way computers talk to one another to how files are stored in a central information warehouse.

Apple's approach is more modular: AppleShare delivers the ability to share a file with another networked user; the AppleTalk protocol controls Mac communications on the network.

The culmination of Apple's file-sharing paradigm came in 1991 with the introduction of System 7. Now aliases let users build one-click network connectivity into the Finder; by creating an alias of an AppleShare server, it is possible to log on without having to deal with the network interface. File-sharing, a set of control panels and extensions integrated into System 7, lets users make any Mac act like an AppleShare server. It's possible in just a few steps to place a whole hard disk or just a single folder at the disposal of an entire network.

Later in 1991, when the PowerBooks were rolled out, Apple added remote networking to its repertoire. Now AppleTalk Remote Access extends the elegance of AppleShare across a dial-up modem connection and opens a huge can of worms for network managers who are concerned about security.

See the Mobile Commuter note below.

⬇

PowerBooks let people do their best work, when they want, where they want, and return to the office to put that information on a network. Once it's on a network, the information helps power collaboration, allowing co-workers to view and respond to one another's work in considerably less time than in the days of inter-office mail.

That idea that people should work together through their computers is reshaping the corporation. Instead of managing people, many companies are finding that they need an expert in managing the flow of information. From the individual's point of view there is only one message: You can be liberated from the confines of a traditional office and still make a valuable contribution to your employer.

Collaboration, however, makes demands on every user. New concepts must be embraced; you have to understand that your computer is becoming a link in a network chain, rather than the rugged individualist you packed onto the electronic frontier. Suddenly, you have to think about security, keeping unauthorized eyes from perusing your company's mission-critical data. Your PowerBook bag will get a little heavier, too, when you begin carrying a LocalTalk cable or a SCSI Port-to-Ethernet adapter (or a PowerLink DeskNet for Duo users) to accommodate the two network connections you encounter most often.

This chapter will focus on how to configure your PowerBook so that it can access an AppleShare server or act as a file server using System 7's file-sharing features. If you want specific advice on connectivity products, electronic mail, and other network-based services, turn to the next part of this section, *A Port for Every Road Warrior*.

The file is in the mail.

File-sharing isn't the only answer to getting a file from one place to another. Electronic mail can be a great alternative for smaller networks, especially when users are on the move all the time.

E-mail, like file-sharing, relies on a server as a repository for files. But e-mail's big advantage is that users don't have to wait for their coworkers to check the server for a newly uploaded file. Instead, e-mail systems deliver the latest draft of a crucial document the moment your coworkers log on to the network. Not only does the file arrive, you can add a message that describes changes you've made and your rationales for making those changes.

You also give up some control over the flow of information when you turn to e-mail. Communication on an e-mail network tends to be rather anarchic, and it's easy to accidentally erase one version of a file when downloading a later draft from the mail server. (Always read your "A newer file..." dialog boxes carefully before clicking *OK.*)

When it comes to support for remote users, most e-mail systems enjoy an advantage over AppleShare—at least without the help of AppleTalk Remote Access. CE Software Inc.'s QuickMail, Microsoft's Mail, and Lotus Development Corporation's cc:Mail all provide client software that lets users dial in to take a look at their mail. We believe remote e-mail can give PowerBook users a more targeted approach to intra-organizational communications than ARA. Logging onto a mail server is an automated process that produces a list of the messages and files that have been sent to you, while ARA requires that you first make the connection, and second, open the Chooser and pick the file servers you want to mount; then you're still left with the job of searching the server to find the file you want. For a smaller company, one that doesn't need to distribute database access to remote users, e-mail is a bargain basement solution to collaboration.

Quick, Robin, to the Bat Cave!

PowerBooks offer myriad networking advantages over PCs, because the modular Macintosh operating system lets you drop in extensions and control panels that support any network protocol to which you need to connect. Extensions and control panels can make your operating system change its network identity, allowing it to handle different protocols (the rules of a network) and different physical connections.

Think of the way Bruce Wayne and Dick Grayson were transformed into Batman and Robin while sliding down the Bat Poles, and you've got an idea about how easy Mac networking can be. From AppleTalk and its derivatives, EtherTalk and TokenTalk, to the proprietary worlds of NetWare and VINES, and even the open standards, TCP/IP and OSI, the Mac is the only computer that can hold up its end of the network mix through a consistent user interface.

You'll view network services as the same kind of icon in the Finder or the Chooser because of Apple's success in lobbying the rest of the computer industry to: first, support the AppleTalk protocol stack; and, second, implement the AppleTalk File Protocol (AFP) on their file servers.

It has been a tough row for Apple to hoe, but the rewards have fallen to their customers. You may need to run a third-party application to gain Mac-like access to a file server, but even this fact drives home the success of AppleTalk, Apple protocol stacks, like MacTCP and MacOSI, and AFP. They allow developers to connect Macs to various computers and translate their exotic filing systems into the familiar Mac graphical interface.

The proof, however, is in the virtual pudding. When you use a Power-Book to access AppleShare, NetWare, VINES, or Network Filing System (NFS, developed by Sun Microsystems Inc.) file servers, you'll see them as double-clickable icons in the Finder. Open the file server, and the files stored there are displayed in folders, just like the files on your local hard disk.

While we cannot hope to present all the possible combinations of software and hardware you can use to grab files from the world's file servers, there are some basics of PowerBook connectivity that you can use to tailor your network to support day-to-day use by Mobile Commuters and Road Warriors alike. If you want more information on Macintosh networking, we suggest you pick up a copy of John Rizzo's *MacUser Guide to Connectivity*, a guide to opening the network doors on your Mac.

The Pieces and the Puzzle

If you want to have ready access to several different networks, a little operating system tailoring is necessary. Flexible connectivity will challenge your creativity, especially if you have very little RAM and a paltry amount of hard disk space in your PowerBook. Every network protocol stack and its control panel or extension gobbles up a bit more memory.

For example, when one of the authors abandoned his desktop Mac in favor of a PowerBook 170, the greatest challenge he faced was maintaining the different network connections he used everyday. Besides the LocalTalk network at *MacWEEK* that connected Mitch to the rest of the editorial staff, he frequently logged onto Internet, a world-wide network of university, military, and research organizations that run on the TCP/IP protocol. TCP/IP is an Ethernet-based protocol, but Mitch was stuck on LocalTalk. At first, he resorted to a simple dial-up service to read his Internet mail and Usenet newsgroups (see Section IV, *Exploring Cyberspace*, for more about Internet), but as time passed, he convinced *MacWEEK*'s network administrator to upgrade a router between the LocalTalk and EtherTalk segments of the newspaper's network, which gave him a window to the Internet from his PowerBook's LocalTalk connection. This required installing the MacTCP protocol stack on the 170 and more than a few loop-de-loops for the net administrator, whose routers suddenly blew up. (This is not meant as a confession, those routers were worn out!)

Even then, the resulting network performance was too slow.

So Mitch finally got a SCSI-to-Ethernet device on his desktop and jumped right onto the TCP/IP network. Now, the network has stabilized and he can wander the Internet at Ethernet's 10-Mbps red line. Lately, he's been trying out *MacWEEK*'s link to the Ziff Communications corporate NetWare networks, which are interconnected by high-speed telephone lines. Yes, they are all visible in the Chooser on his PowerBook, because he's using a NetMounter, a control panel made by Dayna Communications Inc.

He pays for these whiz-bang network connections. The files that provide AppleShare, TCP/IP, and NetWare support consume approximately 910 Kbytes of disk space, and the operating system requires at least 550 Kbytes of additional RAM when running, compared to a system without any network access capabilities.

When building your own system, keep in mind the tradeoffs you make when you add support for additional network protocols. First-generation PowerBooks, because they can handle only 8 Mbytes of RAM and ship with small hard disks, may not be the machines for the multi-protocol

Road Warrior. PowerBook 160, 180, and Duo owners who don't install extra RAM will be in a similar jam, but don't despair. Your computers can be tuned to become the digital equivalent of the big-muscle street machines that headed out to the drag strip on Saturday nights of yore.

Jacking In—The Basics

If you own a PowerBook and use a network, it's most likely a LocalTalk- or Ethernet-based system, which predominate in Macintosh offices.

LocalTalk grew out of the original Macintosh and is beginning to show its age as networks get larger. Nevertheless, its simplicity and low price point (it runs on the same unshielded phone cable you use in your home) have sustained its place in small and medium-sized groups of networked systems. The problem with LocalTalk is its lack of bandwidth. If you think of a network as a highway, bandwidth is the number of lanes traffic can drive on. LocalTalk's 230.4-Kbps speed is the equivalent of a two-lane road, but that's understandable because it dates from the age of the Model A, as computers go. (The Model T of personal computers was the Apple II. The PS/1, from IBM, finds its analog in the steam-powered horseless carriage. For a complete list of car-to-computer metaphors, e-mail us from your PowerBook Miata.)

Ethernet, on the other hand, is a ten-lane digital autobahn where traffic flies along at 10 Mbps, approximately 43 times faster than on bumpy, old LocalTalk. Understandably, companies with more than 50 networked computers have tended to adopt Ethernet.

You have several choices of Ethernet media or cabling. Thick and thin coaxial cable and shielded twisted-pair telephone cabling are the most popular options for Ethernet traffic.

How do you connect to the network? Let's take a look first at the physical connections.

LocalTalk runs over ordinary telephone wire or over a printer cable if it has the mini DIN-8 connector on both ends (like the cable used to connect to an Apple ImageWriter II). Don't make the mistake, however, of plugging your LocalTalk network into the RJ-11 modem port on your Power-Book. Ask your Apple dealer for a LocalTalk Connector or one of the Farallon-type PhoneNet connectors that are compatible with LocalTalk. These devices plug into the printer serial port on PowerBooks and Duo Docks or the Duo's single serial port.

See the
Road Warrior
note below.

Ethernet requires an external adapter. PowerBook 100, 140, 145, 160, 170, or 180 users will need an external adapter that plugs into the SCSI port, such as Dayna Communications Inc.'s DaynaPort SCSI/Link or Asanté Technologies Inc.'s EN/SC adapters. An Ethernet-to-serial port adapter, the DaynaPort E/Z, is also available. But we recommend this device as a solution of last resort, because the PowerBook serial port doesn't have the capacity to handle Ethernet's 10-Mbps transmission speeds. This isn't a problem most of the time, because the DaynaPort E/Z has buffer memory that holds the data that can't get through the serial port. When traffic is especially heavy, like those times you want to copy a 2Mbyte file from the server to your PowerBook, there's a chance you'll exceed the buffer's capacity and cause the file transfer to fail.

The Duo link to Ethernet is available through adapter cards installed in the Duo Dock, or you can use one of the third-party docks, such as the PowerLink DeskNet dock from E-Machines, that include a built-in Ethernet transceiver.

A lot of PowerBook users never get around to shutting down their computer but just go from place to place with a sleeping portable tucked under their arm. If you will be frequently connecting and disconnecting from a network, it's a good idea to get in the habit of rebooting the PowerBook each time you do so. AppleTalk networks assign a unique network address to connected Macs when they boot. If your computer wasn't connected to a network when you turned it on and therefore didn't get an address, connecting it to a network while it's sleeping will cause a lot of confusion. The first time your PowerBook tries to access the network, it will get a message that translates from computerese as something like, "Who the hell are you?" Not only does your PowerBook become confused, the whole network can get bogged down, as Macs and routers begin asking each other, "Who the hell is that?"

The same goes for disconnecting a PowerBook from a network. AppleTalk uses Dynamic Node Addressing, which means it assigns an address that is free at the time the computer boots up. (A Mac asks if a number is taken, and if it doesn't receive an affirmative response along the lines of "Hey, that's my address," it uses that number as its own address.) If your computer wakes up thinking it has an address that was claimed by another Mac while you were off the network, the network generates a lot of traffic trying to straighten out the disagreement, and may suffer the computer equivalent of the bends that a deep sea diver gets when too much carbon dioxide accumulates in his bloodstream.

Now that you've got a physical connection, you need to tell your Power-Book which kind of network you are using. Doing so means you step up from the nuts and bolts of network connections into your PowerBook's operating system.

The Doorway to Heaven

Everyone has probably heard some variant of the riddle about the two doors. One leads to heaven, the other to hell, and guarding the doors are two guards, one who always tells the truth and one who always lies.

You only get to ask one guard one question to figure out which door is which. So the challenge of the riddle is to figure out the one question you could ask to find which door leads to heaven.

The ports on your PowerBook are like those two doors. In order to enter the network, you must always connect to the printer port; only that port is LocalTalk-enabled (it's also faster than the modem port). The printer port is sometimes referred to as port B.

There is one PowerBook where this isn't true, the Duo. The Duo only has one serial port on it, and it is designated as port A, normally the slower modem port that doesn't support LocalTalk. But with a little silicon magic, Apple's Duo engineers have managed to make port A perform like the printer port—it supports LocalTalk and the higher throughput necessary for networking.

What's really neat about the Duo serial port is, when docked to a Duo Dock or MiniDock, the port designations revert, and the ports on the docks behave normally: the modem port (port A) is slow and doesn't support networking; the printer port (port B) does.

Okay, comparing PowerBook ports to the door riddle was a bit of a stretch. By the way, the answer, or rather the question is, "Which would the other guard say is the door to heaven?"

Network Control Panel

The Mac operating system uses small blocks of code called network drivers to control the physical connection to a network. A LocalTalk driver is built in to the computer's system software, others must be added using the Apple Installer. When you first start your computer, it loads the LocalTalk driver, on the assumption that you are using a LocalTalk network. If you want to change the connection to Ethernet, open the Network control panel.

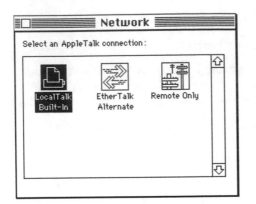

Figure 1. Network Control Panel

An icon representing each installed driver appears in the control panel; when you open it for the first time, the LocalTalk driver will be highlighted. To change your network connection, simply click the driver you want to use. Until you choose another driver or until the connection fails on startup, the computer will continue to use the network connection you selected.

If you are, for example, using EtherTalk and a SCSI-to-Ethernet adapter at your office, and you arrive home and restart your PowerBook, the connection will fail. The computer will look for the Ethernet network, which is no longer available, and warn you that it is going to default back to LocalTalk. The next time you go to the office, you'll have to open the Network control panel and select the EtherTalk driver.

That's all you need to know about working with the wired network links in your PowerBook. Let's move on to the software that enables different kinds of file-sharing.

AppleShare Extension

The AppleShare extension makes the blind PowerBook see file servers.

See the Mobile Commuter note below.

⬇

AppleShare doesn't run on your PowerBook—it is a program that resides on a server somewhere on the network. Most AppleShare servers, in fact, live in closets or under someone's desk, which is the fate of a computer that does little more than store files and user profiles.

The AppleShare extension is a sort of over-glorified network driver. Its only job is interacting with AppleShare servers on a network. Once this extension is installed, the AppleShare icon will appear in your Chooser, letting you mount a server and have it appear on your desktop as an icon. Once a server appears in the Finder, it acts just like a hard disk; you can double-click it to see folders and files, and many of those documents can be opened with a mouse click. There are some files, however, that you'll not be able to open or, perhaps, even see when logged onto an AppleShare server. Security features in the server allow a network administrator to lock and hide some files or simply prevent users from making changes to the document that appears on the server.

Before you can use an AppleShare server, you will need to contact your network administrator to have her create a user account for you. There is a Guest access feature that allows users to log onto an AppleShare server, but most network administrators disable Guest accounts to prevent unauthorized access.

AppleShare and Its Limits

Sharing is a time-consuming business for a computer. The more users you connect to an AppleShare file server, the more CPU cycles you'll expend on administratrivia within the computer. Why? Because the server has to think about each user separately, and it can't do more than one job at a time. This is the reason that Apple tells companies not to connect more than 120 users to a single AppleShare server.

Let's not mince words, though. If all 120 users on a network were to log onto a server and try to copy files to their desktop simultaneously, that server's back is going to break like that of an old plowhorse whipped beyond its limits. Practically speaking, you can probably safely support between 40 and 65 concurrent users on a single AppleShare server— although you should still pray that they are not collectively seized with the desire to copy files.

If you're an ordinary user, one who doesn't have to maintain a network, the closest you'll ever come to an AppleShare server is the icon on your desktop. The AppleShare application runs best on 68030-based Macintoshes, which are usually stowed out of sight in an air-conditioned telephone closet. We find that the SE/30 is a favorite for its compact size and CPU speed.

Remember, too, that not all digital nomads will want to keep the Apple-Share extension in their system folder. Intentional Tourists who never use anything but floppies and SCSI Disk Mode to transfer files to a desktop Macintosh will probably find better uses for the disk space and RAM saved by excising the AppleShare extension and other file-sharing-related resources.

You still must make a few critical changes before you can access a file server. You make those changes in the Chooser.

The Chooser: Window to the Network World

Apple leveraged the value of its built-in networking with a new idea in network interfacing, the Chooser. A vast improvement over the PC and Unix windows on networking, which require the user to commit to memory a lexicon of archaic commands to switch drivers and identify a target printer or server, the Chooser lets you select whatever printer or server you like by clicking on an icon and a name.

Using the Chooser is usually a two- or three-click job. When you open the Chooser from the Apple Menu, begin by clicking in the window at the upper left on the icon for the service you want to access, be it an Apple-Share server, a printer, or something more exotic. Your choices will appear in the window on the right or, if you are on a multi-zone network, the selections will be limited to those available in the local zone. You can switch your view to other zones by clicking on the zone names in the AppleTalk Zones window on the lower left of the Chooser interface (see Figure 2).

Setting up an AppleShare connection requires that you first enable AppleTalk and select the server you want to bring onto the desktop. After getting your account and password, you must:

1. Open the Chooser.

2. Turn on AppleTalk by clicking the radio button in the lower right corner of the Chooser window.

3. Reboot your computer.

4. Open the Chooser, again.

5. Click the AppleShare icon. A list of available servers will appear in the window to the right of the icon.

6. Select the server you want by double-clicking its name in the list.

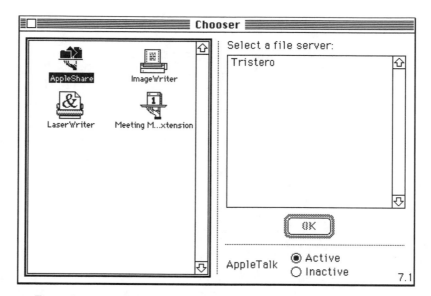

Figure 2. The Chooser

7. Once you've made a selection, a password dialog box appears—this is what happens when you log onto an AppleShare server or another Mac. Type your password and name and click the OK button. It should be noted that once you've set up your name in the Mac, you won't have to type it again unless you want to log in under a different user name.

   If no password is required, just click *OK.*

8. Yet another dialog box opens. Chances are, that the server incorporates several mounted volumes, so the Chooser presents a second window in which those volumes are listed. You can choose the volumes you want by holding down the shift key as you click on the volume names in the list. Click *OK.*

   This dialog box also gives you the option of having the operating system open the server automatically when you reboot your computer. We recommend that you don't click the radio button that enables this feature, because every time you boot when disconnected from the server you'll get a warning dialog telling you the server could not be found.

See the Digital Nomad note below.

9. You're back in the original Chooser window. Just close it, and you'll see the server icon(s) on your desktop.

Since PowerBook users are switching network and printer connections quite often, it's important to remember that documents may not look exactly the same when printed on different printers. Incorrect printer settings also affect the look of text on your PowerBook display. In fact, it is not unusual to find that a document that's displayed with the ImageWriter driver is as much as a quarter-page longer on screen than the same document displayed while the LaserWriter driver is enabled.

When you select a new printer in the Chooser, you'll be prompted to choose *Page Setup* in all open applications. This guarantees that the changes necessary to accommodate the printer you choose are reflected in the layout of your documents.

Alias Smith and Jones

System 7's aliasing feature can slash the number of trips you take to the Chooser, automating the entire process of logging onto file servers. Just as you can create an alias that tracks down and launches an oft-used document or application, you can use aliases to reach across a network and access a server.

Road Warriors and Mobile Commuters, in particular, who might access file servers on two or three different networks in a given week or month, can live more comfortably under an alias.

A file server alias can be double-clicked, which brings you directly to the password dialog in Step 7 of the Chooser directions above. All you need do is enter the password, and the operating system will take you directly to your destination. If you're an especially granular person who wants to keep aliases for individual documents or folders on a server, go ahead. The sign-on process works just the same for files and folders as it does for the whole server.

We suggest that you create a folder on the PowerBook desktop for each network you typically use and store aliases for frequently used servers, folders, and documents for those networks (use the command-N key sequence to create a new folder).

When you put a first-generation PowerBook to sleep or disconnect it from a network, it normally dismounts any servers or shared volumes you might have on your desktop. The next-generation PowerBooks deliver AutoRemounter, an answer to the automatic dismount.

AutoRemounter is a System 7.1 control panel that lets your computer search the network for shared volumes and servers that were available before it went to sleep and then automatically log onto them (see Figure 3). If AutoRemounter can't find the volumes because the network connection has been lost, the usual message appears announcing that the file server is no longer available.

You can set the controls to remount shared disks whenever the Power-Book wakes (by selecting *After Sleep*) or whenever the computer wakes or restarts (*Always*). There's a security concern here, because you can set your PowerBook to remount servers with or without a password. If you are concerned about keeping files on the server private, we suggest you require a password whenever AutoRemounter does its thing.

The bad news is that the AutoRemounter control panel ships only with the second-generation PowerBooks. The really bad news is that it doesn't work with first-generation PowerBooks (100s, 140s, 145s, and 170s).

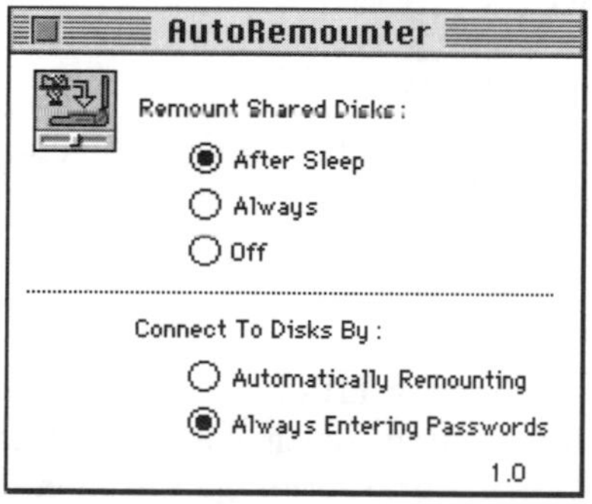

Figure 3. AutoRemounter is the automatic door to network resources.

Sharing Your Space

System 7 lets you set up your PowerBook as a file server. Be forewarned, though, because personal file-sharing in System 7 opens your computer like an all-night grocery. Folks can just drop in and look around your hard disk whenever you want, unless you take some time and learn about the security features of the Macintosh operating system. This section looks at the control panels and Finder commands that let users build relatively sophisticated levels of file access into their networked computers.

Reining in unauthorized users who might try to log onto your networked PowerBook must be a high priority for Mobile Commuters and

Road Warriors who keep sensitive information on their hard disks. At the same time, you need to share that information with key people in your organization.

Solving the security versus access conundrum begins with a little bit of thought. It's obvious that you don't need to share information with everyone you work with, nor would you want a file to be accessible to a stranger. Make a list of the people with whom you need to share files, then try to put them into groups.

There are two criteria you might use to group people together. If you tend to work with different people on different projects, put folks and the files that you normally share with them in the same group. Or, if your organization has a rigid hierarchy, try grouping people by lines of authority, combining decision-makers with the information they need. Now, go to your desktop and create folders into which you put all the documents for each group of people with whom you'll be sharing files on your hard disk. Later in this section, when you are learning to set privileges for folders, refer to the lists you've just made.

Sharing Setup and Users & Groups

These are the most powerful lines of defense in the Macintosh operating system, so learn to use them wisely.

Sharing Setup

When you unpack and boot your PowerBook for the first time, it's completely closed to network connections, even if you've already plugged a LocalTalk adapter into the serial port. Outgoing links, which let you view servers and files on the rest of the network, must be made in the Chooser (see above). Incoming network links, which open your PowerBook's hard disk to other networked users, are disabled by the default setting in the Sharing Setup control panel.

Before initiating file-sharing on your hard disk, you must open Sharing Setup and do a little computer housekeeping (see Figure 4).

First, fill in the Owner Name field with your name.

Be sure to type a password into the Owner Password field; otherwise anyone on the network who tries to log onto your PowerBook can access all your files, using only your name as identification. We suggest you use a password of at least seven letters (the limit is eight), mixing upper- and lowercase characters. Try to avoid predictable words (like your daughter's name or the model car you drive) in order to foil an intruder who might make a lucky guess. (For an extended discussion of network security, see Section II, Part 3, *A Port for Every Road Warrior*.)

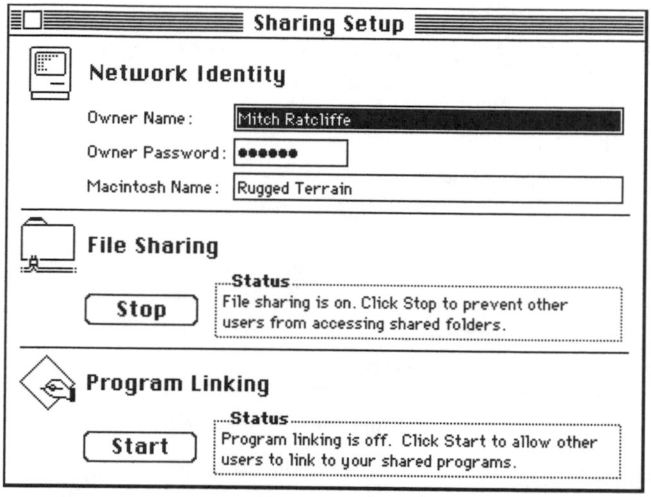

Figure 4. Sharing Setup opens PowerBooks to network file-sharing.

After typing in your PowerBook's name, you're ready to enable file-sharing. Just click the Start button under *File Sharing*. What happens? Your PowerBook appears by the name you just entered in the Chooser for all users on the network (see "Users & Groups" below). Be sure to pick a clever name; systems administrators especially like names that bear as little relationship to the computer they belong to as possible. Actually, it drives them nuts to have all these weird PowerBook names popping up and down on the network like an electronic "Whack-A-Mole" game.

Program Linking, the other radio button in the Sharing Setup control panel, will allow applications running on a network to communicate with one another. An Apple events-dependent feature, you'll probably want to leave it off unless your office has a shared contact database that uses your address book as a resource.

Users & Groups

Until you use this control panel to build a list of people who can log onto your computer, your PowerBook is wide open to intrusion—and by enabling file-sharing, you've just hung out a virtual invitation that shows up on the network for all to see.

When you open Users & Groups, two icons that resemble an unlikely humanoid profile appear in a Finder window (Apple's idealized user must be the space alien reported in the tabloids to be buddying up to U.S. politicians). One of these little guys has your name, and the other is called "<Guest>" (see Figure 5).

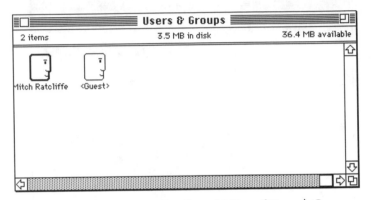

Figure 5. The Innocuous But Powerful Face of Users & Groups

First, open the <Guest> icon by double-clicking. You have only two choices to make, but they are critical to building a wall between your personal data and the office snoop (see Figure 6).

Guest is a standard access account built into almost all network-savvy computer operating systems. The idea is to facilitate coworkers who need a quick look into a colleague's files. Say the boss needs to grab the latest copy of your quarterly sales analysis. She just opens her Chooser, selects your PowerBook, and clicks the Guest radio button in the dialog box that appears. She's into your hard disk without having to enter a password or even identifying herself.

Guest is also the hole that intruders count on you to leave open; it's the oversight that butters the bread of most of the hackers who have broken into major computer networks. In other systems, like Digital Equipment Corporation's VMS and most flavors of UNIX, there are numerous variations on Guest that are designed to let system administrators get access to a computer.

The default setting for Guest is off. Leave it that way, and you will foil the efforts of any intruder who might try to sneak onto your networked PowerBook.

If someone needs access to your computer, they should first ask you to create an account for them (see below). It's safer for all concerned. As for Program Linking, you'll want to enable this only if your network is out on the leading edge with Apple events-savvy applications.

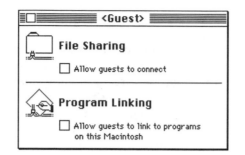

Figure 6. Shutting down the Guest connection isn't bad manners.

When you enable file-sharing, you have to play traffic cop with regard to the comings and goings on your hard disk. This is what you do when you create user accounts and assign privileges in the Users & Groups control panel.

In order to understand more about user accounts, let's look at the user icon with your name on it. Double-click this icon to set the access you will have if you try to log onto your own PowerBook from another Mac on your office network (see Figure 7).

It's not unusual at *MacWEEK* for one of the staff to sit down with an editor without a copy of an important file. Rather than run back to their desk, open the file, and print it out, they just open the editor's Chooser and select their own Mac. With a couple of mouse clicks, the reporter can have the document open for reference. The conference goes on unimpeded, since Macs let us manipulate network connections so easily.

When the user account window opens, you will see that under the File Sharing icon are three check boxes:

- **Allow user to connect**   If you check this, you can log onto your PowerBook from another Macintosh by using your own name and the password you entered in the Sharing Setup control panel.

- **Allow user to change password**   We recommend that you disable this function to eliminate any edge it might give an intruder who gains access to your PowerBook by posing as its owner, you. This checkbox lets you change your password while logged onto your PowerBook from a different Mac.

- **Allow user to see entire disk**   Here's a practical question that forces you to balance security against convenience: should a disk be wide open or should the files stored there be viewable only by users with specific permission to see them? When it comes to your own access, the authors suggest that you keep your view as wide as possible. But only if you have added a password in Sharing Setup.

If you have installed AppleTalk Remote Access, you'll see another section in User Profiles that controls access to your PowerBook by systems that dial in using a modem. This controls direct access to the computer, which can occur only if your PowerBook is connected to a phone line and is configured to answer incoming calls (see below for more ARA-related information). Checking these Remote Access boxes does not limit the access of remote users who dial in through another Macintosh on the network; if they have a user account, or if you've forgotten to disable the Guest account, they can still log on to your computer.

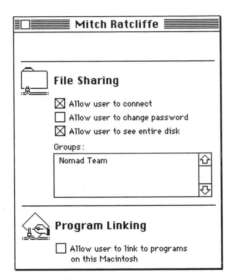

Figure 7. The User Control Panel

The Groups list provides an accounting of all the file-sharing groups that have access to your PowerBook. Each group can have a specific set of privileges that allows for customization of the information flow for co-workers collaborating on different projects.

Before you can create groups, you have to dole out some new user accounts. The process begins in the Users & Groups window. Select *New User* under the File menu to create a new user icon named, aptly enough, New User. Change the name of the icon to the name of the person whose account it will represent.

Open the icon. The window is a little different than the one that describes your own account (see Figure 8). You can and should assign a password to the user. The control panel won't let you grant access to all of your PowerBook's hard disk within a single checkbox. (By golly, Apple is watching out for your interests, after all!) In our example, Stephen Howard, who did the technical editing on this book, is allowed to log onto the Power-Book, and he can change his password, if he likes. What you don't see are the file-sharing privileges Stephen has, which are attached to his identity as a member of the Nomad Team group (see below).

It's possible to disable a user account without dragging it into the trash; just remove the check from the "Allow user to connect" box. It pays to save user account files, because you may want to enable and disable a particular person's account as the projects on which you collaborate come and go.

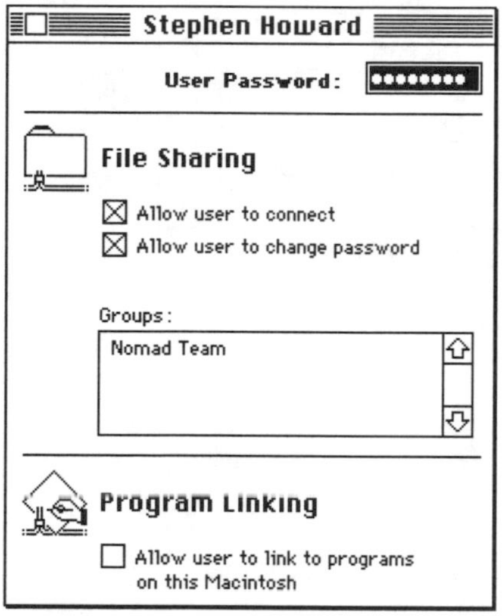

Figure 8. User accounts set the limits of network access.

Now that you have set up a couple of accounts for your coworkers, you may want to group them together so that you can set access privileges by project team, department, or security clearance. While in the Users & Groups window, click on the File menu and select *New Group*. A two-user profile icon (a group of blockheaded users) appears; but when you click on the icon, it opens into an empty window because the group still doesn't have any members.

You don't have to hold an election to get someone into your new group; just click the user icons you want included and drag them onto the group icon. What you've done is create aliases of the user accounts that are included in the new group. Now, if you double-click on the group icon, you'll see blockhead portrait icons for each user account you included (see Figure 9).

Want to evict someone from a group? Just drag their portrait icon from the Group window into the trash. Groups, too, can go the way of the waste basket once you finish a project. Icons from Users & Groups windows cannot be dragged into other folders or onto the desktop, because they are not real files but are preferences stored in a master file that resides in the Preferences folder in the System folder.

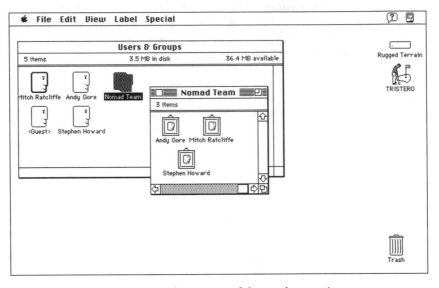

Figure 9. A group icon rounds up copies of the usual suspects' user accounts.

The journey toward safe and sane file-sharing is almost complete. But there's one more step necessary after closing the Users & Groups control panel. Once you have returned to the Finder, highlight your hard disk icon and click on the File menu. Select *Sharing*, and a dialog box appears, where you can set different levels of access to your hard disk (see Figure 10).

Checking only the "Share this item and its contents" box beneath the hard disk icon lays open all the files on the disk to anyone with a user account on your PowerBook. You may want to take the next step and narrow the access to the disk. Use the User/Group pop-up menu, a list of all user and group accounts installed on the PowerBook, to grant privileges to a specific group of people.

Privileges at the hard disk level are very arbitrary, because you can assign access to only one user or group at a time. Conversely, you can throw the doors open by checking the See Folders, See Files, and Make Changes boxes in the Everyone row. We think you'll agree that an all-or-nothing choice is restrictive when all you want to do is give different groups their own access privileges to files stored on the PowerBook disk.

- **See Folders**   Checking this box allows people to see and open folders; unchecking it makes folders invisible. You can see a folder but be unable to open it only when both See Folders and See Files have been unchecked—the Finder doesn't even bother to open it. And if you can't see some of the contents of a folder, the Finder won't copy the whole folder.

- **See Files**   Users can open documents stored on your hard disk but cannot make changes to those files. Instead, they can save a copy of the file to their own disk, leaving the original untouched.

- **Make Changes**   Not only can your coworkers open your documents, they can make changes and save them to your hard disk, close the documents, and log off your computer without leaving a hint that they've been there.

```
┌─────────────────────────────────────────────┐
│▤□▧▨▨▨▨▨▨   Rugged Terrain  ▨▨▨▨▨▨▨▨▨│
│                                             │
│    Where:         Rugged Terrain, SCSI 0    │
│   ┌───────┐                                 │
│   └───────┘                                 │
│                                             │
│  ⊠ Share this item and its contents         │
│                                             │
│  ─────────────────────────────────────────  │
│                       See    See   Make     │
│                     Folders  Files Changes  │
│    Owner: ┌─Mitch Ratcliffe ▼┐  ⊠   ⊠   ⊠   │
│ User/Group: ┌─Nomad Team  ▼─┐   ⊠   ⊠   ⊠   │
│              Everyone           ⊠   ⊠   ⊠   │
│  ┌─┐                                        │
│  └─┘ Make all currently enclosed folders like this one │
│                                             │
└─────────────────────────────────────────────┘
```

Figure 10. ***The Sharing Dialog: Lop-sided Privileges*** *It may look like the Nomad Team is the only User/Group that has sharing privileges for this hard disk. However, the checks in the See Folders, See Files, and Make Changes boxes grant access to all users.*

We suggest that instead of sharing the whole disk, you should set up individual folders for each user or group with whom you want to share. Although users will see the your PowerBook's hard disk in the Chooser, once they enter their password, they'll be given access only to those folders you allow, and the rest of the disk will be invisible (a shared folder appears in the Finder as a file server icon). The Sharing dialog can be used to share any folder or nested folder on your hard disk. This is an ideal mechanism for creating project repositories or distributing data to your department.

Remember that controlling the number of changes made to files on your hard disk is critical to your own organizational sanity. Take special care with the Make Changes privilege or you can face the potential for embarrassment or disaster.

For example, imagine that your entire hard disk is shared, and the Make Changes box in Sharing is checked. Your partner needs to change a spreadsheet called "Gross vs. Net Profits" that resides on your PowerBook.

While you are tied up in a meeting with your accountants, he logs onto your computer, finds the file, and begins to work. As he pours in his revised profit projections, he includes a small mistake that makes your company's financial statement look like the subject of a Ross Perot half-hour infomercial on the national debt. Before you know it, he's out to lunch, and you decide to haul your PowerBook and the spreadsheet into that accounting meeting to show off the latest numbers. There's nothing about the icon or filename to indicate that it's been changed since you put the final polish on it over breakfast—you double-click the file and doom your Small Business Administration loans for the next century.

Here's a scenario that makes more sense: Don't share the whole disk; instead, you should create two folders on the top level of your hard disk, calling one "Outgoing." Turn off the Make Changes privilege for the Outgoing folder. Use this as a distribution point, allowing coworkers to copy files out of the folder to their own hard disks. This is the place that your partner should have gone to grab the Gross vs. Net Profits file.

Call the second folder "Incoming," then select *Sharing* in the File menu and uncheck the button "Same as enclosing folder." Then check the Make Changes box. This special folder (and any folders inside it) will then be writable. If you want to be more secure, you could uncheck the See Files and See Folders buttons, making this special folder into a drop box. People would be able to copy files into it, but no one could see what was there. Your partner can drag a file called "Updated Gross vs. Net Profits" onto your hard disk during a file-sharing session, and then you can review it during your next free moment, leaving your original work—and your corporate audit trails—intact.

Now, a Scenario That Will Entertain Our Friends and Annoy Our Enemies

Real people don't have just one job, nor are they wrapped up in only one project at a time. Their lives are complex and so is the information they need to share. Let's say you are the division manager at a small lumber company, and you need to do three things every day: one, let the salespeople know the latest Redwood prices; two, nag your lobbyist to keep the pressure on local politicians to win big tax breaks for the sawmills; three, issue orders to your security people about which tree-and-owl-hugging environmentalist you want harassed. You like to write these memos using your PowerBook at home, when the kids are in bed and your rifle is freshly oiled. But how to distribute your orders?

With a PowerBook, it's a piece of cake. To enable sharing of these files follow these instructions:

1. Do not share your disk. Instead, create folders for each group of environment-ravaging toadies you order around.

2. Create user accounts and collect them into groups, like Sales, Scam (for your lobbyists), and Security (what most corporate gangsters call their thugs), that coincide with the names of the folders you just created.

3. Highlight one of the folder icons in the Finder. Let's use the Sales folder as an example.

4. Select *Sharing* in the File Menu.

5. When the Sharing window for the Sales folder opens, check the "Share this item and its contents" box (see Figure 11).

6. Using the User/Group pop-up menu, select the Sales group.

7. Disable the Everyone and the Make Changes checkboxes.

8. If you want to include other information for each group, you can take advantage of the fact that all the nested folders are automatically shared. For instance, folders inside the Sales folder can be shared with the sales staff.

Use the "Make all currently enclosed folders like this one" button to build different levels of security for nested folders. It sets the privileges for nested folders, instead of having them inherit the privileges of the topmost folder. For instance, you could share a folder full of folders by setting the topmost to See Files, See Folders, and Make Changes. When you click "Make all enclosed folders like this one," each nested folder will be stamped with these wide-open privileges. Then, change the topmost folder to just See Folders and close the sharing window. Now the users cannot change the names or contents of that topmost layer (nor can they see any files hanging around up there), but inside any of the nest folders, they have free rein. If you hadn't checked the "Make all enclosed..." button, then the nested folders would have inherited the more-restricted privileges as soon as you closed the Sharing window.

9. If you want to keep users from trashing your outrageously venal, closed-minded, anti-environment orders that are stored in nested folders, check the "Can't be moved, renamed or deleted" button. You only need to check this box if the folder is inside a folder that has Make Changes enabled. In other words, this allows you to secure against renaming or trashing an item that would otherwise be open to anything. It's not necessary if you've disabled Make Changes at the layer above.

```
┌─────────────────────────────────────────────┐
│ ▨▨▨▨▨▨▨▨▨▨▨▨ Rugged Terrain ▨▨▨▨▨▨▨▨▨▨▨▨ │
│                                               │
│  ⬛  Where:      Rugged Terrain, SCSI 0        │
│                                               │
│  ☒ Share this item and its contents           │
│  ─────────────────────────────────────────    │
│                    See      See     Make       │
│                   Folders   Files  Changes     │
│                                                │
│   Owner:  [ Red-baiting R... ▼]  ☒   ☒   ☒     │
│                                                │
│   User/Group: [ Sales      ▼]    ☒   ☒   ☒     │
│                                                │
│              Everyone            ☐   ☐   ☐     │
│  ─────────────────────────────────────────    │
│  ☐ Make all currently enclosed folders like this one │
│                                                │
└─────────────────────────────────────────────┘
```

Figure 11. Folders can be shared individually.

Now, when you compose your maniacally short-sighted, destructive orders, just drag them into the appropriate folder and head for the office. When your PowerBook is plugged into the office network and the Sales, Scam, and Security staffs log on in the morning, they will be able to open only the folder that coincides with their responsibilities.

Shared folders also offer a convenient sharing monitor feature (see below) in the Finder. The Group icon is superimposed on a folder when users are logged on to your PowerBook.

File-Sharing Monitor

This is a Mobile Commuter-class control panel that we suggest Intentional Tourists can do without, unless you plan to enable System 7's file-sharing capabilities. As we explained above, file-sharing lets networked Mac users log onto your PowerBook and open a file. While they are working on that document, you don't have any access. One consolation of being the subject of a file-sharing session is that you never give up ultimate control of the file, since it is stored on your hard disk.

But responsibility comes with control, since you don't want to shut down your PowerBook and cut off your comrades at mid-rewrite while they are using files on your computer. The File Sharing Monitor lets you check who is connected to your computer, giving you the opportunity to shout out a warning before powering down (see Figure 12).

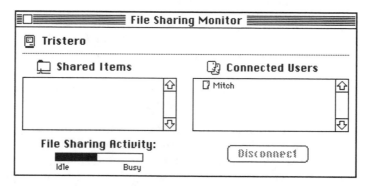

Figure 12. File Sharing Monitor displays a list of connected users.

If you don't bother to check for users before you shut down, you still receive a warning dialog that lets you send out a message to connected users telling them how long you'll keep the link live. However, that's no consolation if you are in a hurry to catch a train, so we recommend that Road Warriors and Mobile Commuters hang onto the monitor.

AppleTalk Remote Access—No Free Rides

One of the technologies on which the authors were most prepared to congratulate Apple is AppleTalk Remote Access, the application that lets a PowerBook user dial into their company's network. For the first year, ARA was free with every PowerBook. Now, ARA will cost you between $150 and $200, because Apple has begun productizing anything that will boost their margins. Result: Users are paying for a technology that made the already-pricey PowerBooks really godawful cool.

ARA is more than some interesting bells and whistles, which is the kind of performance we've come to expect from bundled software. With ARA in place, the *MacWEEK* editorial staff has transformed the way we cover events in cities far from our San Francisco headquarters.

For example, during the Fall '92 Macworld Expo in Boston, eight MacWEEKers were able to set up a remote news operation, using ARA as the network link between Room 724 at the Boston Four Seasons and 301 Howard Street in San Francisco. Not only were we able to send stories

back to our office, editors in Boston were able to grab copies of stories written in California from *MacWEEK*'s AppleShare servers. In the days before
ARA, the data stream was a one-way affair; traveling writers and editors
sent stories to San Francisco, and occasionally a story was faxed back. But
in 1992, we managed the entire editorial process electronically—all because of that bundled ARA software.

Well, we can't say ARA isn't worth the price it carries today. Go out and
buy it, if you haven't already got it. Licensing for each ARA package gives
you the right to install the software on three computers: your PowerBook,
an ARA host on a local area network, and your home computer. Remember that, unless you have an ARA server, like the LanRover/L from Shiva
Corporation, you will need to install the software on two computers.

ARA requires that you have a user account on the host you'll be dialing
into (similarly, the accounts you created in the Users & Groups control
panel let people dial into your PowerBook). Contact the network administrator in your office to get your account, and to learn the phone number
for the ARA host (see Figure 13). The application will remember your
password, but we suggest that you do not check the "Save my password"
box. It's safer to enter it each time you log on.

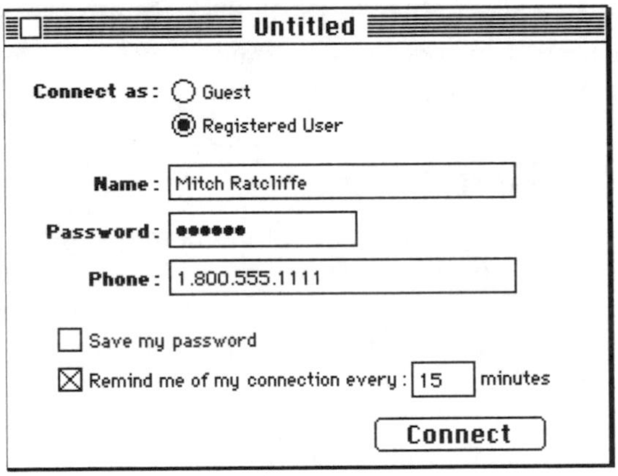

Figure 13. AppleTalk Remote Access Connection Controls

A status window will tell you when the ARA connection has been made.
Nothing else will happen, but that doesn't mean you've got computer
problems. Open the Chooser, and you'll see the services that are available
on the network, including file servers, printers, and application servers. If
the ARA server is configured to give you only limited access to the network
it resides on, possibly the only thing you'll see in your Chooser is the Mac
you dialed into.

Not only does ARA do a good job of supporting file-sharing, it supports any networked application as though it were running on a local area network. Electronic mail, databases, group scheduling, and dozens of other software categories operate splendidly. ARA is truly a means for expanding your network to the far corners of the world, using only the public telephone network.

See the
Road Warrior
note below.
⬇

If ARA is going to be your latest, greatest thing, get ready to make a couple of significant upgrades to your PowerBook and your local area network (for more information on the office end of the ARA equation, turn to the next part, *A Port for Every Road Warrior*). For now, let's focus on the PowerBook part of the equation.

If it ain't fast, it ain't file-sharing.

AppleTalk Remote Access works so well because Apple's engineers found a way to slice the fat off of network communications.

Your local area network, whether it's LocalTalk, Ethernet, or fiberoptic, gets bogged down in overhead, all the extra information attached to every piece of data, which tells the network where that data is going. Adding to the congestion is a lot of conversation among devices on the network—computers checking in with the network to make sure the connection is still alive (you've probably seen a Mac "hang," this is what happens when the computer tries to use the network and nothing comes back) and routers gossiping to one another about the networks and routers to which they are connected (in AppleTalk parlance, this is known as exchanging routing tables).

AppleTalk Remote Access wipes out all this chatter, passing only the most essential information between the remote computer and the network. More bandwidth is left for important data, like pieces of files or database queries.

Off of what traffic does cross the telephonic void, ARA shaves the most it can, using software-based V.42 error correction and V.42bis and MNP-5 compression protocols. Nevertheless, you'll want to use ARA conservatively. Be sure to compress files before dragging them from your PowerBook to the remote server icon or vice versa. (Aladdin Systems Inc.'s StuffIt is a good compression choice; it's the most efficient program we've used.)   *(continued)*

If it ain't fast, it ain't file-sharing. (continued)

Optimization can't handle all the responsibility for good ARA performance. A high-speed modem is an absolute necessity, at both ends of the telephone connection. We recommend that you set the modem speed bar at a minimum of 9,600 baud, else you will pay the price with sluggish, tedious, mind-numbing ARA performance. If you can afford the upgrade, or if your boss can be made to understand that you are unproductive while waiting for a file to transfer, get 14.4-Kbps modems for your PowerBook and your ARA host.

Some crazed souls have made the claim that ARA is useful at 2,400 baud. These are the same people who claimed George Bush still had a shot at re-election on November 4, 1992.

Remote Access Setup

Most of the time, you'll be dialing into a network with your PowerBook. The Remote Access Setup control panel lets you use pop-up menus to configure the modem and your connection to the modem. A collection of drivers install with ARA; they will appear in the Modem menu when you click on it. In the interest of disk space conservation, we suggest that after loading ARA, you go into your System Folder to clean out unneeded modem drivers.

Should you want to let a remote user dial into your PowerBook or a network connected to your PowerBook, you'll need to configure the settings in the lower half of the Remote Access Setup control panel. Obviously, you'll need to check the Answer Calls box, but more important is the setting for maximum connection times. We suggest that you limit call lengths, allowing time for the tasks you intend but preventing unbridled browsing and downloading of your hard disk.

The last choice in the control panel consists of two radio buttons that allow access to an entire network or only the Macintosh on which the ARA software is running. Clicking the "Entire network" button will let a remote user utilize your PowerBook as a gateway to fileservers and other network resources, which we suggest you do. After all, your PowerBook will usually be travelling with you, unlike a desktop Mac, which is like an unguarded door to the network. When someone calls your PowerBook for an ARA session, and it's sitting in your hotel room, it is the entire network. If you've taken the time to set up user accounts, you're not likely to lose data to a stranger.

Back to Users & Groups

Even if a coworker does dial into your PowerBook, they won't be able to see your files if they do not have an user account set for ARA.

Let's say the project you're heading at work is at a critical juncture, dangling between glorious success and failure, when the boss calls and asks for a briefing. But you are in Topeka with the analysis on your PowerBook, while the rest of the team is in Seattle.

Using ARA, you can put your entire team to work on the analysis during your dinner hour. You hook your PowerBook up to the telephone line at your brother's house (did we mention that you have a brother in Topeka?) and sit down to pot roast. The phone rings, your computer answers. Within minutes, a member of the team has logged onto the PowerBook and copied the analysis back to his Macintosh in Seattle. Half an hour later, the phone rings again, and the completed presentation file is uploaded to your hard disk for your review.

The reason these calls can happen successfully is that you've already given your coworkers accounts on your computer. If not, their calls would fall on deaf ears, so to speak.

After you install ARA, open your User & Groups control panel. A new section will have been added, called Remote Access (see Figure 14). Check the box that lets each user dial in. Now, when a user dials in, he'll have to enter his password before gaining access to your PowerBook or the network it's connected to.

Adding a level of security to ARA is very easy. The call-back box lets the computer launch a routine when a remote user calls in. It's a little dance that goes like this:

1. The remote user enters their name and password in the ARA control dialog and dials your PowerBook.

2. A short conversation ensues between the two modems, during which the name and password of the remote user is sent to your PowerBook. If the name/password combination matches a user account you've created, your PowerBook hangs up and calls the number listed in the call-back box.

3. This time, the remote user's Macintosh or networked ARA server answers the phone, and the computer connection is established.

Call-back security is only marginally useful for Mobile Commuters and Road Warriors, because they will very seldom call from the same number for more than a couple of days. Even more difficult is the hotel room-to-ARA connection. The front desk always gets in the way of the call-back.

Think about it: You call from the Tampa Bay Westin, and the ARA host recognizes your account information and hangs up; when it tries to call back (assuming it even has the right number), the hotel operator can't route the call to your room because he doesn't happen to speak screaming modemese.

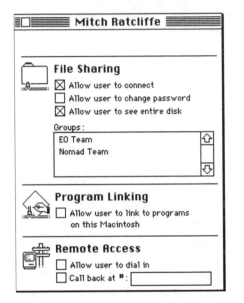

Figure 14. ARA adds dial-back controls for individual user accounts.

Smoother ARA connections may depend on the hotel industry coming to accept new telecommunications technologies by allowing direct connections to guest rooms. But we believe the solution may rest in wireless telecommunications, especially cellular data networks. The day will come when our telephones will travel with us all the time and when cellular service is almost as affordable as regular wired telephone service.

Data networks are clearly one of the key growth industries for the 1990s. With the election of Bill Clinton, the U.S. may be committing to providing simple, affordable voice and data connectivity wherever you travel, from Portland, Maine to Portland, Oregon. Apple's operating system is already showing signs of these trends.

1993: The message is "collaborate."

Messaging will take a leap forward in coming years, especially as Apple continues to innovate on the AppleShare and AppleTalk Remote Access paradigms.

During 1993, Apple will transform the file-sharing concept by intro-ducing its Open Collaboration Environment, or OCE. This project, which has been cooking in one of the most innovative technological kitch-ens at Apple for the past three and a half years, turns on the idea that file-sharing should be automated at the user level. OCE relies on a set of mes-saging technologies (electronic mail taken to a new level) that dovetail with the Mac operating system and applications. Instead of waiting for your coworkers to grab a file from an AppleShare file server, you'll be able to send it directly to them while you continue working. The message will ap-pear in the other user's Finder, in a new window, called the Compound Mailbox. They just have to double-click the file to open it.

Apple's engineers have gone much further than that simple description makes it sound. OCE will store a message when the recipient's Mac is turned off and send it when the target Mac returns to the network. It will also let you sign a document with a unique mathematical signature that will prove you were the author and that the document has not been altered since you signed it.

Versatile network connectivity will be the hallmark of the OCE inter-face. A new kind of file, called a Business Card, will be traded by OCE us-ers over the network or on floppies. When you meet someone, you'll walk away from the encounter with an electronic list of network and telephone connections that can be used by your PowerBook to send that person a message. Each OCE-enabled Mac will also be able to build a directory of every device and user on your network at a given moment, so you can find an address easily and quickly, when you need it.

PowerBooks figure prominently in the OCE scheme. The "store-and-forward" nature of OCE (the ability to hold a message until the recipient's Mac reappears on the network), will let PowerBook users compose docu-ments all day long, even when they are roaming across the country, and send them in a single batch when they connect to the network in the evening. AppleTalk Remote Access will let you interact with an OCE net-work by telephone, making Road Warriors an integral part of the office work-flow at all times. Conversely, OCE will also keep work flowing with-in your office when you are travelling. Imagine that you have been out at meetings all day—when you return and plug into the network, all the com-munications that have been sent to you will be available instantly. With a little thought and a few keystrokes, you'll be managing your staff or meet-ing your deadlines much more quickly than ever before.

PART

3

A PORT FOR EVERY
ROAD WARRIOR

197

You've been working under the hood long enough. With your system configured and your networks connected, you're ready for the big, bad world. But PowerBooks, like people, need a place to roost, a port in a storm after a hard day on the road.

Actually, a PowerBook needs two homes, one at the office and the other at that place you probably don't see much, you know, where you sleep some nights and the people who live there all look vaguely familiar. Each location needs a few special accouterments that should make bringing your PowerBook inside like easing into a comfortable chair.

Statistics don't lie (they only exaggerate). If you're like most PowerBook users, a Mac IIsi or more powerful computer is sitting on your desk at work, and a Mac Plus, SE, SE/30, Classic, or LC is probably waiting for you at home. Extrapolating a little further on Mac demographics, your office computer is probably connected to a network, while your homebound CPU is standing all alone, save for the company of a printer and perhaps a modem.

If you happen to be one of those lucky few whose job description includes providing support for Mac users, you may be wondering what all this PowerBook mobility means for your company. What hardware and software can you buy that will help employees with PowerBooks be more productive? What can you do to make connecting to the office from the road easier? And what do you need to make sure a stampeding herd of telecommunicating laptops doesn't overload your network infrastructure?

You could be one of the roughly 25 percent of PowerBook owners who've never owned a Macintosh before. Many of you choose to straddle the gap between the ubiquitous PC and the best portable solution available today (in our own and John Sculley's humble opinions). How do you keep your portable and desktop computers talking? It's a strange kind of détente you'll need to practice as a cross-platform dresser (sorry, couldn't resist).

Perhaps you've even thought of dumping your desktop system altogether in favor of a PowerBook.

For all you do, this chapter's for you.

The proliferation of products that has hit the market in the wake of the PowerBooks' runaway success makes it impossible to account for every mobile Mac product here. And like world overpopulation, the number of PowerBook gadgets is growing geometrically. Everything is marketed as a PowerBook product these days, from screen cleaners to word processors. We're not joking—version 5.1 of Microsoft Word has a special PowerBook installation that takes up less space on the hard disk. It also has a battery indicator and supposedly spins up the hard drive less often, although we've seen little evidence to back up that particular claim.

So rather than try to cover everything, we'll discuss a broad sampling of products that may help you assess the choices confronting you down at the local computer dealer. We'll also give you a few tips on combining add-ons to construct a port of call ideal for Intentional Tourists, Mobile Commuters, and Road Warriors.

We should note that there are many excellent products available for PowerBooks not covered in this chapter or elsewhere in the *Guide*. We chose to highlight the products we did because we've have had personal experience with them, not necessarily because they are the only, or even the best, solutions available.

And for those of you who must have the latest on PowerBook add-ons, we'd recommend subscribing to *Nomad Notes,* our quarterly newsletter for digital nomads. You get the first issue free by registering your copy of the *Guide* with Random House (see the coupon at the back of the book).

The PC and the PowerBook

A Floppy Love Story

Compatibility has been critical to Apple's marketing for the past half decade, and yet it is still a chore to share files with an IBM-compatible PC, unless you have assembled a small armament of software to grease the cross-platform skids. For the digital nomad, this can be a deadly shortfall. As you travel, you're more likely to encounter someone with one of those infernal machines who wants to share files. There are a lot of those DOS- and Windows-crippled minds out there, and, unfortunately, we have to work with them! (Isn't the hubris of Mac users amazing?)

First off, your PowerBook, if it has a floppy drive, can read a DOS floppy. The external floppy drives for the PowerBook 100 and Duos also can deal with PC disks. However, you're going to need some software to make any sense of what the diskette drive reads.

There are several ways to go about this.

With its system software Apple includes an application called Apple File Exchange that lets you insert and view the contents of a DOS floppy. This is something of a kludge, because you have to launch File Exchange before your PowerBook will recognize a DOS disk instead of telling you that it is unreadable and asking if you would like to initialize it. Even then, all you get is a list of DOS files, no icons. That's not even slightly intuitive, especially after years of hearing that Macs are DOS-compatible. Sorry, Apple, users should see DOS files in the same graphical environment as they do Mac files when a floppy slides into the drive.

That's why Apple and several third parties now offer software add-ons that allow your PowerBook to read a DOS-formatted diskette as easily as it reads a Macintosh floppy.

Apple's commercial system extension that lets a Mac read a DOS disk is called Macintosh PC Exchange. Available since the middle of 1992, Macintosh PC Exchange allows you to insert a PC floppy and copy files back and forth between the DOS disk and the PowerBook hard drive by dragging files in the Finder. You can open PC files, if you have the Mac analog to the PC application that created the file you want to open. An extension-mapping feature that lets you link certain PC files to the appropriate Mac application is needed to open it.

We like Dayna Communications Inc.'s DOS Mounter extension better than Apple's because it works equally well on floppies, hard drives, and CD-ROMs formatted for DOS; Macintosh PC Exchange is a bit brain-dead, because it digests only floppies. The Apple product borrows heavily from Dayna's, which was the first to provide the ability to view the contents of a DOS disk as folders and icons. DOS Mounter's extension-mapping capabilities let you link DOS files to Mac applications, displaying each DOS file on the disk as a double-clickable Mac document icon; that is, PC text files can appear as Microsoft Word files on the Mac desktop (see Figure 1).

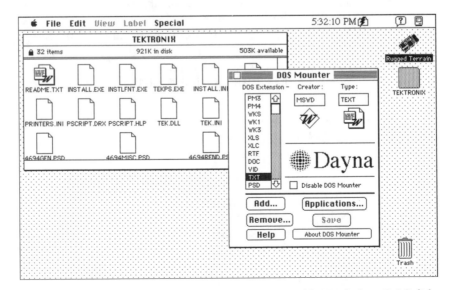

Figure 1. Dayna Communications' DOS Mounter adds Mac looks to DOS disks.

Insignia Solutions Inc.'s AccessPC is another choice for DOS compatibility. It's also more versatile than Apple's Macintosh PC Exchange, working with any type of disk. It also allows you to see DOS files as icons in the Finder.

You may also want to take a look at Argosy Software Inc.'s RunPC, an integrated set of programs that let you mount DOS disks, transfer files between a PowerBook and a PC, and control a PC remotely from your computer. Here's an application that lives for a hard-wired connection to a DOS machine.

There's a wire in your life.

A serial connection, a cable stretched between your PowerBook's serial port and the RS-232 port on a PC, can be the fastest and most efficient way to exchange files with a PC user. A serial link can work at speeds of up to 57.6 Kbps, six times faster than a 9,600-baud modem, but you'll find that some software can't support more than 19.2-Kbps communications.

Of the two kinds of software available for serial communications, terminal emulation and file-translation programs, we urge you to make the investment in translation software. Even if you've already got a terminal emulator, translators let you give a transferred file a file-type identity in the target computer's file system, so that it can masquerade as a native document in that system.

Developed by Apple spin-off Claris Corporation, XTND is a technology that lets you add translators to the Claris folder in your System Folder. Once in place, those translators can be used by numerous applications to translate to and from various file formats, whether those files come by way of a floppy or wire. Some applications, like Microsoft Excel and Word, come with their own file translation engine built in.

See the Mobile Commuter note below.

⬇

Even if you've got XTND or another translation engine, you may still need another file translator to handle files that fall outside the bounds of your applications' translation capabilities. The choices available are Argosy's RunPC, which includes an application called Software Bridge/Mac, DataViz Inc.'s MacLinkPlus/PC, MasterSoft's MasterWord, or LapLink/Mac from Traveling Software, which also sells a serial accelerator add-on that speeds transfers to 700 or so Kbps.

We recommend MacLinkPlus/PC, an XTND-compatible application that automates translations and includes a battery of translators that can tackle almost any compatibility problem. It supports the fastest serial connections and is the easiest to set up, in our opinion. A translators-only version of MacLinkPlus, intended for use with XTND applications, is also available. And to top that, you get Dayna's DOS Mounter free with either version (although this version of DOS Mounter only works with floppy diskettes).

Let's say you've already solved the file translation problem. Sometimes, you'll just need to construct a quick link to a PC. Unfortunately, Power-Book users will almost always need to count on their DOS-bound coworkers for the connection.

PCs users can set up for roaming PowerBooks by installing a Farallon Computing Inc.'s PhoneNET Talk card and drivers (you can buy them separately), which add support for AppleTalk communications to a AT-bus or Micro Channel-bus computer. With one of these cards in place, you can string a LocalTalk cable between your PowerBook and the PC. Timbuktu 5.0, a remote control product (also from Farallon), can give you the ability to operate the PC using your PowerBook's trackball and keyboard, an easy way to grab copies of the files you need from a PC, even if it is running Windows (see Figure 2).

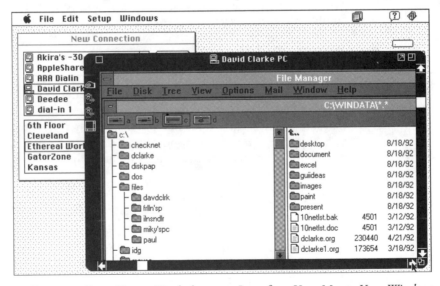

Figure 2. From Here to Timbuktu or at Least from Your Mac to Your Windows System

XTND in the Ether

Claris developed XTND and for a while marketed it by licensing the translation technology to other vendors to bundle with their applications and by bundling XTND with its own suite of programs. But there was a fly in Claris' ointment: the company reserved some of the most useful translators, like the one that opens Word files saved with the Fast Save option, for bundling only with their products, giving them a competitive edge over other developers.

It became obvious to Apple that XTND or something very much like it needed to be part of system software, so that all developers' products could capitalize on automated file translation. Therefore, to resolve the inequity in how Claris licensed XTND, Apple took over development and licensing of the XTND engine and many of its most important translators. (Claris is a wholly-owned subsidiary of Apple, by the way.)

Now Apple is working on the Translation Manager, sometimes referred to as "XTND Pro." However, until the Translation Manager ships (Apple may or may not choose to include it with System 7), the only way to get XTND is to buy a product that has the engine bundled with it. Getting the translators you need can also be a challenge, unless you buy DataViz Inc.'s MacLinkPlus/PC, which comes with a pile of file translators.

Apple Pack

DOS and Windows users, Apple wants you! The fact that many of you have been willing to use a PowerBook as a portable, even if you're married to a desktop PC, is not a point lost on Apple's marketing gurus. So, to make connecting your portable Mac to a PC easier, Apple has bundled several of the products we discuss here, plus a PowerBook-to-VGA display solution, into one convenient package.

The bundle is called The PowerBook/DOS Companion and includes Apple's Macintosh PC Exchange, DataViz's MacLinkPlus/PC, and GDT Software's Power Print (see the next topic). It also comes with MacVGA, an adapter made by James Engineering that lets PowerBook 160 and 180 users connect to most VGA and SVGA PC monitors.

The bundle is reasonably priced at about $200, less than half what those products would cost to purchase separately.

We expect that if the Companion bundle is successful, Apple will follow it with other bundles targeted at specific uses, including PowerBook to PC networking and perhaps cross-platform application bundles, such as Lotus 1-2-3 and WordPerfect for Mac and Windows.

And Now, Output from Our Sponsor

Printing is the first and last problem you absolutely have to deal with as a PowerBook user. Whatever else you do, there's nothing more important than getting your ideas on paper so you can present them to that vast non-computing portion of humanity. They would never know computers existed were it not for the advent of the neatly published laser printer-produced page.

Carrying a LaserWriter along to Tucson isn't going to fly, so you've got to find a way to use any printer you can find—or you can carry along a small, high-resolution printer. Below, we discuss a few key products to solve the PowerBook printer problem.

The Software Solutions

An absolute must is GDT Softworks Inc.'s Power Print, a veritable printer hound's pocketful of magic. Power Print includes drivers for more than 850 printer, which you can drop into your System Folder to add compatibility with the printers you encounter. It also comes with adapter cables that let you make the physical connection. Road Warriors shouldn't leave home without Power Print.

If you'll be wandering into UNIX territory, take along InterCon Systems Corporation's InterPrint, a protocol stack that will give you access to Adobe PostScript printers attached to TCP/IP networks. It also lets you use the worldwide Internet network to select a printer in a distant office to process your print job, kind of like network-powered faxing. But, you'll need to connect to a TCP/IP network to use InterPrint, which is sometimes a trick unto itself.

Grappler IIsp

You rush in from the first snowstorm to hit Tucson in the past 22 years and find that the office you've entered has nary a LaserWriter or ImageWriter, just a Hewlett-Packard LaserJet. With only ten minutes before your meeting and in desperate need of handouts for your talk, you reach into your bag to withdraw a Grappler IIsp, a small adapter that plugs into your PowerBook's serial port and the parallel port on the printer. In a moment, the LaserJet starts to churn out the pages you need.

Orange Micro Inc.'s Grappler combines the adapter and a set of print drivers that work with LaserJet and Epson LQ emulations. It includes a built-in print spooler that frees your PowerBook, letting you work in another application as the printing continues.

The Littlest Printers

The Grappler IIsp lets you use several very compact portable printers that are available for DOS laptops, including the four-pound Canon BubbleJet 10ex, the Citizen PN48 (a three-pounder that's less than half the size of a PowerBook), and the 5.5-lb. Kodak Diconix 701. All provide at least 300-dpi output and will operate on battery power only.

There's also a PowerBook companion printer, the GCC Technologies Inc. WriteMove II, which weighs in at just two and a half pounds and connects with an ordinary serial cable. Battery-operated yet still capable of producing near-laser-quality output, the WriteMove II ships with Adobe Type Manager (an extension that wipes away the jaggies) and 21 Adobe fonts. It's also the same slate gray as your PowerBook—so hip.

We tested the WriteMove II and found it to be most satisfactory in terms of quality, speed, battery life, and its adaptability for use almost anywhere. The only problems were its inability to accept more than one page at a time (you have to hand-feed the little printer) and the fact that it eats up its tiny ribbon cartridges at an appalling rate. We rarely got more than 25 pages of $8\frac{1}{2}$-by-11-inch output before it was time to chuck the cartridge for a fresh ribbon.

From Desktop to Eternity

The connection to a network is the first step out into a bustling world full of information. Network hardware that fills various roles is available from a variety of companies; let's take a look at a few of our favorites. By the way, we refrain from listing prices because they are more prone to change than a country suffering from twelve years of Republican leadership.

PowerBooks don't leave you any room for a network interface card, such as those that fit inside a desktop Macintosh. So the next best connection to an Ethernet network will come through the SCSI port (Duo Dock owners can install an ordinary Ethernet card in one of the Dock's NuBus slots).

See the Mobile Commuter note below.

Asanté Technologies Inc. offers two SCSI-to-Ethernet adapters that we've had good luck with at *MacWEEK*. The EN/SC PB delivers a connection to all three types of Ethernet cabling: thick and thin coaxial and 10 BASE T (unshielded twisted-pair). The EN/SC-10T PB provides only a 10 BASE T port. When buying these adapters, make sure you get boxes that include "PB" in the name, as they come with the proper HDI-30 SCSI cables for a PowerBook.

Dayna Communications Inc. is another developer with which we've had good luck. The DaynaPORT SCSI/Link-3 PB is a three-in-one (thick and thin coaxial and 10 BASE T) adapter. Their other offering is a thin coaxial and 10 BASE T adapter called the DaynaPORT SCSI/Link PB. Both adapters ship with an HDI-30 SCSI cable.

TechWorks Inc. also ships a three-in-one, SCSI-to-Ethernet adapter with an HDI-30 cable, called the Ethernet SC. Chesapeake Systems Inc. offers single-media and three-in-one Ethernet-to-SCSI connections in its GeoBook connectors.

The least expensive connectors on the market come from Focus Inc., which ships the EtherLAN SC and EtherLAN SC-T with support for thin coaxial and 10 BASE T cabling, respectively. If you want to save the most money, you'll want to look at these. But because Focus merely acquired these products from a company that quit the Mac networking business last year, be sure to check support policies (such as availability of driver upgrades, refunds, etc.) before buying.

Delivering Network Data to the Proper SCSI Address

If you use an SCSI-to-Ethernet adapter, you must be sure that you place the device in the proper place on the SCSI chain (the string of peripherals attached to the port) and that you give it an SCSI address that doesn't conflict with your PowerBook and hard drive.

For example, the Asanté EN/SC PB can sit anywhere in an SCSI chain, though the company says the adapter is optimized to be the first in line. It also ships with the SCSI address set to *2*, which should not conflict with the standard PowerBook setup. If, however, you are using an external disk, make sure it's not also set on *2*, as the address conflict can cause your system significant distress.

Some adapters and peripherals aren't so tolerant as regards their location on an SCSI chain. It's not an attitude problem. The last device in an SCSI chain—even if you have only one SCSI device connected to your computer—must be terminated. Some vendors solve the problem by requiring their device be the last link in the chain; these devices have built-in termination. The Asanté adapters include automatic termination capabilities that work when an adapter is placed at the beginning or end of an SCSI chain.   *(continued)*

Delivering Network Data to the Proper SCSI Address (continued)

Others, like the DaynaPORT SCSI/Link, let you turn the termination function on and off, depending on where you place the device. Termination should be enabled only in the first and last device in an SCSI chain. Unlike desktop Macs, PowerBooks have no internal termination.

Travelling in Foreign LANs

Roving PowerBooks will be faced with foreign network protocols, like Novell Inc.'s NetWare or Sitka Corporation's TOPS. Some of these networks require that you install extra software, and there are a few shortcuts that can smooth the way to cross-platform file-sharing. If parts of your network speak in UNIX (not a biblical language but the multi-threaded, multitasking operating system), you'll need to plug into the TCP/IP network by adding Apple's TCP/IP communications stack, MacTCP, and UNIX-savvy applications.

NetWare

Novell's network operating system runs on IBM and IBM-compatible PCs; however, Mac users can still access and store files on NetWare servers. Most NetWare sites you'll be stopping by will probably have the NetWare for Macintosh NLM (NetWare-Loadable Module) installed on the server, which provides the PC with the ability to communicate with Mac clients, like you and your little PowerBook, even though you aren't running any additional software.

The Mac NLM lets the NetWare server describe the contents of its disk in the AppleTalk File Protocol (AFP). That means directories show up in the Mac Finder as folders and documents as double-clickable icons. NetWare servers appear as AppleShare servers in the Chooser. Mac users can also download a desk accessory that lets them view their NetWare access privileges, send text-only E-mail, and print to printers connected to the Novell server.

Unfortunately, not every NetWare network you encounter will be so Mac-friendly. Some companies just don't feel the need to support useful computers like those that Apple makes, or maybe they just don't want to pay the $1,995 that Novell charges for the Mac NLM.

It times like these, when you encounter such a close-minded network, that Dayna Communications' NetMounter will come in handy. When you use NetMounter, files and PC servers will appear in the Finder, as though

Mac NLM were running on the NetWare server. This control panel lets your PowerBook grab network data in plain-vanilla NetWare form and translate it into AFP. An extension-mapping tool, which lets you choose what Mac applications will open particular DOS and Windows file formats, lets you control how files on the NetWare server will appear on your desktop.

Dayna can perform this bit of magic because the company worked with Novell to develop the original NetWare for Macintosh. In return, they got the Mac keys to the Novell servers.

There are less elegant solutions for NetWare access. For instance, you can combine SoftPC and SoftNode from Insignia Solutions Inc. on your PowerBook to present a PC face to NetWare server. Along with a large swath cutting across your RAM budget to support both Insignia programs, you get stuck with the same dreary command-line interface a DOS user has to deal with.

We suggest that you're better off keeping a copy of NetMounter on your PowerBook. When you need to grab a file from a strange NetWare server, just drag NetMounter into your System Folder and restart your computer. One thing to keep in mind: regardless of how you make the software connection to NetWare, you need a user account and the proper cable before you can log on to the server.

Banyan VINES

Currently, there's no easy, inexpensive NetMounter-like access to VINES, a UNIX-based network operating system that provides universal directory services. (*Universal directory services*: Imagine being able to bring up a list of all the users in your corporation, then search by first name and office location to pick out that guy you chatted with at a sales meeting, but whose last name you can never remember.)

As with NetWare, you'll need to have some expensive Macintosh software installed on the VINES server in your office, as well as a user account, before you can log on. VINES software for Mac clients gives them access to those great directory services, called StreetTalk, and VINES mail applications. Servers and files are presented through AFP.

VAX Hacks

Digital Equipment Corporation's VAX minicomputers are the granddaddies of distributed computing systems. The Mac has been a favored client of VAX systems since 1988, when DEC and Apple collaborated to create the Pathworks for Macintosh network connection. That project netted a few key tools that deliver VAX connectivity for terminal emulation, file-sharing, and electronic mail programs.

If terminal emulation is your favored VAX connection, our favorites are Synergy Software's VersaTerm-PRO, Software Ventures Inc.'s Micro-Phone Pro, and PacerTerm, made by Pacer Software.

VersaTerm-PRO provides a journeyman's view of the VAX world. It allows you to cut and paste text to and from a terminal window and even lets you use System 7's publish and subscribe features to deliver automatic updates of terminal data to, say, a Mac spreadsheet. You can also run multiple terminal sessions concurrently.

MicroPhone and PacerTerm offer much more sophisticated scripting features, which let you go through the work of logging on just once. After the script is in place, it can run automatically, while you grab some coffee or work in another application.

VAX e-mail and file-sharing require installation of software on the server, but you'll get a Mac's view of the contents and messages, rather than having to wrestle with the command-line cryptology of straight DEC computing. Check out DEC's Pathworks, Pacer's PacerShare, and AlisaTalk from Alisa Systems. When installed on a server, these programs support AFP-enabled file-sharing, Chooser-selectable services, and support for e-mail.

UNIX

Macs need a special translator to talk with UNIX workstations over a network. MacTCP, Apple's TCP/IP protocol stack, gives Macs the UNIX smarts they need. We'll talk more about this in Section IV, *Exploring Cyberspace.*

TOPS

Sitka Corporation hasn't made a much noise in the market for quite a while, but there are still a substantial number of machines using TOPS to share files. Like System 7 file-sharing, TOPS lets users share files stored on their hard disk with other users on the Mac network, but you get the added advantage of file-sharing with PCs and Sun Microsystems workstations (you'll also be able to share files with pen-based systems using GO Corporation's PenPoint OS, thanks to PenTOPS).

TOPS software must be installed on every Mac, PC, and Sun workstation on the network you want to share files with. It gives users the ability to "publish" their hard disk as a shared volume and browse other published drives. There's also a modicum of security.

If you don't need TOPS software to access a cross-platform network, we recommend that you leave this network operating system where it belongs: in the past. Sitka will announce a new version of its network, called Open-TOPS, in 1993.

Remote Access at Your Service

The biggest drawback of AppleTalk Remote Access is that you lose the Mac it is running on while a remote user is logged on. That makes for an expensive doorway to your network by anyone's reckoning. For the first nine months after Apple shipped ARA, the expense of dedicating Macs to manage each wide-area connection was a barrier to many companies looking to make remote file-sharing, printing, e-mail, and groupware applications a reality for their PowerBook users.

Several vendors have already solved this problem, and many more are on the way to putting ARA into relatively inexpensive boxes that can sit on a network to act as a remote access server. PowerBook users dialing into the network won't be able to tell the difference between a Mac running ARA and one of these devices.

Shiva's LanRover

The very first developer out of the gate with a remote access server was Shiva Corporation. At press time, the one-port LanRover/L still cost more than $500, but that's a far sight less than sticking a Mac into a closet to support a single ARA connection. The device has two critical limitations: it only connects to a LocalTalk network, and, as noted above, it only has one port. In order to use the LanRover/L, companies that have moved onto Ethernet will have to take a step back into the network Bronze Age and install a router to link the two cabling eras. LanRover/L users will also need to purchase multiple 'Rovers if they want to have more than one Power-Book connecting to the network simultaneously.

Shiva addressed both these limitations in late 1992 when it shipped four-port and eight-port Ethernet-compatible 'Rovers, called LanRover/4E and LanRover/8E. Nevertheless, the per-port cost of the new remote access servers still hasn't dropped much below the $500 mark.

Cayman Systems Inc.

GatorLink, a three-port ARA server that connects to an Ethernet network, was the second such device to appear on the scene. Today, Cayman is working to expand the number of modem ports its GatorLink can support and is rumored to be on its way toward delivering more than a dozen ports sometime in 1993.

Unfortunately, the technology used by both Cayman and Shiva seems doomed to produce pricey devices. For the best price/performance ratio, you'll want access to the kind of device that grew up on UNIX networks, the terminal server.

Centrum Communications Inc., Cisco Systems Inc., and Xylogics Inc.

These companies will build support for ARA into their multiport terminal servers by the summer of 1993. Terminal servers are network devices that have their own CPUs to handle the protocol processing for a bank of modem ports that serve as gateways between remote users and network services. However, Apple must ship an upgrade to ARA before these gadgets can get to work.

Terminal servers were developed to provide remote access to mainframes and large TCP/IP networks, but they tend to rely on common protocols to enable the modem connection. The two predominant terminal server protocols have been the Point-to-Point Protocol (PPP) and its predecessor, the Serial Line Interface Protocol (SLIP). Connections established using PPP let most network protocols piggyback on PPP to get from the remote user to a router somewhere on the network. In other words, the PPP connection is a broad virtual bridge between two modems, and it looks to the network and computer just like a regular network connection.

The Apple approach to remote access diverged from this norm in order to tightly integrate ARA protocols with AppleTalk. If you'll pardon another simile, ARA is like a thread tossed across a chasm. In its current iteration it is just wide and strong enough to handle a small slice of the AppleTalk traffic that courses through the typical corporate network.

ARA 2.0, the multi-protocol version of Apple's remote access software required to make ARA palatable to terminal servers, is due in the spring of 1993. Once you can get your hands on that software, count on seeing a flood of terminal server hardware that supports ARA.

Xylogics' MicroAnnex XL and Annex 3 terminal servers are scheduled to include ARA support, as is the CentrumRemote Access Server from Centrum Communications. Networking giant Cisco will also build a PPP-enabled ARA server into its 500 CS terminal server, a 112-port data access juggernaut.

Even Apple will get in on the action with multiport terminal cards that will install in the NuBus slot on a Mac. But you'll still have to closet the Mac that runs one of these cards, because the computer will be fully employed just keeping up with ARA sessions.

The important thing to remember when investing in ARA servers is the per-port cost, which should include the price of a dedicated Mac if required. Something under $200 a port would represent a real bargain.

Security Trade

Guarding the Network Frontier

The British spy Sidney Riley died when he intercepted a bullet from a Bolshevik security agent's rifle on the Russian frontier, but we know plenty of hackers who have crossed corporate network boundaries without receiving a scratch. And they'll keep it up just as long as you let them.

Now, we don't want to propagate the myth of the dark side hacker, an ashen-faced, antisocial teenager with a misdirected, hormonal passion for other people's computers. However, we do want to point out, without magnifying the legend, that a network with remote access capabilities is like an unattended liquor store at the edge of a high school campus—someone's going to wander in now and again.

That's why it's important that you use passwords and dial-back security on ARA connections. Combined, the two will virtually eliminate the threat of break-ins. Some companies, especially those with employees who travel frequently from place to place, can't use dial-back, because the remote user's number is continually changing.

During 1993, Apple reportedly will address this problem with a new version of Security Dynamics' ACE Server, which will run in firmware (reprogrammable flash memory) on its ARA-enabled NuBus cards. Cayman Systems and Shiva have already announced a version of the ACE Server that runs over their ARA servers. But these implementations require that you have a UNIX server running on your network to support ACE security.

In an ACE environment, every user is given a credit card-sized device called a SecurID with a small LCD display (although it fits easily in a your wallet, storing it there risks damaging the card). Once each minute, the number on the SecurID changes. This apparently random number is your access code. The ACE Server uses a special algorithm that allows the server, and no one else, to know what number is on the card at any given moment. When dialing up an ARA connection, you just wait until the number changes, type it in and hit Connect (remember, the number will change in 60 seconds, so give yourself the maximum amount of time). The server, recognizing the number as your legal access code, will establish the connection on the first dial.

We have talked with several hackers who tell us that they consider the ACE Server the most challenging security scheme available today. They claimed that no one had yet broken the ACE system, and it makes sense that this should be so. The chances against choosing the appropriate Secur-ID number for the appropriate user account in the appropriate moment are astronomical. But kids these days are awfully resourceful, aren't they? Experience tells us that whatever you do, you must assume that one day the brightest young minds will find a way in.

Enigma Device

The second line of defense is encryption software, which scrambles the contents of your hard disk, locking out anyone who doesn't know the correct password. This could be a critical precaution for digital nomads who carry sensitive information on their PowerBooks. If the computer does grow legs and walk away, you'll be secure in the knowledge that no one is browsing your payroll data, product plans, or the details of an unannounced merger.

But while encryption software is probably the most secure way to lock your data, there are two risks associated with it. First, no encryption product is 100-percent reliable; in the process of scrambling your data, it may so thoroughly confuse the bytes that even with the correct password it won't be able to untangle the resulting mess. And second, because the data is scrambled, if you forget the password, the only salvation for your files is a trip to the encryption software vendor, who can unlock them for you.

As always, back up your critical data on diskettes or backup tapes and store them in a safe, preferably lockable container. Make sure you have unencrypted backups or risk kissing your files good-bye!

Look for file security software that lets you assign different levels of security to different folders and files, or that allows you to hide some folders completely. It is also important to have the PowerBook protected in its entirety, so do not purchase security software that can be overridden by inserting a system floppy disk at startup.

The authors, in their pursuit of confidentiality for sources, have used Kent Marsh Inc.'s FinderBolt and MacSafe II with success. Remember, however, not to get too creative with passwords—pare the list of passwords you use to only one or two, or you're likely to forget them.

Lock Down

Even if your PowerBook is secure from electronic snooping, you probably want it to stay put when you do.

The PowerBook 160, 180, and Duos include a Kensington security slot that lets you lock the computer to a desk or bed frame. The slot supports the Kensington MicroSaver lock and a variety of other shackles. For pre-slot PowerBooks, CMG Inc. put the kibosh on PowerBook lids with its PowerLock, a keyed bracket that slips onto the side of a closed PowerBook to hold it shut; it also includes a cable for use in lashing the computer to a desk.

There's even a mercury-switch motion detector available from Quorum International, Ltd. If anyone tries moving the PowerBook without first deactivating the alarm, the Elert (once armed) will emit a 107-decibel scream for 30 seconds.

Asphalt Software

The postman always gongs twice.

Electronic mail (e-mail) is the avatar of network communications. So far, it's the only network-based application that has garnered broad adoption by millions of computer users. In many companies, e-mail is the second or third most-used program and has driven the installation of many networks. E-mail comes the closest of all collaborative programs to emulating a communications medium we're all familiar and comfortable with: inter-office mail.

The Mac's ubiquitous networking (every Mac ever shipped has at least come with LocalTalk built-in) provided an early and friendly platform for e-mail. From the silly forms that can be created in CE Software Inc.'s QuickMail to the file translation in Lotus Development Corporation's cc:Mail, the Mac's built-in networking has spawned a rich array of mail choices.

We describe the leading packages below.

QuickMail

The most popular e-mail solution on the Mac is QuickMail, an easy-to-use application that installs on Macs and PowerBooks to allow them to log on to a server and collect, send, or archive their mail. If you don't keep the client-to-server ratio relatively low (approximately 60 clients per server is pushing the limits), your network will probably suffer from poor performance. QuickMail is available for both Macs and PCs, though the PC version is a relatively recent innovation. As a result, few cross-platform networks are currently running QuickMail.

As we've already mentioned, one of the most attractive aspects of QuickMail is the ability to create forms. We've seen everything from a crazed, nose-picking Calvin of the comic strip *Calvin and Hobbes* to the downright pornographic (this may seem, at first blush, a matter of [bad] taste, but the argument can be made that an obscene QuickMail form is a type of sexual harassment—be warned, cement-headed sexists).

QuickMail's remote access capabilities helped secure its lead in the Mac e-mail market during the past year. Even before the PowerBook came along, QuickMail users could log in from home or hotel to read and send messages. A special version of the application, called QM Remote, must be installed on your PowerBook. It delivers a convenient way to work remotely, allowing you to compose messages and send them when you log on to your office network. When travelling, for instance, you can compose messages throughout the day and store them in the QM Remote Outbox. When you connect to the network, all the mail in the Outbox will be sent and the application will let you read and respond to messages sent to you (see Figure 3).

Figure 3. The QuickMail User Interface

You can also use Netstrategy's ARA-Link QM and Apple's ARA to replace QM Remote. ARA-Link can be configured to initiate an ARA connection when you open the QuickMail desk accessory. It logs onto your network, allowing you to browse your mail. The connection is closed automatically when you close QuickMail. You can also create scripts that let ARA-Link QM maintain relationships with multiple QuickMail servers.

But there is a major drawback to using QuickMail and ARA-Link QM—you will not be able to compose mail offline, save it in the Outbox, and send it when connected.

During the past year, CE and Apple have gone round and round over the Macintosh Communications Toolbox tool that QuickMail uses to transfer files from the mail server to the remote user and vice versa. If you have problems with QuickMail, make sure that you have the latest Apple Modem Tool (version 1.1.1) and version 2.5.1 of the mail administration software installed on your PowerBook and your QuickMail server. This should remedy the problem.

Microsoft Mail

This e-mail package runs a close second to QuickMail in popularity, but its real strengths shine through on cross-platform networks. Microsoft's natural advantage as the leading Mac software developer and creator of Windows has made it possible for the company to integrate its mail software into any Microsoft application (Windows or Mac), so that files can be sent without leaving the work you are already doing.

Microsoft's e-mail also delivers better performance than QuickMail. The MS Mail server supports more clients, with greater performance, than CE's servers. MS Mail also has the ability to update an entire network as user lists change. For example, when an employee quits, a network manager only needs to change the user list on a single server to update every server and client on the network.

Like QuickMail, MS Mail includes the ability to compose messages while disconnected from the network and upload them to the server when you arrive back at the office or by dialing in over ARA.

cc:Mail

Lotus Development's mail package runs on more platforms than QuickMail or MS Mail, but it also took the longest to develop a full-blown Mac interface. Earlier versions looked suspiciously like a Windows, or worse yet, a DOS application.

cc:Mail is the first Mac e-mail package with a full-text search feature, which lets you search incoming and stored messages for particular words, and it's also the first to present enclosed files in the e-mail interface as full-sized, double-clickable icons. While these are nice capabilities, there are three significant drawbacks to cc:Mail that should give PowerBook users cause to pause before buying into the system.

cc:Mail runs as an application that requires more than a megabyte of RAM, way too much for PowerBooks with only 4 or 8 Mbytes of memory.

Although you can reduce the memory allocation to as little as 800K, performance will suffer.

Speed is something cc:Mail could use more of; it won't be winning any benchmark contests. It's a dog on a PowerBook 100 and only marginally better on the 140. That's problem number two.

Third, cc:Mail mobility doesn't come cheap. While you can run the application over an ARA link, its basic performance problems will only be magnified by the presence of a modem. A dial-up client is also available, but unlike the other mail vendors, Lotus charges extra for its remote mail software.

Networks plus people equals groupware.

Digital nomads probably won't stay in one place all the time, but while you are in the office, wouldn't it be nice to use the network to share your schedule, critical information, and ideas with your coworkers? A category of software known as groupware, which has struggled for legitimacy for several years, may at last find a following in PowerBook users.

Groupware attempts to address the problem of variations in people's schedules, differences that prevent them from communicating face to face. What does that mean in terms of real experience? Groupware hopes to mend the gap that opens between you and your peers when you can't walk down the hall to their office to set a meeting or when you can't get them on the phone. A groupware application lets you do your work—whether that's just entering the name of a new sales lead in your address book or pounding out a draft document for the next briefing your team has to give to the CEO—and share the results with others who are responsible for knowing and commenting on your work.

Groupware is automated collaboration when it works right and organized chaos when it fails.

It seemed to fail a lot when people used applications to share data that was just as easy to exchange in person. For instance, many companies, *MacWEEK* included, tried using network software to route draft proposals and planning documents around the office. When an editor came up with a story list for *MacWEEK*, for instance, they posted a copy of the list to the groupware server, and the rest of the staff was expected to open the document, add their own comments, and, well, we were going to *get organized*. The problem with that scenario is that it is just as easy to look up and talk about an idea with a coworker. When folks came back from a trip, they generally were brought up to date on projects during a meeting and not through groupware.

But, now that many of us travel with a PowerBook, we can use groupware to continue our planning while on the road and then share those ideas with other members of the staff when we return. Using AppleTalk Remote Access, we can even collaborate over the phone.

So, you see, groupware was a little ahead of its time. As corporate structures get more flexible, and as more work moves out of the office and onto the road or into the home, groupware's ability to overcome differences in time and space ("I'm not available when you are in the office," or "You can never get me on the phone, just leave some voice mail") will make it a more valuable addition to the company's computing arsenal.

Some of the software we've tried is described below.

Meeting Maker

ON Technology Inc.'s scheduling application has been a staple at *MacWEEK* for the past year, and it's also used by many of the Apple legion we know. The company's software requires that you have a server on the network, where everyone's schedule can be stored. Individual users are able to log on in the morning and keep their calendars open in the background. As meetings are proposed, each invitee receives a notice detailing who will be there, the location, and the agenda (see Figure 4). You can also attach a document to the invitation to allow folks to review materials that will be presented at the meeting. If someone is busy at the time you select for a meeting, Meeting Maker will search for the next time your invitees can attend. The application also lets you select proxies, who can log on and view your public calendar when making appointments.

Personal calendars can coexist with professional ones in Meeting Maker. When scheduling a personal activity, like a doctor's appointment, you can check a box that displays the time as scheduled, but without any details, in your public calendar. Your own schedule will contain all the information when you log on or receive a reminder.

Meeting Maker 2.0, which is the first cross-platform version (both Macs and PCs can use it), lets you carry your personal calendar along with you on your PowerBook. You can make changes and propose new meetings that will be delivered to the server the next time you connect to the network with the personal version of Meeting Maker; such flexibility offers an exciting new dimension to mobile commuting. Also, with Meeting Maker's more distributed architecture, your ability to set up appointments won't be hobbled every time the Meeting Maker server goes down (a common problem in Cupertino).

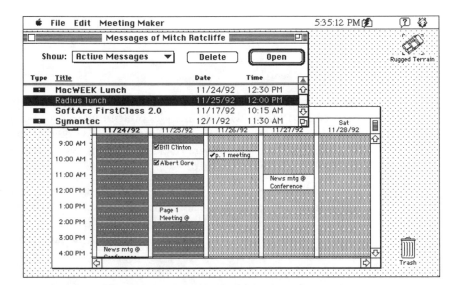

Figure 4. Phone tag and conference room conflicts are things of the past with Meeting Maker.

Microsoft Schedule+

If you're already using Microsoft Mail as your e-mail application, you'll want to add Schedule+, a group scheduler that uses the MS Mail server. Its interface is not as elegant as Meeting Maker's, but it does let you dial in to your network to set up meetings with your coworkers or to schedule company resources, such as conference rooms. It also works with Windows for Workgroups networks, so you can call in to set meetings with Windows users.

Up-to-Date

Now Software Inc.'s group calendar doles out some of the basic information that can keep a group operating on a common schedule. It does not, however, offer the kind of automation you'll get with Meeting Maker. It does excel in its simplicity, a commodity that is often in short supply in software these days.

Networked Up-to-Date users can scan one another's calendars when scheduling appointments, but they cannot issue invitations to meetings. On the network you'll also need to install server software that keeps track of the appointments scheduled by individual users.

When you burst from the mooring of the network, your Up-to-Date schedule goes with you. As you collect new appointments, you simply add them to the calendar on your PowerBook. Once you return home, the up-dated calendar is uploaded to the server for sharing with others.

Instant Update

Also from ON Technology, this is a groupware integrated application. The server-based Instant Update includes built-in word processing and graph-ics capabilities that let you share ideas with coworkers who can edit and alter your work. The software tracks activity for each document and flags items that have been changed.

We found the interface a mite too Spartan, lacking as it does many of the formatting features that are standard in even the least expensive word processors, for instance. Also, the way that Instant Update reconciles changes when two or more users are modifying the same document at the same time can be downright mystifying. (We've seen it merge multiple changes to a single document without removing the information the changes were meant to replace, creating an indecipherable mess.)

Instant Update has the potential to be a real hit in the era of Apple's Open Collaboration Environment, when it could conceivably run beneath existing word processing, graphics, and spreadsheet applications, among others. If ON can build on OCE's mail and directory services to provide a clear picture of how the current version of a document got that way, they'll have a cool tool for PowerBook users, who, after returning from a trip, need to learn what's been going on in their absence.

WordPerfect Office 4.0

This application combines the features of electronic mail, to-do lists, group scheduling, and shared notepads to facilitate collaboration, and, best of all, it integrates into WordPerfect Corporation's word processing program.

Like Meeting Maker, WordPerfect Office needs a server; at press time a Mac version of the server was unavailable but was planned for spring 1993. Office spans many more operating system platforms than other collabora-tive applications: Besides the Mac, it runs on DOS, Windows, OS/2, UNIX, and VAX/VMS hardware. If yours is a complex network of users who thrive on a diversity of platforms, Office may be the best choice for you.

We've been especially impressed with the features of the latest version, which includes the ability to route a message around the network (this lets you create a memo with a check-off system to ensure that each person who needs to will see it) and to build a set of filters that grabs messages related to specific subjects and incorporates the information into schedules and to-do lists.

InForum and PacerForum

These applications, from MacVONK USA and Pacer Software, respectively, give your network the same look and feel as some of the graphical online systems, such as America Online. The idea is to create a network conferencing system, where you can create topics for people to discuss, and around which a long series of messages will collect that newcomers can use to bring themselves up to date on a subject.

Lotus Notes

Lotus Development's collaborative environment shell for OS/2 and Windows workstations will reach the Mac in 1993. Because it incorporates a store-and-forward engine, meaning that the application can hold a message addressed to you while you're away and deliver it when you return, it may be a real boon to companies that need to support PowerBook users.

But the Notes pay-off may be limited to companies that mix Macs and PCs. In and of itself, Notes is little more than a new layer of software on which you can build groupware applications. You'll get that same capability with Apple's OCE, which will be getting a Mac-to-Windows gateway shortly after it appears in the spring of 1993.

PIMs: The point is management.

PIM stands for Personal Information Manager, a broad description for a class of applications that people use to organize their lives. It's only natural that after having applied electronics to our typing, calculating, and desktop publishing, people have turned to the more mundane but labyrinthine problem of keeping track of everything they do.

This brings us to an observation that perhaps only computer journalists are capable of making after surviving a thousand hours of product demonstrations. Every week, we see two or three people traipse into *MacWEEK*'s offices carrying their latest software. They sit down and run the application, talking back over their shoulders as they navigate through a maze of menus and commands, showing us how they accomplished something miraculous, like building a calendar for the week or a flowchart that describes the best route to eliminating the national debt.

They invariably offer a copy of the software for us to evaluate, which many people on staff (including the authors) endeavor to squeeze in time to try out.

After adding a list of meetings and deadlines to the application's database our lives should, we think, run more smoothly for the remainder of the day, if not an entire week. But such is rarely the case. It usually turns out that what we witnessed was a demonstration of how a programmer managed to map into his software his own way of looking at the world. He was able to navigate through the Byzantine interface he created, talking all the while about the great philosophical questions of personal information management, because the application *is* his brain incarnated as software. The mistake these people make is in trying to automate a unique process, instead of building a tool that can be customized to fit many different, personal organizational styles.

Well, we're not aware of a single creative person who can thrive by following someone else's model of organization.

However, there are a select few applications that avoided this pitfall and have built in enough flexibility to make them useful to a broad spectrum of users. These programs seem to focus primarily on one of three critical areas: contact management, to-do lists, and time-tracking.

Contact Management

Dynodex   We've included an earlier version of this excellent contact management application, so you can try out the idea of an electronic Rolodex for yourself. If you decide you like it, we suggest you upgrade to version 3.0 to gain the ability to update your contact data between a desktop Mac and the PowerBook. This allows you to add names and numbers for people you meet on the road and, on your return, add that information to the Dynodex database on your desktop machine. It cuts both ways, giving you the most up-to-date information when you head out for a long trip, as well.

Dynodex is a great example of an application that focuses on doing one thing and doing it right. You won't be able to set appointments with this contact manager (although with Apple events, you may be able to call up a Dynodex contact record from within a separate calendar program). But you will be able to do almost anything you might want to do with a contacts list, including search and sort on multiple criteria, print labels, and easily import and export contact data.

INtouch   The power of information in many organizations depends upon who has access to it. For example, if it is going to provide acceptable service to customers calling in for information, a sales team needs to know who the latest prospects are and the status of their orders.

Advanced Software Inc.'s INtouch lets networked PowerBooks and Macs share information about people and companies. For each record there is a note field that is large enough so that you can include comments on the status of orders that can be used by your coworkers to answer questions when you're out. INtouch is server-based but doesn't support updates from

PowerBooks that have strayed from the network. We found that because the application lumps so much information that must be searched into just two fields in the interface, it takes a while to dig up the data you are searching for.

TouchBASE The latest version of After Hours Software Inc.'s contact management software is network-savvy and plenty fast when it comes to retrieving a record. TouchBASE takes a more conventional tack when you're sharing databases. Instead of requiring a server, you only have to place your data into a shared folder on an AppleShare server or make your contacts file available to other Macs on the network, and then others can log on and use it.

Updating your central database after a spell on the road is problematic. You must select the records you've added and altered while away, then export those records from your PowerBook. After importing them to your shared database, you must go through the data to remove the earlier versions of data altered while you were travelling. For instance, if you changed the telephone number for Bob Smith after importing the update, you'll end up with two copies of the Bob Smith record in the shared database. The old record has to go, which adds an extra step to the process.

Contact Ease WestWare Inc.'s contact manager incorporates sales-tracking functions and support for roaming users. Besides a database of names and addresses, users can create a to-do list for each individual customer and use mail-merge features to write and print sales letters at each step in the sales cycle.

Contact Ease also solves a major problem that PowerBook users have with other contact managers: it synchronizes private contact databases with a master list, adding updates collected while a PowerBook was in the field. Its ability to maintain separate to-do lists for individual records and a master to-do list for each user catapults Contact Ease beyond the ordinary PIM and into the realm of sales automation tools.

To-Do Lists

Active Memory Sharing a to-do list between yourself and your secretary would probably double your productivity, because any list maintained by only one person can suffer because of your short memory.

ASD Software Inc.'s Active Memory puts a shared to-do list and automated reminders on small and medium-sized Mac networks. It lets you create a list of deadlines in a point-and-click interface and can remind you when deadlines arrive, even if the application is turned off. We found the interface, which looks a little like a spreadsheet and offers few intuitive guides for creating an event, somewhat daunting. Nevertheless, Active Memory is worth a try-out on your network; its sophisticated use of Apple events and System 7 publish and subscribe features, as well as its inclusion of a monthly calendar and easy-to-use printing capabilities, combine many functions that previously were only available separately.

DayMaker   Although Pastel Development Corporation's DayMaker is a standalone program, it certainly deserves mention as a excellent organizer for PowerBook users who work alone. It includes a calendar, to-do list and alarms in an interface that is easy to navigate and use, to create a customized view of what you have to accomplish each day.

In Control   Although, technically, it isn't a groupware program, In Control ultimately displaced Instant Update at *MacWEEK* as our project organizer of choice. Although its interface is somewhat reminiscent of a spreadsheet, a row of large, easy-to-understand buttons at the top of the screen makes it much easier to set up and modify an In Control document than any spreadsheet we've ever used (see Figure 5).

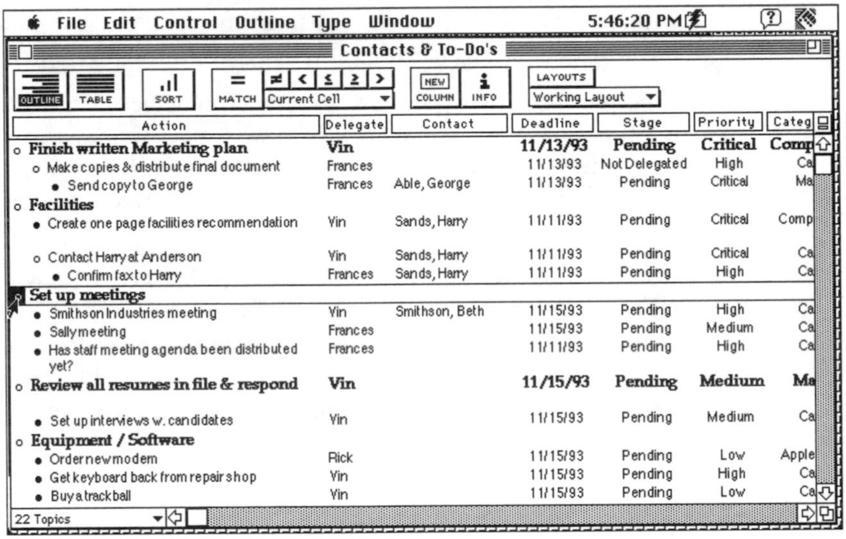

Figure 5. In Control allows for fast and flexible to-do list management.

You can create multiple, resizable columns with a single click, allowing the construction of to-do lists to take place at lightning speed. The ability create pop-up lists of standard entries or to auto-enter words or phrases into a cell based on just a few keystrokes is also a nice touch. In Control to-do lists can toggle between a hierarchical outline or table format. The program has the ability to quickly sort rows by a number of criteria, including dates.

To call In Control a to-do list manager is to drastically understate its flexibility. We've used the program for a number of things not normally considered to-do list territory, including the outline for this *Guide.* One of the authors is currently using In Control to construct a screenplay, complete with collapsible subheads so that character backgrounds, scenes, or whole acts can be hidden from view.

Time-Tracking

Many PowerBook users are billing for their time. Creative folks, lawyers, writers, marketeers, consultants, analysts, and service technicians, to name just a few, need to account for their time in segments that can be billed to a particular client. There are two good choices for keeping tabs on your time.

Timeslips and Laptrack Timeslips Corporation's Timeslips has been around for several years, but it requires a server that PowerBook users won't always be able to reach. For the digital nomad there is Laptrack, an application that lets you create a record of time spent on each project and compare that to preliminary budgets in reports. Laptrack can also log on to and use a Timeslips server to download information used to prepare billing statements.

You've got to get in the habit of opening Laptrack to start and stop the meter as you go from project to project during the day, but the results are solid, professional billing statements that back up your hard work.

TimeLog This control panel works in the background whenever you have your PowerBook running, tracking every move you make between the Finder and various applications, folders, and documents. There's no forgetting to start the timer on a project.

How do you know you are billing for the right project at any given time? Simply create a folder for each client or project; that way you'll naturally move from place to place as you work, leaving a record of the time you spent in each folder. TimeLog records can be exported to a spreadsheet for use in documenting billable hours.

Packing Hardware

A View to a Thrill

Video output has been something of a holy grail for PowerBook users who want to display their work on a color or grayscale monitor. With the latest generation of PowerBooks, video output is no longer a problem, unless you want to display more than 8-bit color on a large screen, in which case your only choice will be a Duo and a Duo Dock or a third-party SCSI video solution.

What follows is a sampling of the video products available.

Internal Organs

Several video-out products are designed to go inside the PowerBook 100, 140, 145, and 170, in the RAM expansion slots. These cards allow you to plug a video display directly into the computer, which improves the speed of the PowerBook in redrawing the image on the screen.

Computer Care Inc. offers three internal video cards. The BookView supports attaching a full-page monochrome monitor to any PowerBook, while the BookView Imperial 100 supports up to two pages of monochrome output specifically for the PowerBook 100. The company's color and grayscale adapter, the BookView Imperial 140/170, can drive an Apple color monitor, VGA, or NTSC (television) display of up to 19 inches in 8-bit color.

Envisio Inc. also opted to go inside the first-generation PowerBooks with its video adapters. The Notebook Display Adapter allows a Power-Book 100 to use monochrome displays as large as 21 inches. A color-capable adapter for the 140, 145, and 170, the Notebook Display Adapter 030, supports up to 256 colors on Apple's 14-inch display or up to 21 inches of monochrome screen.

Sigma Designs Inc. and RasterOps Corporation came up with a hybrid PowerBook video solution when they installed the video card inside their monitors. These monochrome displays connect to the SCSI port on a PowerBook and, therefore, suffer the same poor performance of other SCSI-based video-out solutions. Sigma Designs' Power Portrait accelerates the video output to provide a little better performance for a 15-inch monochrome screen. RasterOps' ClearVue/SD21 offers a vast spread of monochrome screen real estate at 21 inches.

External Attachments

That little miracle, the SCSI bus, is the conduit for a passel of external video adapters. As stated above, these external devices don't enjoy the same kind of throughput as an internal adapter, and they can cause problems if you combine them with an SCSI Ethernet adapter and an external drive or two. However, they are more reliable than many internal cards, and installing one doesn't void the Apple warranty, which many internal video cards do.

And tricks abound in the video trade to kick up SCSI video performance. Lapis Technologies Inc., for instance, has built their SCSI adapters around a 16MHz 68000 CPU that reportedly accelerates the screen refresh rate. The only problem is that even a dedicated CPU is only going to help so much—as most of the SCSI video bottleneck is at the SCSI bus itself. Radius Inc.'s PowerView SCSI video adapter may do a slightly better job of improving video performance—it uses compression and a digital signal processing chip to push as much data as possible across the SCSI bus (it's still somewhat slower than the Sigma Designs Power Portrait mentioned above, however).

The Lapis DisplayServer SCSI adapter supports monochrome output for PowerBook 100s, 140s, 145s, and 170s. The Lapis ColorServer supports color for the 140, 145, and 170 to Apple, VGA, and NTSC screens. The company's PowerBase I, a monochrome SCSI adapter, ships with three video connectors to support multiple displays.

Radius's PowerView adapter drives Apple's 13- and 14-inch color monitors, VGA displays, and the company's own full-page screens, as well as the monochrome Pivot and Color Pivot in portrait mode.

Duo Vision

Perhaps one of the nicest things about the Duo is the ability to mix and match docks for various purposes. For example, you can add Apple's Mini-Dock to get 8-bit video-out, or you can attach E-Machines' PowerLink Presentor to use a TV set as a monitor that can display 8-bit, convoluted color (convoluted basically means that the dock compensates for signal differences between computers and televisions, producing "flicker-free" viewing).

You can also use any number of excellent 24-bit accelerated color video boards designed for use with desktop Macs, such as SuperMac's Thunder card, in a Duo Dock. This gets you the best and fastest color video imaging possible for desktop publishing, image manipulation, or multimedia.

SCSI isn't an insult.

We could dedicate a whole section of the *Guide* to the intricacies of using the SCSI bus with PowerBooks and not run out of things to say. But, because we didn't want to write a book so thick it would crush punier coffee tables, we'll try to cover SCSI connections briefly here.

SCSI Habits

First, avoid the temptation to crowd your external SCSI chain with lots of devices. For instance, if at all possible, don't use an external hard drive.

Opt instead for a larger internal drive, so you can always have your files with you. Also, if you choose to connect your PowerBook to another Mac in SCSI Disk Mode, you'll lose access to an external drive.

Second, avoid adding extraneous SCSI devices wherever possible. For example, we recommend going for an internal video-out solution instead of an SCSI -based product. The reasons? Easier portability, better performance, and the fact that you won't be taking up an SCSI address.

Internal SCSI Devices

Most users who purchase PowerBooks today will get a drive from Apple large enough that they won't be tempted to trade in for a another drive until there is a big jump in internal capacity. However, for owners of PowerBooks with 40- or (gasp!) 20-Mbyte drives, there are a variety of internal third-party hard drive upgrades you may want to consider.

We've been using an 80-Mbyte Roadrunner drive from Microtech International for sometime now and have been quite pleased with its performance. There are cheaper no-name internal drives available through some mailorder suppliers (check the ads in *MacWEEK* or *MacUser*), and Apple service also offers drive and memory upgrade kits.

External SCSI Devices

There are dozens of devices you can connect to the SCSI bus of your PowerBook. In addition to Ethernet adapters and video-out solutions, you can add: high-speed and/or high-capacity external storage drives, such as those available from MicroNet Technology; CD-ROM drives (we recommend getting one of the new dual-speed drives such as the AppleCD 300); and removable storage drives, for instance, a Bernoulli or SyQuest cartridge drive or a magneto-optical drive, such as PLI's 3.5-inch MO drive, which can store 128 Mbytes of data on a disk the size of a floppy. You can also add DAT (Digital Audio Tape) drives for making fast backups of your storage (although by using a utility like Dantz Development Corporation's Retrospect, you can get automatic backup to a tape drive over the network); you can even connect a color scanner to this flexible bus.

SCSI Addresses

The only thing you need to remember about SCSI addresses is that you don't want two devices to have the same one. There are a couple of ways to check this—you can look at the address indicator on the device in question, which is usually located near its SCSI connector (remember, your

PowerBook internal drive will always have 0 as its address, and the Power-Book itself will take 7 for its address). The other way is to use a small free-ware program called SCSIProbe, which will scan the SCSI bus and display all the devices and their addresses. SCSIProbe can also be used to manually mount SCSI devices that don't appear on your desktop (see Figure 6). You can get SCSIProbe from most online services and Mac user groups. (Your local full-service Apple dealer should also have the utility.)

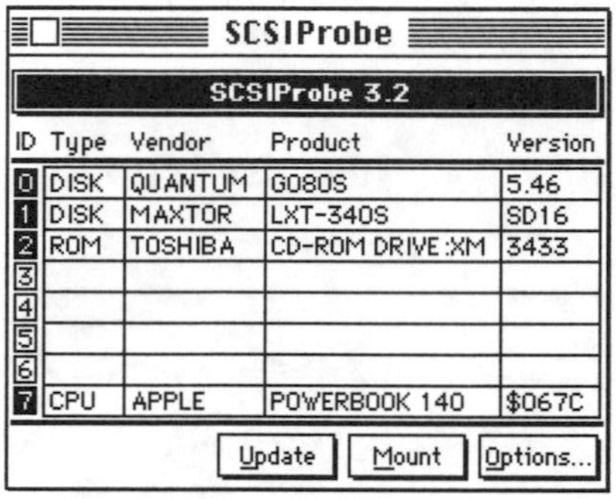

Figure 6. SCSIProbe can quickly locate your SCSI devices and mount them as well.

The Terminator

If you do attach one or more SCSI devices to your PowerBook, there are three things you'll need: an HDI-30 SCSI system cable (this converts the PowerBook's tiny SCSI port to the standard 50-pin connector used by most SCSI devices) and two terminators, unless you have a Duo, in which case you'll need only one terminator.

A terminator is a short 50-pin-female-to-50-pin male adapter that pro-tects the SCSI bus from "echoing back" signals or getting confused be-tween devices. PowerBooks (except the Duos) have no internal termina-tion and as a result will usually require that two terminators be located on the external SCSI chain whenever you attach a device. Duos are internally terminated and only require one terminator as a result. Terminators come in two colors, black and gray. Black terminators were created to deal with the Mac IIfx's finicky SCSI controllers, which didn't always like the gray terminator. Because you can sometimes run into trouble mixing termina-tor colors, we recommend only using gray terminators—they're easier to find and cheaper than the black ones.

Termination is a tricky business at best. Some drives are internally terminated, while others aren't. Still others can have their termination turned on and off. Check to see if the device you're connecting is terminated when configuring a chain and remember that you shouldn't have more than two terminators on the SCSI chain at one time (Duos need only one external terminator). Although you don't have to attach SCSI devices in address order, you do need to make sure one terminator is at the beginning of the chain and the other is at the end. With Duos, the one terminator should be located at the end of the SCSI chain (see Figure 7).

See the
Digital Nomad
note below.

⬇

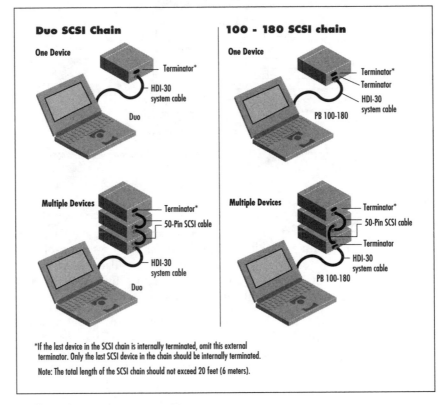

Figure 7. SCSI Chains and Terminators

SCSI Difficulties

So, you followed our good advice and still can't get your PowerBook to recognize that it has a CD-ROM drive hangin' off its backside? Well, we're not surprised. Like we said, SCSI is one temperamental bus.

Here are a few things to try when you run into problems. First, check to be sure any special drivers for the device in question are installed in the System Folder (CD-ROM drives may require that several files reside in the System Folder before they'll operate properly). Next, try swapping the position of devices on the chain, if you have more than one. If that doesn't work, remove one or both of the terminators. If that still doesn't help, try changing SCSI addresses (remember to avoid duplicate addressees).

If none of this helps, it's time to take your PowerBook and its companion devices down to the dealer for testing. Also bring your cables and terminators—one of these may be faulty.

Above all, when swapping drives and cables to test your system, make sure your PowerBook is shut down and isn't asleep. If the SCSI chain changes while your PowerBook is sleeping, it can get mighty grumpy about it when it wakes up!

SCSI Disk Mode

Compared to building a complex SCSI chain, hooking your 100, 160, 180, or Duo up to another Mac so it can access its hard drive is simple. You need to have the HDI-30 disk adapter cable; you can't use the HDI-30 SCSI system cable to make the connection. If you're connecting to a desktop Mac, you'll need a Macintosh 25-pin to standard 50-pin male connector to match up with the disk adapter cable's standard 50-pin female connector. If you're connecting in Disk Mode to another PowerBook, it'll need the HDI-30 SCSI system cable.

Your PowerBook must be the last device in the SCSI chain. Depending on which PowerBook is acting as a slave to which master system, you'll need different termination (see Figure 8).

While in SCSI disk mode, your PowerBook will constantly spin the hard drive, which will be hard on your battery if you don't plug the PowerBook in. Use the Portable or PowerBook control panel to assign an SCSI address to your PowerBook, remembering to avoid address conflicts. While in Disk Mode, an SCSI icon will march across the screen of the slave PowerBook that displays its address.

Figure 8. Termination in SCSI Disk Mode

	100, 160, and 180 in Disk Mode	*Duo in Disk Mode*
Connected to a:		
Desktop Mac or Duo	1 terminator	No terminator
100 through 180	2 terminators[*]	1 terminator

[*] In order to install two terminators between two PowerBooks, you'll need to connect two terminators together and place them between the 50-pin plugs on the end of each PowerBook's HDI-30 SCSI system cable.

Adding RAM

RAM is perhaps the ultimate commodity product. You only need to make sure that you've got the right RAM card and speed for your particular PowerBook (refer to Section I, Part 1, "Concerning RAM," for more information on PowerBook RAM requirements) and that the vendor you're buying RAM from guarantees its quality. Otherwise, shop the mailorder ads for the best deal.

Adding Add-ons

Finally, we turn to one of the greatest shortfalls of the PowerBooks: They are lousy adding machines, so dreadful that they make accountants weep and keen for the luxury of a keypad. Plugging an extended keyboard into the PowerBook Apple Desktop Bus (ADB) port can solve the problem, as long as you're hanging around the office, but no one wants to schlep an unwieldy keyboard along with their cool computer. Luckily, there's more than one choice for add-on keypads.

Plusware Inc. is shipping a ninja-class, 23-key numeric keypad that combines simple math keys with a full complement of function and screen navigation keys. Key options are invoked by depressing a locking second function key. An ADB device, the Plusware Numeric Keypad is an excellent choice for clerical work or even a keyboard-controlled video game.

Kensington Microware Ltd.'s 22-key ADB keypad includes the same array of numeric, mathematical, function, and navigation keys. An LED lights when the function key is depressed, indicating which set of key options are operational.

Digital Nomad Office Infrastructure Rundowns

No one we know has gotten away with purchasing a PowerBook without following the initial investment with a long series of trips back to the dealer for more goodies. The extra purchases always make sense at the time, but the accumulation of gadgetry usually leads to all sorts of functional redundancy. Pretty soon, you end up with three different address book applications—and what for?

It's best to start with a plan, just as you should start with a user strategy in mind, when you begin shaping your operating system. For example, if you're a doctor who wants to track your billing from the comforts of a home office, there's no need to buy an Ethernet adapter. Look over the jobs your PowerBook will be doing, plan on adding software or hardware that will enhance your ability to do that work, and leave the rest of the stuff at the computer store. After all, a tool that is supposed to magnify your intelligence shouldn't wind up making you feel stupid about buying a lot of junk you didn't need!

Thus, with a rasher of information in one hand and a bundle of cash in the other, you're ready to brave the dealer show floor.

The Intentional Tourist at Home and on the Road

You don't rely much on the PowerBook 145 you got last fall and still keep it under the desk most of the time. When you travel, the PowerBook goes along. A Kensington keypad that's crucial to working spreadsheets gets stuffed in your briefcase, as does a well-worn address book that sits beside your desktop Mac. You've been entering contact information into Touch-BASE for months, but you can't quite break your DayTimer dependency.

Another thing that you wish you could take with you is e-mail (but you haven't yet learned the secrets of telecommunications, even though there's a modem in your computer). This stuff is great! Since the company added QuickMail, the volume of information flowing between you and the advertising group has doubled—and your own productivity seems to be higher now that you can tap into conversations about long-term planning.

Still a creature of the paper schedule, your company's system administrator purchased a copy of DayMaker for your use. He told you how great it would be to get everyone to automate their schedules, but when you tried DayMaker on your desktop Mac, nothing clicked, because you like to be able to check your schedule while you're at home, too.

If you brought your PowerBook home, you'd leave it in the entry hall. It's just not the same working on a spreadsheet with that murky screen. Your address book and DayTimer book are out on the kitchen table most evenings and all weekend, ready to answer your questions. Who needs more automation?

Indeed, who does? Well, we predict that if you were to install the following, some changes for the better would come about.

At the Office

Ask your system administrator for an Asanté Technologies EN/SC PB SCSI-to-Ethernet adapter for your PowerBook. Get in the habit of connecting the PowerBook to the network, and leave it asleep if you don't use it. Just keep it connected.

Install Dynodex 3.0 on your desktop Mac and the PowerBook; you can easily export your TouchBASE records to Dynodex. Now, when you add an address while at your desk, you can update the file on your PowerBook with a few mouse clicks.

Ask for a copy of QM Remote, which is free with QuickMail. Find out what telephone number you need to dial to reach your company's mail server. Dial in from home to try out the remote e-mail system, you'll see that the flow of information you value can follow you anywhere.

At Home

Get a Lapis ColorServer and an Apple 14-inch color monitor. This lets you use a color screen to work on pressing projects, and since you'll have access to the same Dynodex and DayMaker information that you previously confined to the office, you can probably risk staying home once in a while to work. You've got QM Remote, so you're still in the information loop.

But, wait, haven't you become a Mobile Commuter?

The Mobile Commuter at Home on the Road

You're a self-employed advertising copywriter, with two clients in whose offices you normally spend one day a week. The rest of the time, you keep in touch by e-mail, logging in to one client's office via cc:Mail's remote client software and to the other client with QM Remote.

The same client who uses cc:Mail has a PC-dominated office and prefers to send and receive files in DOS format. You receive these files, mostly MS Word for Windows documents, on diskette in the mail and convert them to Mac Word format, using DOS Mounter and Word's built-in translation abilities. After editing the file, you stride into the PC den with your PowerBook 160 and a serial cable, which you plug into the DOS machine your client leaves for your use. You launch MacLinkPlus/PC on the PowerBook and its PC counterpart on the dusty DOS machine, and, with a couple mouse clicks, MacLink blasts the files into the PC, converted back to Word for Windows format and ready to use.

Should you need to print a document out for a quick read-over by the client, you carry the Grappler IIsp so that you can plug into the Hewlett-Packard LaserJet beside his desk.

Your other client is a lot more fun. A Mac shop, they specialize in multimedia presentations for trade show booths. There's always a lot of action when you stroll in. Connecting to the network is easy: you just pull out a length of phone cabling and a Farallon PhoneNET Connector and you're in. Since you're such a familiar face around here, the network administrator has given you access to the company's Now Up-To-Date public calendars, which you check for any upcoming meetings you should attend.

As you're browsing around the network, a Contact Ease reminder window pops up on the PowerBook screen. Seems you forgot to send out a letter asking for payment on an overdue invoice sent to another client two months ago. After searching the 160's hard drive, you decide that the copy of the invoice must be on your Mac at home. Time for AppleTalk Remote Access.

You dial your Mac at home, using one of the two account names you have on the machine, and smile as the modems scream a hasty negotiation. After a moment, the line goes dead. Someone sitting nearby comments on how technology never works.

But technology works just fine. Because you configured ARA on your home Mac, whenever someone calls using the account name you entered, it hangs up and dials the desk where you are now. You use a second account to trigger call-backs to your other client's office. In this case, you're using the technology to add some much-needed security to ARA.

After downloading the invoice, you return to Contact Ease to paste the document into a letter, which you quickly mail-merge with the client's address and send off to a nearby LaserWriter. Bringing up a Laptrack time-slip, you click a button that checks you in on a project for the client whose office you're visiting. Now you begin work.

At 3:00 PM, you join the trade show team in a meeting, where a graphic artist shows his latest animation on a PowerBook 170 with an internal Envisio Notebook Display Adapter 030. Pulling out your PhoneNET cable, you ask for a copy of the file, which she promptly copies from her hard disk to yours through System 7's file-sharing. By 4:30, you're off the client's time and back home, where you download the animation file and your Laptrack files for the day to a Quadra 700, which pulls triple duty as an ARA server, a Timeslips server, and multimedia workstation.

The Road Warrior without a Home

The Duo 230 is a four-and-a-half pound tank, armed to the teeth with the software you need to keep in constant touch with your company's critical data. You are a salesman and Road Warrior.

You're at O'Hare, it's 6:30 AM, and there's not a decent cup of Joe to be had anywhere in Chicago. That thought leaves you dreaming of Seattle and its orgiastic celebration of coffee; if you were in Seattle, you'd be ready to face the day, mug in hand.

You will be in Seattle by 10:00 AM—Meeting Maker says so. It also tells you that another flight to another city waits after that.

Seattle. You have 35 minutes to cross the city for a meeting in Bothell. You flip the Duo open on the seat beside you and acknowledge the three reminders that Active Memory has raised since this morning. After reviewing your presentation in the cab's backseat, you recall that you need to meet with all the regional sales managers this evening. Opening Meeting Maker, you slice out the hour between 6:30 and 7:30 PM. Just then, you roll into the parking lot.

There's barely time to set up your Duo and plug your PowerLink Presentor into the large-screen television at the head of the conference table. The senior staff has assembled, so you launch PowerPoint and your first slide appears on the screen: Yolanda McKinney-McConnel, National Sales Manager, First Carcass and Bunting. As you talk, you read from a script on the Duo screen, while the presentation slides play on the big display. In 40 minutes you've closed the deal.

"Would you mind if I used your phone?" A few minutes later, you are cloistered with your Duo in a quiet office. A few mouse clicks launch AppleTalk Remote Access, and in a modem blast you're onto the home office's network. It's a bit disconcerting to get in so easily, but you have the number for one of two LanRover/L ARA servers that don't have dial-back security enabled.

You've got a lot of work to do, and you have to do it pretty fast. Now that you're on the network, you launch Meeting Maker, which immediately issues your invitation to the meeting at 6:30. Two meeting proposals arrive. The first is a new weekly planning meeting, which you reject out of hand. The second invitation includes an agenda that you open and glance over. Looks good, there will be a briefing by one of the industry's top analysts in your company's conference room next Tuesday. Meeting Maker says you'll be available. You accept. Now to QuickMail, the contents are almost uniformly uninteresting, except for a message from the chief financial officer, who informs you that the company's investment in technology is expected to raise productivity by twelve percent this year. How couldn't it, you smile to yourself.

You log off ARA, and, in a matter of moments, you are logged onto the database back at your office. You need the details on availability of the bunting these people just bought and, damn, you're fresh out of carcass. What will you tell them? Back to QuickMail to send a message to the Carcass Division—we need more carcasses! How can we call ourselves First Carcass and Bunting if we've got no carcasses. Geez!

You've got a plane to catch—it's back to the airport. When you arrive in Sacramento, the boss greets you at the door.

"How'd it go?"

"I sold a lot of carcass, but bunting was a little slow."

"Carcass," the boss exclaims, "We're a little short on carcasses right now. I suppose Bothell wants their order filled immediately?"

You hurry to your desk together. This time the Duo combines with a Duo Dock, complete with an Asanté Ethernet NuBus card. Restarting your computer takes a moment, but soon the 21-inch color screen springs to life (it's got a Radius 24-bit color video card as well). You've got to check the supplies in Boseman, Hibbing, and Juneau. Opening the Chooser, you select the Dayna NetMounter icon, and a string of Novell NetWare servers appears in the window. Clicking on Hibbing, you enter your password and begin to search the server for the carcass report. The report was written in WordPerfect for Windows, and when you drag it onto your desktop, NetMounter automatically converts it to Microsoft Word.

There's no carcass in Hibbing, nor does the same process yield even a single moldy carcass in Boseman. The last chance you have is Juneau, where there's little more than a PC and modem in the office; you can't reach it through the network.

Modem connected to the phone line, you fire up the connection and launch Farallon's Timbuktu 5.0 and take control of the remote PC. The boss looks tense, a bead of sweat dripping down the bridge of his nose as he watches you navigate through the Windows directories until, thank God, you find Juneau's carcass report. This time, when you drag the file to your Duo's desktop, DOS Mounter performs the translation as the document lands in Sacramento. The file opens in Microsoft Word, and you have your answer.

"There's carcass in Juneau!"

The boss looks pensive and then ventures his question timidly.

"Can we get it through this computer or do we have to ship it?"

SECTION III

TIPS FOR THE OPEN ROAD

Another airport, another strip search.

I walked up to the security gate. A woman in a blue uniform, who looked like she'd enjoy alligator circumcision as a hobby, stepped in front of me.

"Tickets!" She demanded.

"Here!" I thrust the packet toward her with military precision. I knew the drill.

She looked through the documents, handed them back and waved me on with an officious, human-sounding grunt.

I walked up to the x-ray machine's conveyor belt. I clutched the Power-Book bag to my side. What should I do? Take the time, not to mention the humiliation, of a manual bag and computer check or play radiation roulette? I've put my PowerBook through x-ray machines dozens of times, but I can never get over the feeling that *this* time the mechanism's devilish rays will wipe my hard disk clean like so much damp linoleum.

I glanced at my watch. I had 45 minutes before my flight. Normally, I would have submitted myself to the degradation of the search, but I wanted to find an airport lounge where I could get a booth with an electrical outlet. My PowerBook and I needed a recharge.

I decided to risk the X-Ray Temple of Doom.

Setting the bag on the conveyor belt, I turned it lengthwise to put more distance between it and the electrical fields emitted by the conveyor belt motor, which were probably more dangerous to my computer's health than the x-rays.

As I stepped through the metal detector, I watched the guard who operated the machine's console. She stopped the belt just as my computer hit the center of the machine. She knitted her brow, obviously trying to determine how much x-ray exposure it would take to get the computer's silicon traces to ionize and paint her otherwise-dull screen with a PowerBook-generated Aurora Borealis.

"Do you mind?" I asked her, panic edging into my voice. She looked at me with dull contempt and turned the conveyor back on.

My PowerBook emerged, but just as I picked it up, another guard demanded that I open up the bag and turn on my computer.

"You've got to be kidding!" I said. "If you were going to manually check my computer, what was the point of that lethal dose of radiation you just exposed it to?"

And then he delivered it, the dreaded answer all Road Warriors fear and loathe: "Procedure."

The dictionary defines the Road as "a way made for travelling between places, especially distant places." For Jack Kerouac, the Road was the way made for getting experience. We suggest a slightly different definition: "The Road is any place where you pay twice the going rate for the privilege of eating food you normally wouldn't give to your dog."

Whichever definition you prefer, you can count on myriad hassles when using your PowerBook on the Road. From a shortage of places to recharge, connect, or in general have any peace while using your laptop, to an abundance of people who look askance at your work. There are two looks in particular that you're sure to be on the receiving end of: the tolerant but pitying gaze, like the Howells of *Gilligan's Island* would give the Professor when he began work on another nutty contraption destined to fail at rescuing them from perpetual reruns; or the sneering condescension directed at establishment lackeys who have traded their soul to the corporation in exchange for a fistful of dollars and a few shiny technological glass beads.

But don't despair, you are a pioneer on the silicon frontier. The networks—those data and telephone webs that wrap the globe—are your home. By early 1993, there will be 500,000+ PowerBook users sharing the airways, conference halls, and back rooms of Cyberspace, so you're bound to find a few kindred spirits every time and every way—real or virtual—you venture from home.

Don't, however, neglect the fact that your nemeses are many. You'll find nothing but primitive facilities combined with Neanderthal attitudes and retrograde official policies concerning your portable usage. Airlines that don't allow you to use the AirFone to send or receive electronic mail. Hotels that have slumbered while the telephone jacks in each room went from outdated to fossilized. Rental cars—even if they come with a cellular phone—that don't let you plug a modem into that latest and greatest techno-convenience.

There are no breaks for the PowerBook traveler.

The narratives that open each section are more than just a little light entertainment to give a smile and help put you in the mood for reading some of the more technically dense parts of the *Guide.* They are based largely on real-life experiences that the authors have had while using our PowerBooks.

For example, the story that opens this section is absolutely true; it happened to both of us while we were travelling together through the United Airlines terminal in Boston's Logan Airport, which has particularly puerile security policies. See "Terminal Cases" in Part 1 of this section for a list of the authors' worst terminals.

Tips for The Open Road is an eclectic collection of advice and uncommon wisdom for getting the most out of your PowerBook while travelling. These tips are taken from the authors' own experiences, plus the accounts of our PowerBook-toting friends and colleagues. To the best of our ability, we have tested this advice and found it worthy. However, not everything in this section will be good council for everyone; as always, use common sense when putting these tips to the test.

PART
1

PLANES, TRAINS, AND AUTOMOBILES

It's amazing how fast a cult classic like the PowerBook can develop its own folklore. Just one year after Apple announced these computers, there is already an extensive mythology about PowerBooks that died in their sleep, batteries that explode and/or caught fire, and power spikes that have destroyed logic boards.

Some of these legends are founded in fact, some are just plain loony, and the rest are born of Apple's own public relations machine.

For example, in the spring of 1992 Apple issued a product alert stating that users who toss a loose, fully-charged PowerBook battery into their briefcase might be toting a fire hazard. Under the right conditions, PowerBook batteries can be shorted out by an errant piece of metal, such as a paperclip, pressed against the exposed battery contacts. If the case is stuffed with documents, the result can be disastrous, because the combination of a searing hot paperclip and a lot of paper could result in a hearty blaze, though not one that's good for toasting marshmallows.

Apple issued this alert after hearing reports of two PowerBook bags that spontaneously combusted, this out of an installed base of about 200,000 users at the time. That puts the odds of having a battery flame-out at about one in 100,000.

So, you've got a slightly better chance of winning a personal damage suit against Apple, after you get out of the burn unit, than you do of having your computer bag catch on fire in the first place. Apple's lawyers are said to have urged the company's PR department to do a full disclosure in order to avoid potential liability suits.

All Apple batteries (except Duo batteries, which have a built-in cut-off switch) are now sold with a sleeve that we recommend you use to store your battery while it isn't in use. After all, you never know when your number might come up and force the fates to militate against you and your PowerBook. Besides preventing fires, the sleeve will help keep the battery's terminals clean, guaranteeing a better charge when the battery is placed in a recharger and more reliable power flow when it's in use.

If you have a battery that doesn't come with the sleeve, not to worry. Just store it in one of your carry bag's sealable pockets and make sure the pocket is paperclip-free. When you've got no battery-sized pockets, simply wrap your extras in lint-free cloth (see "The PowerBook Checklist" below) and secure them with a couple of rubber bands or drop them in a Zip-Lock sandwich bag.

To Sleep Perchance to Crash?

One of the great myths in the PowerBook user community revolves around the dangers of transporting a sleeping PowerBook.

The fear is that the jostling your PowerBook takes when you are running to catch a departing flight or crowding onto a train will cause a key to be knocked with sufficient force to wake your computer up. The Power-Book sometimes spins up its hard disk when it wakes, and a spinning disk is easy to damage. A good jarring while the drive is trying to access can corrupt files, damage the surface of the disk so that it cannot store data in that area, or simply cause your PowerBook to crash. Any one of these can cost you lost work and downtime (see "More Restful Sleep" in Part 2 of this section for more advice on the care and feeding of a sleepy PowerBook).

This time the ever-conservative Apple compounded the mythos by recommending that users shut down their PowerBooks when moving them from place to place. Well, that kind of shoots down the portable computer paradigm to some degree because productivity shouldn't have to wait while your PowerBook boots (imagine having to go through the boot cycle every time you need to look up a phone number).

While we suppose that it is theoretically possible for a PowerBook to be awakened in this manner, both authors have travelled extensively with our sleeping computers stuffed under our arms or into overcrowded bags, and we have never once had this happen. Our PowerBooks have crossed cities, bio-regions, states, countries, and oceans, by plane, automobile, and train, five, six, and seven days a week. In fact, one of the authors (Andy) ran his PowerBook in a single continuous session for almost three months, without once shutting down and without any mishaps or lost data.

One of our PowerBooks even took a nasty fall in a parking lot, hitting the pavement hard enough to jam the battery door shut so that we had to take the whole computer apart to free the battery. The PowerBook was asleep at the time but failed to be awakened by the bone-jarring shock!

However, if you are one of those folks who worries about the last inspection date of every elevator you board, it might be better for your peace of mind to shut down the PowerBook before moving it. It all depends on how far out on the edge you want to play. This makes us think of the story of the hypochondriac who, when told that all his ailments were in his head, exclaimed, "How awful that they should all be there!" Some people just cannot be consoled.

See the Intentional Tourist note below.

⬇
You know your limits, but the sleeping PowerBook myth has been stretched beyond the bounds of credibility, as far as we're concerned.

Wonderin' about 100s

It's nearly impossible for a shut-down PowerBook 140, 145, 170, 160, 180, or Duo to start up because of a sudden impact while in transit. That's why Apple recommends that you shut down your PowerBook before hitting the road (figuratively or literally).

However, because you start up a PowerBook 100 from the keyboard rather than by pressing a button on the rear panel or inside the clamshell (like other PowerBook models), it's just as likely to start up from a shock as any PowerBook is to wake after a bump. As a result, it's probably more advisable to transport a 100 while it's asleep rather than when it's shut down. When the 100 starts up as the result of jostling, it's guaranteed the drive will spin, exposing the device to considerable risk of damage. However, if your sleeping 100 should wake as the result of a shock, at least there's a chance the drive won't spin up.

Southern Fried Portables

Finally, let's talk about the rumor that PowerBook logic boards could fry as the result of a power spike.

Any electrical component is in perpetual danger of damage from excess and/or unregulated power while in use. PowerBooks are especially susceptible to this problem, not because of any inferiority in their circuitry, but because they will, by the nature of their use, be exposed to a variety of power environments.

We asked an engineer friend of ours about this. He said that while he didn't have extensive empirical research to back up his hunch, he guessed that the condition of voltage, especially in major hotels in large cities, could fluctuate wildly as a result of the demands put on most cities' electrical infrastructure or by the hotel's central air conditioning, for example. Massive overloads on the power system create "dirty current," electricity marked by jagged spikes and power fall-offs as deep as the Grand Canyon. With that in mind, he suggested that staying in smaller hotels in towns where there has not been a construction boom since the last major upgrade to the local power grid is probably the safest for PowerBooks.

He added that the power supply that comes with Apple's portables has more than enough built-in protection to prevent all but the most severe power fluxes from harming a PowerBook. And you can eliminate this small risk by running your PowerBook on batteries.

We have only heard of one case where a PowerBook may have failed as the result of dirty current. Even then, the power spike diagnosis was a guess made by the repair technician who had eliminated all the alternative causes; there was no hard evidence.

If you feel concerned over the quality of power in a city where you are staying, this is what we'd recommend. Plug in your PowerBook only when recharging your batteries, not to run the computer. Remember not to plug in the power when your PowerBook is asleep, because some current will still be flowing to the logic board. If your computer has been shut down, current won't be flowing through most of the delicate components on the logic board. When plugged into a questionable power source, restore your batteries to full vitality first and then run the PowerBook when it is safely disconnected.

See the Intentional Tourist note below.

⬇

Carrying Protection

You can also take a surge protector along with you when travelling, for that added bit of power security. There are a variety of available surge protectors that will suit the PowerBook just fine; most electronics stores sell protectors in a several sizes, shapes, and prices. As always, you get what you pay for. A power strip that comes with a half-dozen outlets but costs only $20 probably isn't going to give you the kind of protection available from a $60, four-outlet box. We recommend protectors that are made specifically for computers and come with as few outlets as possible. At most, you'll need maybe two outlets, one for your PowerBook and one for a portable printer. Also, fewer plugs translates into less crowding in your PowerBook bag and less weight to haul around.

Panamax Inc. in San Rafael, Calif. offers a family of surge protectors built especially for computers. The company guarantees their protectors will keep your computer from being damaged by bad current; if your PowerBook is ever fried because the Panamax device failed to stop a surge, Panamax will buy you a new portable. The company also offers surge protectors that guard modems from power fluxes on the phone lines.

Surge protectors are an especially good idea when travelling abroad; the power in many of the grand old cities of Europe is of highly questionable integrity. In fact, we would go as far as to say you probably don't want to plug in your PowerBook overseas without the stopgap safety provided by a surge protector.

The PowerBook Checklist

The following list contains the items you want to have before you head out the door with your PowerBook. Some items are things you'd want whether you're going around the corner or around the world, such as an extra battery or a good bag. Others, such as extra ribbons for a portable printer or a voltage converter kit for accessing foreign power sources, will depend on what you plan to do while on the road.

As every good scout knows, planning ahead is what will make the difference between a hassle-free trip and a nightmare adventure of biblical proportions. It's the campers with extra bug spray who come home with the fewest ticks, as they say.

We'd recommend taking a quick look through this checklist each time you venture out the door with your PowerBook. Even the experienced Road Warrior will occasionally overlook some small detail; the checklist can act as a tickler so that forgetfulness doesn't lead to problems.

The checklist is divided into three parts. "Call Ahead" covers things the Intentional Tourist will want to confirm about their destination when embarking on a long trip. "The Basics" covers the minimum equipment every digital nomad will want to have every time they venture out with their PowerBook. And "Special Considerations" covers those items that most users won't want to drag along unless they are needed for a particular task.

Call Ahead

- Contact the hotel or motel where you're staying and make sure the phone system supports some kind of modem hookup (alternately called data or computer ports by some hotels). Don't assume the person taking your reservation understands what you're talking about. If having a telecommunications link is critical for your trip, you should insist on talking to one of the hotel's facilities managers; they should know for sure what kind of telecommunications support is available, if any.

See the
Road Warrior
note below.

What you want to make sure of is the availability of a telephone outlet that will let you plug in an RJ-11 phone jack from your modem. That might mean plugging directly into the wall or into a special data port on the side of the room's phone.

See the
Intentional
Tourist
note below.

If you can't find anyone at the hotel who has the foggiest idea what you're talking about (a good indication that they don't support modems on their phone system), ask how long it's been since the hotel's phone system has been upgraded. If that period is more than seven years and the hotel is large (over 300 rooms) it's probably a safe bet the phone system is "telecom-hostile."

If you determine that the hotel is telecom-hostile, you don't necessarily have to change to another hotel. Refer to "Hot-Wiring Your Hotel" below for tips on how to bypass inaccessible phone systems.

- While buying tickets on an airline that you haven't flown before or for an overseas route, double-check the policy concerning computer use on that flight. See "Airline Rules" below for more information on laptop policies and flying.

- If you're going by train, you should check to see if the train has outlets in the passenger cabins. For an overnight ride, you especially need a power source.

- If you're going to another country, you may want to check that nation's policies concerning bringing in a computer. Most countries won't have a problem with your PowerBook. But a few, notably those in South America, can be a bit strange and startlingly restrictive with regard to their technology importation policies. Your travel agent should be able to warn you about any special tariffs or restrictions.

- If you'll be working out of a branch office of your company or another company's offices, you'll want to check ahead about the facilities before you go. For example, if you're depending on having access to a printer or phone line, you should make sure they have the correct cable or plug for your PowerBook, and you'll want to make sure you've got the correct printer drivers. Power Print from GDT Softworks supplies a number of drivers for connecting printers designed for IBM PCs and compatibles and includes an adapter cable that will work with most PC printers. GDT claims its printer driver software will connect your PowerBook to over 850 different models.

- If the purpose of the trip is to give a presentation from your 160, 180, or Duo, you should check ahead to see what sort of display will be available. Apple's video-out-equipped PowerBooks are very flexible and can even use VGA and SVGA PC monitors, but you must come prepared with the correct cable to make the connection.

Don't forget that a third-party dock that supports NTSC video-out, like E-Machines' PowerLink Presentor, will allow you to use your Duo and any standard U.S. television for presentations. However, circumstances might make it more sensible to bring along an LCD projection panel, such as one built by nView Corporation, that can be laid on an old-fashioned overhead projector. Be sure to check the size of your audience as well—a 13-inch screen isn't going to do much for 200 people.

In all cases, make no assumptions about there being a video adapter cable for your PowerBook; bring your own!

The Business Center Follies

Some hotels want to have it both ways, offering their telecommunications-savvy guests the impression that they support dial-up modem connections while steadfastly refusing to bring their telephone system into the twentieth Century.

How do you spot these two-faced inn-keepers? Listen for the Business Center Follies. When you ask if your room will accommodate a modem, they'll say "no," and launch into a sermon on the virtues of their modern business center, an office for executives on the road that comes complete with computer (rest assured it's a DOS machine), modems (also PC-compatible, a possible problem for you), and fax machines. What they've done is upgrade only a sliver of the phone system, leaving all their computer-toting guests a few data lines in a corner of the lobby.

Business centers are no answer to the Road Warrior's problems. They require that you drag your PowerBook downstairs each time you want to send or receive data, a far cry from the ballyhooed convenience of mobile computing. Even more insidious is that most hotel business centers operate as a separate profit center. Phone lines and fax connections are offered at incredible premiums; seven outgoing fax pages can cost as much as $30, compared to the few dollars it would cost to send the information from your PowerBook via a room-based phone line.

There is some solace in the presence of a business center, however, because they indicate that some of the rooms in the hotel may have been upgraded when the phone system was overhauled. Ask if there are modem-ready rooms (now might be a good time to get the facilities manager on the phone).

What a Hoser!

We can't stress strongly enough the need to call ahead for telecommunications. On a trip to Toronto for Macworld Expo/Canada, one of the authors was so unprepared he almost didn't get into the country. (I assumed because U.S. citizens can enter or leave Canada by car without a passport that the same held true for flying in and out. Wrong!—Andy)

(continued)

What a Hoser! (continued)

After an hour of explanations (and a little gratuitous begging) at Canada's immigration service desk, Andy finally managed to get into the country. Upon arriving at the hotel he found that one of Toronto's premier hotels, L'Hotel, had an ancient phone system where the cables were bolted into the walls. He didn't have his hot-wiring kit, so even though Canada uses RJ-11 jacks, he couldn't get access to a phone line to send important files back to *MacWEEK.*

Luckily, he was only in Toronto for 36 hours, so the lack of accessible communications wasn't more than an inconvenience. But on another day in another week, that inaccessible phone system could have spelled disaster!

The Basics

- Make sure you've got a *reinforced bag* that will accommodate your PowerBook and assorted paraphernalia. On airline flights in particular, it might make sense to use a larger bag that can hold your papers as well, so you won't have problems with the "two pieces of carry on luggage" rule enforced on most of today's overcrowded flights. See the "Little Black Bag" discussion below for more information on picking out the right PowerBook bag.

- At least one *extra battery.* Maybe two, if you think it'll be a long time between recharges or if you're going to want to use your laptop most of each day you'll be on the road.

- Your *PowerBook AC power supply.* Okay, it's obvious. But if you forgot it on a long trip, imagine the troubles you'd have.

- *Two LocalTalk or two PhoneNet connectors,* for those times when you want to connect to another Mac. Farallon's StarConnectors make an even better choice for RJ-11-based wiring, because they're cheaper than PhoneNet connectors and less than half the size.

See the
Intentional
Tourist
note below.

- A *two-prong extension cord.* The cord serves two purposes: it gives you more reach from a hotel room plug, and it can help you connect to a crowded outlet.

- A *three-pin AC ground adapter.* You won't need this to plug in your PowerBook, but if you carry a printer with you or need to plug a monitor into a wall for use in a presentation, these adapters can be life-savers. They'll also be helpful if you need to plug in a the three-prong Duo power supply.

- A *pen-style screwdriver* with a slotted head on one end and a Phillips head on the other. This little tool can be put to a variety of uses—from unjamming a stuck RJ-11 jack to fishing out a paperclip from between the keys. Avoid screwdrivers with magnetized heads; there is a minute chance it could foul up your PowerBook's innards.

- A *lint-free cloth.* This can be used for everything from getting the dust off your PowerBook screen to quickly sopping up spills. Alternately, you can use the dry tissues intended for cleaning eyeglasses.

- A *boot disk* with a stripped-down copy of System 7.0.1 or 7.1. See Part 3 of this section for information on constructing a boot disk.

- An *emergency recovery disk,* such as the one that comes with Symantec Corporation's Norton Utilities for Macintosh or Central Point Software's MacTools, that can replace a boot disk.

- *Back-up disk(s).* It's a good idea to back up important data files to diskettes before embarking on a trip, just in case your PowerBook is damaged or stolen. You may also want to back up one or two key programs to floppies. All PowerBooks can use high-density (1.44-Mbyte) diskettes, so you should be able to store your essentials on two or three floppies. Be sure to keep those diskettes handy so you can put them on the plastic tray at the airport security scanner, thus avoiding both x-rays and the metal detector.

- A *list of emergency phone numbers,* including Apple's field service number (1-800-SOS-APPL, which translates to 1-800-767-2775).

See the Intentional Tourist note below.

⬇

- *Stereo earplugs* that use a "miniplug" style jack. This can be used to hear your PowerBook's sound output privately when you're in a public place. Because the PowerBook speaker shuts off automatically when you plug into the sound-out port, you can use the earplugs to keep the computer's beeps from disturbing passengers around you.

Outlet Roulette

It seems there is only one rule in hotel architecture: to make things as inconvenient for the laptop-toting guest as possible without being completely obvious about it.

Case in point: hotel room power outlets. Even the most modern hotels always seem to have exactly one less outlet than what is needed for all the room's lamps and appliances and your PowerBook. Even if there is an open plug, it'll be behind the bed or davenport and will require Herculean strength and a contortionist's flexibility to reach. *(continued)*

Outlet Roulette (continued)

Once you reach the outlet, you can also depend on it being positioned in such a way that it prevents you from attaching the fat block of the AC adapter that comes with most PowerBooks.

That's why we suggest that you carry an extension cord. It's small defense against a world filled with hostile hotel designers.

Radio-Free Airplanes

The reason for carrying stereo earplugs, even though the PowerBook only outputs sound in mono, is that you can also use the earplugs with almost all airplane audio systems. You should find a miniplug on the armrest next to or near the twin sockets for those uncomfortable plastic headsets the airline company usually charges $4 for the privilege of using. Not only can you avoid the headset charge, you'll get better audio quality for in-flight movies and other audio entertainment.

Special Considerations

- **For Duo Users**   Make sure you've got the appropriate dock and floppy dongle for access to diskettes, video-out, or extra ports. Always carry a three-to-two-prong power plug adapter, as many hotels and other public places won't have three-prong plugs.

- **For 100 Users**   Make sure you've got your floppy drive.

- **International Travellers**   Bring along the appropriate voltage converters, plug adapters, and phone cable adapters (ask your travel agent for this information, or call the embassy of the country that you are planning to visit).

  Also, make sure you've got the correct modem scripts for the country you'll be visiting. Most communications programs will require special scripts for accessing local communications nodes (see "France on Five Kilowatts a Day" below for more information on international travel).

- **Telecommunications Connections**   When travelling outside your local calling area, make sure you've got a list of access numbers for your online services, such as CompuServe or America Online. These numbers, which let you make a connection to your telecommunications network from where you are staying, can save you a lot of extra money that you might otherwise spend on long-distance charges.

- **Using a Portable Printer?**   Remember to bring an extra battery, plenty of extra ribbons, and some blank paper. While printers like GCC Technologies' WriteMove II are very nice luxuries, they gobble their tiny ribbons like machine guns going through shells. Also, store blank paper inside a stiff folder that will fit inside your briefcase or PowerBook bag. There's nothing worse than going to the trouble of lugging along a letter-quality printer and then having nothing but battered and wrinkled stationery to print on.

- **For the Security-Conscious**   The new PowerBooks have security slots that can be used with compatible third-party lock-down kits. We recommend carrying along one of the cable-style kits, so you can lock down your unattended PowerBook by wrapping the cable around a table leg or the coat-hanger rod in the closet. Better yet, don't leave your PowerBook unattended.

You may also want to consider using some security software to protect the data inside your PowerBook. See Section II, Part 3, "Security Trade," for more information on third-party security products.

Black-Bagging It

Let's face it, there's no such thing as the perfect bag. The PowerBook bag you pick will depend largely on how you use your computer, and you may need to use different bags for different purposes.

Don't assume that because it says its a PowerBook bag, it's going to be good for your PowerBook. We've seen an amazing assortment of mediocre PC bags sold as specially-made for PowerBooks. Often, general-purpose luggage will work fine and cost less.

Whatever you do, don't buy bags mailorder, unless you've tested out the bag in person.

Search out bags made of tear-proof, impact-resistant nylon. Dark colors are better (we like black) because they hide wear, tear, and dirt better. Also, pick a bag with multiple compartments, an outside pocket, and places for things like pens, diskettes, and cables. A bag should accommodate not just your computer but the rest of your life—important papers, magazines, books, or whatever you like to carry along.

What follows is a quick breakdown of the bags we recommend for the three PowerBook user types.

Staying in Tourist Class

Despite the inconvenience of lugging around a larger case, Intentional Tourists are probably better off with larger bags, perhaps even one of those rigid-construction metal briefcases. Larger cases have the advantage of being able to carry your PowerBook and supplies—all the peripherals, paper files, cables, and equipment you might need on the road—in one place. A rigid case gives you the added security of a nearly indestructible vessel for your PowerBook.

A large bag or a case will help you pass the two-bag limit for most airlines, besides keeping your overall load lighter. Both authors like to avoid baggage claim delays by just taking a suit carrier and a large PowerBook bag along on trips. If we had to carry an additional bag, a flight attendant could use that as an excuse for forcing us to check our suit carrier on crowded flights.

For an Intentional Tourist who doesn't carry a PowerBook everywhere, a larger bag can be great, because you can throw everything you need into it and forget about doing a travel check-off; your travelling office will always be ready. It's only when you carry a PowerBook every day that you need to begin to consider weight before utility.

The Daily Grind

Mobile Commuters will want the tiniest, most form-fitting bag they can get. A reinforced sack with a shoulder strap and handle is what this class of user will probably like best. With complete PowerBook habitats at home and at the office, Mobile Commuters can keep the weight they carry back and forth to a minimum. A pocket for a few paper files and a diskette or two would also be nice.

For the real minimalist who wants to forsake a bag altogether, a shoulder strap that attaches to the PowerBook foot anchors, like the one sold by Premier Technology, will fit the bill.

Your Mobile Home

Road Warriors will probably opt for something between the Mobile Commuter and Intentional Tourist bags. This is because they need to carry some of their peripherals when they are away from the office, since they are gone so often, but they also need something relatively light, because this same bag may spend just as much time commuting as it does seeing the world. We recommend a bag designed so that you can unzip its cover and open the PowerBook without having to remove the portable. These offices for the road should also be able to store enough paper and pens to let you get your work done, wherever you find the time to do a little brainstorming. Road Warriors may want to carry a separate "junk" bag, where they can stow their assorted dongles, cables, and various paraphernalia.

Planes

Most PowerBook users will spend the majority of their travel time in airports and on airplanes. Unfortunately, the combination of overzealous, undertrained security guards and paltry facilities makes airports one of the worst places for PowerBook users to spend time.

However, with a little preparation and a lot of patience, the clever digital nomad can make the time waiting for the next flight productive.

Airport Security

X-Ray Scanners

It isn't the x-rays you have to worry about, it's the motors that drive the conveyor belts. These motors create an electromagnetic field (EMF) that can wreak havoc with your hard drive. The x-rays themselves are harmless —our PowerBooks have been through scanners more than 90 times (collectively) without incident.

Even the conveyor belt motors probably won't give you any grief, as long as you follow this simple rule: Lay your PowerBook bag down lengthwise (short side toward the x-ray machine's rubber curtain) and as close to the scanner's entrance as possible. This should help limit exposure to EMF.

Manual Checks

If you have the time, you can submit your computer to a manual inspection. This involves turning on the computer to demonstrate that it works and, therefore, doesn't contain an explosive device. It's a good idea to keep your PowerBook asleep, instead of shut down, for this inspection, as you can more quickly get to a working screen that will satisfy the guard.

If your PowerBook is turned off, turn it on while holding down the Shift key; this bypasses loading system extensions and speeds the startup process. Users of Connectix's CPU PowerBook utility can use that program's Airport Shutdown feature, which lets you quickly get to the "Welcome to Macintosh" smile and be on your way with a keystroke.

Terminal Cases

It should be noted that some airport terminals have a policy of doing the manual computer check even if you submitted your PowerBook to an x-ray scan. We tried contacting airports around the country to determine why this was true of some terminals and not others, but we found that the airport security officers who answered the phone were most unresponsive, although the creativity of their rude suggestions was unparalleled.

Our totally unscientific and informal survey (in other words, based on the airports where we have been hassled) shows that this mandatory manual check rule seems most prevalent east of the Mississippi. Terminals where we were checked twice, by x-ray and by guards, included Boston's Logan Airport, New York's Kennedy Airport (although not LaGuardia, even when flying to another country), Chicago's O'Hare Airport, and Washington's Dulles and National Airports.

Backups

If you've prepared backup diskettes (something we recommend for especially important data files), place them on the plastic tray before going through the metal detector. Don't put them through the x-ray machine, or they could be erased (floppies are slightly more susceptible to erasure, because the polymers they are made of are less stable than metal hard disks).

You should put your boot disk on the tray too, along with any other emergency floppies you have. Some of the concerns about x-ray machines have been raised regarding metal detectors as well. Although we've both crossed the magnetic threshold many times without first placing our diskettes on the tray, we've never had a problem.

By the way, a couple of diskettes won't set off most airport metal detectors, so if you are feeling brave, you don't need to empty all your pockets.

Inside the Terminal

Once you're past the security gauntlet, there's little left to do but check in for your flight, and if there's time, relax in one of those incredibly over-priced rubber cuisine restaurants that populate most airport terminals. Or you may decide to grab a bag of Peanut M&Ms and the latest copy of *SPY* magazine and retire to the waiting area near your gate.

If your flight's been delayed or you're one of those people who likes to be at the gate an hour ahead of time "just in case" (of what, we don't know), you may want to unbag and wake your PowerBook to get some work done.

Whatever your pleasure, we recommend a quick search to find a power outlet. Especially if you're between connecting flights, you can grab a little extra computing time by plugging in your PowerBook while you wait to board the flight.

- **The Waiting Area**   Most airport waiting areas have power outlets for use by maintenance equipment. Look around the base of pillars or along moldings for metal plates, which are more often than not hidden behind trash cans. Sometimes, you can find available sockets next to vending machines or near a ticket counter. Of course, before you plug into the outlet near a ticket-taker, you might want to ask permission.

- **The Restaurant**   The place to look is along walls or in booths. If you can find a table and an outlet near each other, grab one and plug into the other.

See the Road Warrior note below.

⬇

- **Making a Fast Connection**   Most airport phones are PowerBook-resistant. There is no place to plug in an RJ-11 jack or to "hot-wire" these heavily armored pay phones. However, some more modem-friendly airports now feature AT&T credit-card phones with digital readouts, keyboards, and modem ports.

  If you find one of these slick new pay phones, you'll need to have a length of phone cable and an internal or external modem to make the connection. But these phones are still not very friendly, since there is seldom a shelf on which you can set your PowerBook.

On the Air

Reason number 437 why cellular modems are just too cool: sending files from airport waiting areas. Using Applied Engineering's external cellular interface, which will connect your internal modem to many standard cellular phones, all you have to do is plug in, switch on, and reach out and telecommunicate to someone.

With the AT&T and McCaw Cellular alliance, it may be that cellular phone networks will even become reliable enough for you to depend on a clean connection from any major airport. This marriage of long-distance and wireless communications giants may also help smooth out some of the bumps most cellular phone users encounter while outside their local cellular provider's calling area (this is called "roaming" and can be expensive and complicated).

On the Plane

In the early days of portable usage, many airlines banned the use of portables on flights, for fear the devices would disrupt the airplane's navigational instruments.

This rather shortsighted policy has since given way to a much more permissive attitude toward laptops. The FAA (Federal Aviation Administration) is fairly vague on rules concerning the use of portables. Currently, PowerBooks fall under the category of electronic devices in the FAR (Federal Aviation Regulations), which the pilot can let you use at his or her own discretion. If something untoward should start happening to the instruments in the cockpit, the captain may request that you shut off your computer and put it away.

The rules get a bit foggier concerning the use of wired communications, such as a LocalTalk connection. Although network connections are not specifically forbidden, we'd recommend leaving your LocalTalk connector in with your carry-on luggage, unless you have a compelling need to use LocalTalk (sorry, a hot network-based game doesn't qualify as a compelling need).

Wireless communications devices such as cellular modems are still definitely against the rules on airplanes.

See the
Intentional
Tourist
note below.

In most other respects, portable computer use on airplanes is becoming a common way to put the monotonous hours of air travel to productive use and is welcomed by all the airlines we contacted.

Mouse-Hand Coordination

If you regularly fly in Coach Class, we'd like to suggest that you practice moving your PowerBook trackball with your thumbs instead of with your fingers.

Not only does this allow you to keep your fingers on the keys for faster typing (no more time wasted moving your hand between the trackball and keys), it also allows you to keep your elbows on your side of the armrest. Moving your hand down to the trackball so you can manipulate it with your fingertips can cause you to reflexively move your elbow up and out—and into the side of the passenger next to you. By mousing with your thumbs, you can avoid this reflex and help protect the fragile peace that exists between passengers on long-haul flights.

One thing we should mention for the benefit of the power addicts out there: You won't get away with taking an hour in the bathroom to charge your batteries. About a year ago, the airlines began to crack down on businesspeople who locked themselves in the head in order to shuffle their spreadsheets on jetliner power. But there's good news on the flip side. We've heard tell of some late-model airliners with power outlets in the armrests for the convenience of portable users!

Trains

The advantage of trains over planes as a way to cover a lot of distance are many. Most modern long-haul trains have easily accessible power outlets and provide comfortable digs, even for passengers travelling in economy class. Train stations have much lighter security, so you don't have to weather a strip search when boarding. Once the train pulls out of the station, using a computer or even a cellular modem is just fine with transit authorities.

The main disadvantage of train travel is the time it takes. However, with the advent of the PowerBook, that time can now be put to productive use. In fact, the quiet, relaxed atmosphere of most passenger trains can make an excellent environment for getting lots of work done.

While train travel may be a seldom-used mode of transportation in the U.S., in most foreign countries trains may be the best, and perhaps only, way to travel between cities. Especially in Europe, trains are fast, elegant, and clean; they are probably the best way to go from Brussels to Frankfurt, für instance.

Short-haul trains are more problematic. It's probably best not to display an expensive piece of equipment like a PowerBook while riding the New York City subway system, no matter how much work you might be able to get done on the long ride from Brooklyn to Manhattan's Upper East Side. Commuter trains are much safer venues for PowerBook use, even though they are unlikely to have amenities like power outlets.

However, if you're a Mobile Commuter who faces an hour-long train ride twice a day, the work you can get done while riding might just be enough to convince your boss to buy you that new 160 you've been asking for. In fact, time spent working productively with your PowerBook might be a good reason to leave the family car in the garage and start taking public transportation.

And Automobiles

Using PowerBooks in cars can be very dangerous. We should know, we do it all the time.

Because we keep our calendars and Rolodexes on our PowerBooks, we sometimes need to keep our computers open on the seat next to us to find an important address or directions to our next meeting.

It's better to have someone else drive while you type or dial a cellular phone to your heart's content. This is the scenario Apple seems to think best; a number of PowerBook promotional materials show users accessing their PowerBooks in the backseats of cars. In fact, Apple ran a commercial in Germany to promote a special version of the PowerBook that comes with a built-in cellular modem (sorry, this configuration is only available in Deutschland), and it showed a German executive lounging in the back of a BMW while using his PowerBook to get online and download his electronic mail. Of course, not many of us have the luxury of a chauffeur to drive us around.

If you're one of those people who does use your PowerBook in the car, park before you type. You should also consider purchasing a cigarette lighter power adapter for your PowerBook, such as the one available from Lind Electronic Design Company of St. Louis Park, Minnesota.

General Security

Imagine that a sign is painted in bright red letters on the side of your PowerBook, saying, "Warning! Ownership of this device is nearly impossible to trace, and it is easily fenced for large sums of cash. Please, do not steal!"

There might as well be such a notice permanently embossed on every PowerBook. Like any overpriced product with lots of snob appeal, PowerBooks are tempting morsels for the petty thieves who frequent transportation hubs, hotels, and other public places. We've heard stories about the magical disappearance of PowerBooks while their owners were waiting on line at the ticket counter, in a restaurant, or even in a public restroom. Most of these tales are punctuated with comments like, "I only turned my back for a minute," or, "I asked the lady in the seat next to me to watch my bag," or, "I locked my room before I left."

Don't leave your PowerBook unattended in a public place. If it seems a drag to have to lug the little beast with you everywhere you go, even the john, balance this against the drag it'll be to buy a new one after the inevitable happens. Treat your PowerBook like it's an adorable, mute child with hundred-dollar bills stapled to its OshKosh B'Gosh overalls. It can't call out to you when a stranger grabs it.

When standing or walking about in public, always keep your PowerBook bag in front of you or slung over your shoulder, your hand firmly grasping the bag's bottom. When sitting, either grasp it between your legs or hold it in your lap. Don't leave it behind in your hotel room and don't lock it inside your car where someone passing by can see and identify it. Never check it into baggage claim.

See the Digital Nomad note below.

Even if you follow these guidelines, you might still find that some day your PowerBook will run off with a nimble-fingered stranger. Against such an occurrence, you can purchase special computer insurance.

A Piece of the Rock

Safeware, The Insurance Agency Inc. of Columbus, Ohio, offers what it calls the Key Computer System plan for PowerBook users. Safeware's computer insurance is especially attractive to home-based businesses, as many homeowner's policies won't cover equipment used in the home for business purposes.

For about $200 a year, you can buy a comprehensive policy that covers losses due to theft, accident, and vandalism, as well as damage due to power spikes, fire, or natural disasters at home and on the road. And, this policy will let you recoup losses for anything that isn't covered under your Apple one-year warranty.

Regardless of how the computer is being used, for business or personal purpose, Safeware will pay for the full replacement cost of your system, including software, up to a maximum of $10,000 (after a $200 deductible). If the damaged computer has been discontinued, the company claims to be able to track down replacements. For an extra $99 a year, Safeware also offers the Gold Key endorsement, covering copiers, phone systems, typewriters, user manuals, and the rental of computers and other expenses incurred as the result of a loss, up to an additional $5,000 over the basic policy.

The Safeware key plan covers losses in the United States only. The company offers a more expensive policy that covers losses outside the U.S. Coverage up to $10,000 under this plan runs $500 annually.

If your PowerBook isn't covered by either your homeowner's policy or your company's insurance, Safeware may be a good option. The company can be contacted at (800) 848-3469 or (614) 262-1714.

And don't neglect your computer's safety when you're at home, either. Check your homeowner's or renter's policy to see whether it covers your

PowerBook. If it doesn't, you may want to consider buying a rider to your policy, assuming one is available. Be sure to check that the rider will cover your computer at home and on the road; a policy that protects your Power-Book only while it's sitting on your desktop isn't going to be much use if you accidentally run over it in a rental car. Before you run out and buy any extra insurance, however, you should check to see if your company's insur-ance covers your PowerBook—it should, if the computer belongs to them. If they don't have the right insurance, you should be able to get them to defray the cost of a policy. After all, it's their investment you're protecting.

If you own one of the new PowerBooks with a security slot, we highly recommend investing in both desktop and mobile security solutions that are compatible with the slot, like those from Kensington Microware.

And never forget that your best insurance against all kinds of disasters is backups. It's also a good idea to store backup diskettes separately from your PowerBook—they won't do you much good if they're stolen with the computer.

Hot-Wiring Your Hotel

Physicists can attest to the fact that the universe is not engineered for be-ginners. Neither are most hotel rooms. Rare is the room that has a phone with a data port into which you can plug your modem. If you do get your-self stuck in a hotel room that's straight out of the era of Alexander Gra-ham Bell, there are still a couple of ways around your telecommunications predicament.

The great advantage of having our nation coast on an infrastructure built by a single, huge company is that workarounds are surprisingly uni-form. Each time you can't simply plug in your modem, remember the simple formula that says red wires should always be connected to red wires, while green wires are intended to be connected to green.

Planning ahead is your key to success. What you need is:

- *Two RJ-11 cables* for your modem. Two are necessary. One six- or eight-foot cable is suitable for connecting your PowerBook to a tele-phone with a data jack or directly to the wall jack. The second should be twenty feet or longer, allowing you to reach the inevitable hidden wall jack in the most remote corner of a luxurious hotel room.

- An *RJ-11 "splitter,"* available from your local Radio Shack, is a one-to-two jack adapter that lets you connect both your PowerBook and the hotel phone at the same time.

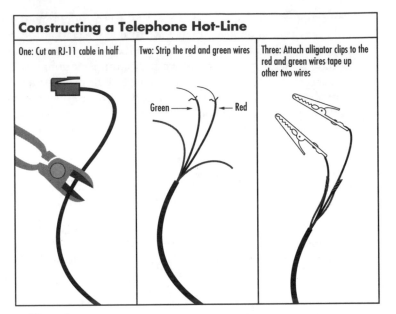

Constructing a Telephone Hot-Line

| One: Cut an RJ-11 cable in half | Two: Strip the red and green wires | Three: Attach alligator clips to the red and green wires tape up other two wires |

Green ⟶ ⟵ Red

Figure 1.

- A *female-to-female RJ-11 connector.* The extraordinary value of the insignificant will become readily apparent the first time you're left holding your twenty-foot RJ-11 cable with two more feet to go before you reach a desk. Take several of these inexpensive connectors, so you can leave them behind without leaving yourself in a jam.

- A *pocket knife or safety razor blade.* When push comes to shove, you're going to need to do a little rewiring that requires stripping the insulation from phone cables.

- An *RJ-11 cable with alligator clips.* This component is the one you have to make. Buy a six-foot RJ-11 cable and cut it in half (you can actually make two of these adapter cables in one sitting, one with each half of the original cable). Strip the red and green wires that are exposed by the cut you make and connect an alligator to each one, taping them on with electrical tape. Just ignore the other wires; seal them with your tape by wrapping them against the finished alligator connections.

With this home-made adapter in hand, you can connect your modem to telephone jacks that don't have an RJ-11 plug.

Worst-Case Scenario #1—The Jackless Wonder

You've been in your room for ten minutes, just enough time to toss your bags on the bed, check the room service menu, and begin setting up shop. To your horror, there's nary a telephone jack to be seen. The phone's only link to the outside world is a cable that emerges from a tiny hole in wall like an electrical snake; there's no faceplate on the wall. Nothing.

It's time to dive into the telephone itself. Beware that you'll be losing the convenience of voice communications, because the phone will need to be rebuilt when you want to make a call. It may be easier to check out and head to another hotel.

Unscrew the mouthpiece of the handset and tip the microphone into your hand. Two wires are soldered to the microphone, one in the center and the other on the outside edge. Take your alligator clip adapter and clip the red wire to the connector on the center of the microphone; clip the green wire to the outside connector.

Some phones will not have wire connectors on the microphone, but rather aluminum contacts that press against the microphone when the mouthpiece is in place. With these phones, you just need to connect the red alligator clip to the contact that is connected to the red wire, and similarly, connect the green clip to the green-wired contact in the handset.

Worst-Case Scenario #2—The Mouthpiece Doesn't Come Off

Most phones made in the past five years don't allow you to unscrew the mouthpiece, so you've got to risk doing a little damage to the phone. We don't suggest vandalism, however... We say the hotel is just asking for this, but you should still be careful to avoid permanent damage.

Take your pen knife and cut a small slit along the cable that connects the handset to the telephone. Keep this cut close to the base unit, since you'll want to be able to lift the handset to answer voice calls without dislodging your handiwork.

Peel the cover back slightly and pry out about a half-inch length from the bundle of wires inside the cable. Again, you are only after the red and green wires. Peel away a small section of the insulation on each wire, being careful to separate the exposed wires to prevent a short-circuit. Attach the alligator clips, red-to-red and green-to-green, and you are all set to connect the other end of the adapter to your PowerBook.

And be good camper—repair the phone before you leave, taping the wires and the cable individually!

Worst-Case Scenario #3—Into the Walls You Go

Alright, the last time you stayed in this dump you received an angry call from the manager two weeks after you got home. Seems she did not like the surgery you performed on the hotel's telephone, so you've got to hide your intrusion better this time.

You spot the faceplate out of which the telephone cable protrudes. Grabbing the trusty screwdriver, you fall to your knees and work the plate off. Inside is the usual collection of wires, among them the expected red and green ones. Carefully strip a bit of the insulation off of each and clip on your home-made adapter. Here's one of the times you'll probably need a female-to-female RJ-11 connector to attach your short adapter cable to a longer one that reaches the desktop.

France on Five Kilowatts a Day

While getting access to the facilities you need in the U.S. can be a challenge worthy of the most seasoned Road Warrior, the variety of conditions you'll encounter overseas is enough to make an ardent isolationist out of the most avid Intentional Tourist. Especially in Europe, where any plot of land larger than a baseball diamond can be declared a sovereign nation with its own proprietary power and communications standards, taking your PowerBook on the road can be a nightmare.

International Online

The great thing about the Information Age is the fact that data services are available to you wherever you go. Local access numbers in Nice and Nantucket alike can give you relatively low-cost data connections to the entire world.

When planning an overseas trip, you should contact the online services where you have electronic mail accounts to get information on the special scripts and telephone numbers needed to access their services from the countries you'll be visiting. Be sure to get complete sign-on instructions for the town you'll be staying in. Not only do the standards vary greatly from country to country, in Europe they can also vary from town to town. Also, some systems, like Apple's AppleLink, require that you enter special codes in the connection dialog to access a foreign network node.

The alternative to dealing with local access rules is to call long distance to the node you use at home, an expensive and difficult means of keeping in touch. The complexity of charging a call by credit card from a foreign country is daunting, but there is a little-known way to avoid the problem.

Call your long-distance provider to ask if they have a local access number in the foreign cities on your itinerary. A few of the largest carriers—AT&T, MCI, and Sprint—are beginning to introduce these Cyberspace doorways from Europe and Asia. If they do, you'll be able to dial a number and get a direct connection to your stateside phone network. It is also possible to create a modem script that will dial the local access number, the number you wish to call in the U.S., and your credit card number.

Many information services, such as America Online, have no local points of presence outside the U.S.; to access these systems you'll have to call home. Also, if you want to dial into your company's network using AppleTalk Remote Access, that's another long-distance call.

It used to be that overseas phone connections were too dirty (static-filled) for reliable data communications. Now, with satellite linkups guaranteeing clear connections, the only thing you need to contend with is the cost.

Foreign Powers

See the
Intentional
Tourist
note below.

The PowerBook's AC power supply is very flexible. Although foreign voltages can vary greatly (up to 240 volts in some countries) your power supply should have no problem getting what it needs from any power source, providing you have the right plug adapter.

If you know you're going overseas, you can acquire a travel adapter kit from almost any general electronics store; it should include all the plug adapters you'll need. Duo users have the advantage of local Macs from which they can steal power cords that will fit their Duo Docks and Mini-Docks, should the correct adapter not be available. Unfortunately, they'll also be under the disadvantage of the third prong (the ground) that most foreign voltage adapter kits will not be able to handle—yet another reason for Duo owners to buy a three- to two-prong plug adapter. If you're concerned about grounding for your Duo (and in foreign lands you should be), you can always run a wire from the prong adapter to the metal screw that holds the outlet's faceplate to the wall.

Don't be surprised if either your PowerBook plug or your voltage adapter plug doesn't fit snugly in the outlet. Apparently, outlet design is an inexact science in many countries, so you shouldn't worry too much if the plug is loose, just so long as you find a way to keep it seated well enough for the power to flow.

As always, it pays to double-check with your travel agency or a friend in the country you're visiting to make sure you've got the right adapter for the job. (This can lead to some interesting conversations, where your friend tries to describe what to them is an ordinary plug.) You might even find yourself in places where there is no AC current, in which case you'll also want to bring along an AC/DC adapter.

Another useful item you may want to have along with you on trips overseas is a surge protector. Foreign power isn't always stable (just ask anyone living in the Baltic Republics), and you wouldn't want your PowerBook to take the heat because the town where you're staying hasn't upgraded its power grid since Truman visited Yalta.

Figure 2.

The Right Currency

While your PowerBook may have no trouble with foreign power, don't assume that your peripherals are similarly immune to problems. The wrong current can cause a lot of damage to delicate electronics. In extreme cases, it can even cause a device to burst into flames!

If the device in question—whether it's a printer or an external modem —uses a transformer (usually a large box that sits somewhere on the power cord), check to see that its voltage range will accommodate the local current. This information is usually printed on a label attached to the transformer box.   *(continued)*

The Right Currency (continued)

If your peripheral doesn't have a transformer, check the product's manual under "Power Requirements" or "Specifications." If you still aren't sure, or if you find out the device can't handle the voltage in question, make sure to use a voltage transformer; these are usually sold as part of a foreign voltage kit. They can also be acquired separately. Be very careful not to mistakenly use a 1,000-watt converter that looks almost identical to a power transformer, should your kit come with one. You may blow more than a fuse if you accidentally use the 1,000-watt box.

NTSC vs. SECAM vs. PAL

Another thing you'll notice when you travel abroad is that many of the televisions use different connectors.

This isn't just fickle design, these countries actually use different television broadcast signals and electronics in their TV sets. Many countries' proprietary TV-signal standards make them incompatible with Power-Book video-out solutions that work with American televisions. If you plan to use a television as a monitor on your next trip, remember that U.S. televisions are tuned to the NTSC scheme and the sets in the destination country likely will not be. If you're going to a country that broadcasts PAL or SECAM television signals, you're out of luck, unless you can find a display that has a multi-standard picture tube or you have a localized version of your PowerBook-video-out-to-TV solution.

Parlez-Vous Adapteur?

If you think finding the right plug can be a problem, just wait until you try to connect your modem to a foreign phone socket. To say there are as many kinds of phone plugs as there are totally repulsive cuisines in the world would not give the phone plugs enough credit. Not only will sockets likely change from nation to nation, in some countries they may also differ between cities (again, Europe seems to be the worst offender in this area).

The best strategy is to wait until you arrive at your destination and then evaluate your situation. Once you know what you're dealing with you can go to the local phone store and buy an American- (also called a modular or RJ-11)-to-PTT adapter.

Germany: "Ich möchte einin modular adapter für das telephon," or "Ich möchte einin Amerikanischen adapter für das telephon."

France: "J'ai besoin d'un raccord moduler pour le téléphone."

Spain (or Spanish speaking countries): "Neccesito un adaptador modular por el teléfono."

England: "Excuse me, old chap, would you happen to have one of those American phone thingies?"

Figure 3. How to Ask for the Right Phone Adapter in Europe

Foreign Intrigues

Not all your problems abroad will come from trying to use a PowerBook. Your problems can start before you ever set foot in your destination.

For example, a friend of ours almost wasn't allowed to bring his computer into Brazil recently. Apparently, the border guard decided, because the computer had software on it and software is a potentially marketable commodity, that our friend might try to make a profit by selling copies of his software during his visit.

He talked his way out of this predicament and was later told by an associate that the guard was probably fishing for a bribe, which the associate said is a common way to remedy customs entanglements at the Brazilian border.

But this is dangerous thinking and the product of a peculiarly American conceit. It is highly inadvisable to offer a bribe to a foreign official. In fact, it is stupid and will probably land you in jail. If you encounter problems with customs or with any other official, call the American Consulate immediately, don't reach for your wallet.

Consider our friend's situation. If he had attempted to bribe that guard, he might very well have confirmed the suspicion that he was up to no good. It is always better and more effective to put professionals to work on your problems—that's what a Consul is for, after all.

You can be prepared for the basic questions when you arrive in a foreign land, even though it's hard to anticipate exactly what kinds of documents you may be asked to produce. At the very minimum, it's a good idea to bring along your bill of sale just to prove you own the computer. Also, check customs requirements with your travel agent before departing.

PART

2

THE CONSERVATION
OF ENERGY

271

Portable power management is not rocket science. You really don't need to know how many volts your PowerBook battery outputs at various points in its discharge cycle or during what power states your laptop's sound chip is drawing electricity to get the most from your PowerBook's battery. The whole point of a portable with a sophisticated power manager like the PowerBook is not having to concern yourself with these things and still getting maximum performance.

However, while we won't waste your time by going through the esoterica of PowerBook power systems, in this section we will discuss all the major factors that contribute to battery life. Getting good performance from your laptop while extending battery life is a balancing act. Anyone can reduce power consumption by moving the PowerBook control panel's performance slider to maximum conservation and cranking down the CPU clockrate to 16 MHz. However, not everyone will enjoy using a $4,000 180 that runs as slow as a $2,000 140, is constantly hanging while the drive spins up or down, and suffers from an extreme case of narcolepsy.

It's like owning a car (will the automotive metaphors never stop?). You can use your PowerBook like it's got an automatic transmission, leaving most of the power conservation decisions, such as when to spin down the internal hard drive, to the computer. As a result, you'll lose both response time and, depending on how often your applications need to access the drive, fuel economy. Automatic transmissions deliver the median performance that many motorists choose over dealing with the complexities of a manual transmission. However, as most stick enthusiasts will tell you, once you become proficient in clutch operation, you have much more control over your vehicle than with an automatic. By balancing the release of the clutch with the flow of fuel, you can choose, at one point, to slowly roll the car forward from a stop, and at another point, to peel rubber, putting down that obnoxious tailgater who thinks he's so hot because he drives a BMW that costs more than most middle-class family homes in Arkansas.

Likewise, by understanding the effect each PowerBook subsystem has on power consumption, you can switch from being the little old lady from Pasadena to being the asphalt warlord cruising the Hollywood Hills' winding canyon roads in a souped-up Chevy with oversized rear wheels big enough to hold up a jumbo jet. Once you understand how each factor changes your PowerBook's battery life, you can make a few small compromises and reap much longer computing sessions. In fact, even without resorting to the extreme of the PowerBook control panel's maximum battery setting, you can get just as long, if not longer, battery life by manually controlling how much current your PowerBook draws. Like driving a manual transmission, once you make conservation a habit, it won't require much more thought than downshifting instead of using the brakes to slow your car.

The Trappings of Power

Your PowerBook is an amazingly flexible device. While delivering all the functionality of a desktop computer, the Apple laptop is also able to operate free from a wall socket for limited periods of time, without forcing many compromises.

The PowerBook power manager is what makes this possible. It controls how power is regulated, partitioning it between charging the battery and powering the PowerBook's subsystems, controlling sleep, processor cycling, and clockrate. Combined with miserly components, long-lived batteries, and super-efficient power supplies, this system can allow PowerBook users to work unattended for several hours without having to change batteries.

Apple even gave its combined power management system a trademarked name, EverWatch (although we have to wonder how the Eveready people feel about this). You only need to know two things about Ever-Watch: one, it is the sum of many parts—internal and external power circuitry, special ASICs (Application-Specific Integrated Circuits), and low-power components; and two, it is one of the key differences that makes your portable stand apart from the ranks of DOS and Windows-based notebooks, most of which use electricity less efficiently.

A Tale of Two Sources

There are two ways that your PowerBook draws its lifeblood, off an external power adapter or off an internal battery. Your PowerBook should always have a battery inside it, even when sucking power off a wall socket, because the battery's integrated door protects the portable's insides from dust contamination. Also, if the battery isn't inside and the power cable comes loose from the back of the portable, anything you're working on and haven't saved will be flushed out into the electromagnetic ozone. This can happen much more easily than you might imagine, as the power adapter's small plug is designed for fast and easy removal. (Also, you're more likely to have a portable power cable strung across the floor, just waiting for the first person to walk by and yank it out with his foot.)

See the Digital Nomad note below.

One of EverWatch's many neat tricks is its ability to instantly switch over to the battery—with no interruption of service—when the AC power source is suddenly cut off, either at the back of the PowerBook or at the wall socket. Feel free to yank the power cord out of your portable any time you want without shutting down or sleeping the computer first. As long as a battery is installed, it should continue to operate without a problem.

There is little reason for you not to have a battery in your PowerBook, because the power adapter charges the internal battery any time you're plugged in, even when you're using the PowerBook. So, taking out the internal battery to place it in an external charger really does nothing to speed up the charging process. (A battery in a charger will recharge a tiny bit faster than it will in a running PowerBook, but the small time savings isn't worth the risk of leaving the portable's battery slot open.)

There are two kinds of power adapters available for Apple's family of PowerBooks: the standard "brick" style, which has two outlet prongs mounted permanently on one side of a rectangular gray box; and the Duo System power supply, which uses a removable three-prong plug adapter to connect its supply to the wall. The brick works with the 100 through 180 models, while the Duo supply only works with Apple's dockables. Do not under any circumstances try to power your PowerBook with anything but the adapter that comes with it. Power adapters may sometimes look alike, but there are subtle yet important differences between the supply you'd use to run your Nintendo video game and your portable. Those differences can be killers.

Unfortunately, you also can't swap the regular PowerBook brick for the Duo supply. They use different plugs and the brick uses a linear power supply, while the Duo supply uses a more efficient switched system. The Duo power supply features several innovations over the brick, including a longer cable that can be wrapped around retractable arms, a modular power plug that lets you switch between hanging the Duo supply on the wall or running a power cable from it to the wall socket, and the ability to connect a two-slot battery charger directly to the supply. With a Duo charger hooked to your power supply, you can charge two batteries in the charger, as well as the battery in the Duo. If you want to run your PowerBook 100 through 180 off a wall socket while one or two other batteries are getting powered up in their external charger, you'll need to purchase a second power supply.

PowerBook chargers are sold separately, so don't look for one in the portable's packaging. You can also buy a third-party charger from companies like Lind Electronic Design. Some third-party chargers offer the ability to deep-discharge a battery before charging it, guaranteeing that the battery gives the best possible performance. If you're going to buy a charger for your PowerBook, we highly recommend going for one of these charger/dischargers. (For more information on deep discharging, see "I remember when…," below; for more on third-party battery products, also see "A Party for Batteries," below.)

You can purchase a 12-volt power adapter for connecting your PowerBook to a car's cigarette lighter. Although we can't recommend using your PowerBook while driving, this can be a convenient way to recharge your internal battery between destinations or to keep your kids entertained on long drives, assuming you're one of those foolhardy types who lets the kids have access to their PowerBook.

Bad Medicine

If you're ever concerned about whether your PowerBook power adapter is functioning properly, there's a very easy way to check it—just run your PowerBook while it's plugged in, call up the Battery DA, and watch what happens. If the power adapter isn't supplying current to your PowerBook, the results should show within fifteen minutes. You should see the battery gauge declining, despite the presence of the lightning-bolt battery icon. Just to be sure you don't have a bad plug, try connecting something that you know works (such as a radio or lamp) to the outlet and switch it on. If you hear music or the room suddenly brightens, then your PowerBook adapter has got problems.

Even if you don't notice that your battery is discharging while plugged in, your PowerBook will eventually figure out that it isn't getting juice. You'll get the "Your battery is not charging" warning; this usually happens when the charge on the power pack is quite low, with less than 25 percent of its charge remaining.

There is one other possibility that may explain why your battery level declines even when your PowerBook is plugged in. Your PowerBook battery may be shot. To test this, shut down your computer and remove the battery without replacing it. (Yes, we know we told you not to do this, but it'll be okay for just a few moments.) Now, try turning on your PowerBook. If the PowerBook starts, then the battery is the culprit and not the supply. Otherwise, it's time to get a new power adapter.

Four of a Kind

As mentioned in Part 1 of Section I, *PowerBook Technical Readouts*, Power-Books use three different types of batteries: lead-acid, nickel cadmium, and nickel hydride. Lead-acid batteries are used only by the PowerBook 100; NiCads are used by the 140 through 180; and NiHys are used by Duos. Like power adapters, batteries are not interchangeable, although they can be shared between compatible PowerBooks (for example, the NiCad battery that comes with a 140 can be used by a 180 and vice versa). Each kind of PowerBook battery has a unique shape and cannot be installed in another portable.

See the
Digital Nomad
note below.

⬇

All PowerBook batteries are rated for about 500 cycles, discharges and recharges. In our experience, this works out to be about a year and a half of usage, when you occasionally condition your battery. If you want to get the most life out of your batteries, we suggest charging and storing them in a cool, dry place. Excessive heat will adversely affect battery life.

Lead-Acid

By far the most primitive of Apple's batteries, the 100 power pack most resembles the battery that runs your car. As with a car battery, it's a very bad idea to ever let your 100 battery completely discharge, as you may never get it to hold a charge again.

This has two implications. First, you obviously want to heed the "battery low" warnings, although in our tests you can go so far as waiting until the ten-second warning before taking action. When you do get the "battery low" warning on the 100, shut down or sleep the computer and plug it in. If it'll be several hours before you can plug it in, use the battery cut-off switch on the back of the 100 to protect the battery from continued drainage, because a shut-down PowerBook still draws small amounts of electricity.

If possible, you should leave your PowerBook 100 plugged in while it is stored or use the cut-off switch to protect its internal battery. And don't trust the cut-off switch to protect your battery for longer than a few months; although lead-acid batteries hold their charge longer than NiCad or NiHy, even they will slowly discharge over time.

Although Apple rates lead-acid batteries as having close to the life of NiCads, our experience is that as they get older, 100 batteries seem to lose holding capacity more quickly than NiCads do. Of course, one compensating factor is that lead-acid batteries don't suffer from power memory.

NiCad

Unlike lead-acid, NiCad and NiHy batteries thrive on occasional deep-discharging. It's okay to store these inside a PowerBook for long periods of time, although we recommend leaving the stored PowerBook plugged in, so the battery is powered up and ready to go when you are. You should also make sure not to allow NiCad, or NiHy, batteries to completely discharge. It could damage the power pack.

A controversy continues over whether NiCads are susceptible to power memory—the inability to charge past a certain level after repeated shallow charges. Our experience is that they are, and we have a year-old Power-Book 140 battery to prove it. We have found that newer batteries seem less likely to exhibit the problem than older ones. According to battery developers we've talked to, this is because they are constantly improving battery technology. However, we suspect the age of the battery is a contributing factor in memory problems.

NiHy

NiHys have many advantages over NiCads. They produce more power with less bulk than NiCads. They are less susceptible to power memory, according to developers—we haven't had a Duo battery long enough to test this theory. Also, NiHy batteries can be charged to 100-percent capacity much more quickly than NiCads.

NiHys are also the only PowerBook batteries that come with their own power cut-off switches. Look for the switch on the side of the battery. The cut-off icons are far from self-explanatory: the partially filled-in battery icon represents the setting for allowing electricity to flow, while the fully filled-in icon represents the cut-off setting. Another advantage of the cut-off switch is that, because it stops electricity from flowing through the contacts, it should eliminate the risk of battery combustion (see Part 1 of this section for more information on flaming power packs).

Backup Batteries

All PowerBooks ship with backup batteries that keep the system clock and other functions alive while you change batteries. The best way to test whether your backup batteries are shot is to disconnect your PowerBook from all power sources and remove the main battery; after a moment, put in a battery or plug in the computer and restart. If the system date has reset to some other era, then the backup battery needs replacing.

The 100 has three lithium cells that are stacked in series (positive terminal touching negative terminal) in a small pull-out drawer in the back of the computer. These batteries are usually good for a couple of years before they need to be replaced. PowerBook 100 backup batteries will allow you to swap a discharged main battery for a fresh one while the computer is asleep (and not plugged into a wall socket) without losing the contents of RAM.

The 140, 145, 160, 170, and 180 have a rechargeable lithium cell soldered to their logic boards, but they do not back up RAM for any period of time.

The Duos have two small lithium cells mounted under the trackball, which will allow you up to four minutes to change the main battery without losing the contents of RAM.

If your PowerBook is disconnected from any viable power source for a long time, a situation that you should avoid as much as possible, the backup batteries will protect the system clock for up to two weeks.

Battery Birth Certificates

A battery comes into this world with only a short march of days before the Grim Reaper comes wielding his scythe. As we said above, PowerBook batteries are good for about 500 charges, or a year and a half of steady use.

To help keep track of when your battery started its working life, we recommend putting a label on it and marking down the date when you start using it. If you have more than one battery (and you will), then we'd also recommend numbering your batteries sequentially. The numbers and the dates will help you keep track of the time that has passed since you bought your battery. So, when your battery starts aging—for example, not holding its charge the way it used to—you'll know it's because the battery is old and not because of some other problem.

Unlike most camcorder batteries, PowerBook batteries don't come with a little colored switch you can change to show whether the power pack is charged. To remedy this problem, you can write the words "charged" and "drained" on opposite sides of the label and then attach a removable sticker (like the ones kids sometimes put on their school notebooks) on whichever side is appropriate to the battery's condition.

The Discharge of the Light Brigade

Many factors can affect the length of time your battery can power your portable before needing a recharge. Power consumption, environmental conditions, and how long the battery was actually attached to the charging power source all influence your battery's lifespan before recharge. The Battery DA and SuperClock! give you only rough estimates of how much power you have. The calibrations on the Battery DA don't represent any exact measure of time; a single click can disappear after 30 minutes or only a minute of run time. The Battery DA isn't a good indicator of whether your battery is charged or not either. It will, in fact, tell you your battery is half-charged after as little as 30 seconds of charge time, even though it takes at least two hours to charge a PowerBook battery.

We've seen two power packs, one with half its charge gone and one with supposedly fully charged batteries, both run the same PowerBook under the same operating conditions for the same length of time. This discrepancy occurs because measuring battery life is an inexact science. Especially with NiCads and NiHys, which produce very consistent current right up until they run out of power altogether, battery-life measurement is a "best guess" business. So, don't take what the Battery DA or any other battery power indicator says as gospel. You could get caught short. Make sure you've fully charged your battery according to the chart below (see Figure 1), and make sure you're regularly discharging and fully recharging your NiCads and NiHys.

Figure 1. PowerBook Battery Charge Times, Starting with a Fully Discharged Battery

	PowerBook 100	PowerBook 140-180	Duo
One battery (to 80%)*	2 hours	2 to 3 hours	N/A
One battery (to 100%)*	4 hours	5 to 7 hours	2 to 3 hours
Two batteries(to 80%)**	6 hours	5 to 6 hours	N/A
Two batteries(to 100%)**	12 hours	10 to 12 hours	4 to 5 hours

*   These recharge times apply to charging your battery either inside your PowerBook or in an external charger. The effect of running your portable while charging an internal battery is negligible.

** These charge times are based on using an external charger.

Getting a Charge

See the Intentional Tourist note below.

To help prevent damaging your NiCad and lead-acid batteries by over-charging them, the PowerBook power manager quickly charges the battery to 80-percent capacity and then slows down the charging process. It can take just as long to get the battery from 80 percent up to 100 percent as it did to get it charged up to 80 percent. Duo batteries don't require shallow charging and hit their 100-percent mark by the time NiCads and lead-acid batteries hit 80 percent.

Once again, battery status software doesn't help much. The Battery DA switches from the charging icon to the standard battery icon once the internal battery hits the 85-percent charged point. SuperClock!, on the other hand, displays the battery with a lightning bolt any time the PowerBook is plugged in, even if the battery has a 100 percent charge (see Figure 2). Because SuperClock! doesn't show battery levels when plugged in, you have to unplug your PowerBook for a few moments to see how far along it thinks the charge is.

This is why it's important to be sure you've allowed the battery time for a full charge; software-based indicators just aren't going to be much help. Especially with NiCads, there's a chance your battery may decide that 80 percent is as full as its going to get—that is, if you don't regularly deep discharge and fully recharge your battery. You probably wouldn't know your battery was stuck at 80 percent, because the indicator would show the partially charged battery as fully charged.

Figure 2. Never trust your PowerBook battery indicator.

We test-charged a PowerBook 140 internal power pack based on what the Battery DA's indicator said was the charge status of the battery. The 140's performance setting was at maximum and backlight dimming was switched off during the test. We used a relatively new, nearly discharged NiCad battery, which we charged in the PowerBook while it was running. Notice the time ticked off on SuperClock!'s stopwatch; it shows how long it took to get each indication.

Going Up...

Here's what Battery DA and SuperClock had to say just before we plugged in:

    00:00:01 ⏱🔋   ⑦
    ┌─────────────────┐
    │ 🔋 E □□□□□□□□ F │
    └─────────────────┘

Miraculously, 30 seconds later we're halfway to a full charge:

    00:00:30 ⏱⚡   ⑦
    ┌─────────────────────┐
    │ □ ⚡ E ■■■■□□□□ F ⌇ │
    └─────────────────────┘

Eight minutes in, and we're nearly there?

    00:08:20 ⏱⚡   ⑦
    ┌──────────────────┐
    │ ⚡ E ■■■■■■■□ F   │
    └──────────────────┘

Wow, it took another sixteen minutes to fill in that last block!

    00:24:00 ⏱⚡   ⑦
    ┌──────────────────┐
    │ ⚡ E ■■■■■■■■ F   │
    └──────────────────┘

After about 50 minutes, even the Battery DA's charge icon went away. That's not supposed to happen until the battery is charged to 85 percent, which should take at least two hours, according to Apple.

    00:50:30 ⏱⚡   ⑦
    ┌──────────────────┐
    │ 🔋 E ■■■■■■■■ F   │
    └──────────────────┘

Well, maybe we had an especially fast charger. Let's see how long it takes to discharge this "nearly-ready" battery.

(continued)

Figure 2. (continued)

Going Down...

Okay, here's our "charged" battery freshly disconnected from the wall socket. We've re-set SuperClock!'s stopwatch (notice that you can now see SuperClock!'s battery-level indicator):

```
00:00:00 ⏱🔋      (?)
   🔋 E ▐▐▐▐▐▐▐▐ F
```

Two notches down in fifteen minutes? This is going to be a short session!

```
00:15:01 ⏱🔋      (?)
   🔋 E ▐▐▐▐▐▐□□ F
```

25 minutes and halfway to the end:

```
00:25:26 ⏱🔋      (?)
   🔋 E ▐▐▐▐□□□□ F
```

Ack! We hit the first "battery almost out" warning in 30 minutes!

```
00:30:34 ⏱🔋      (?)
   🔋 E □□□□□□□□ F
```

Second warning; it's all downhill from here:

```
00:33:13 ⏱🔋      (?)
   🔋 E □□□□□□□□ F
```

Last warning. Ten seconds later our PowerBook put itself to sleep:

```
00:34:39 ⏱🔋      (?)
   🔋 E □□□□□□□□ F
```

Note that it only took four minutes to get from the first to the last "battery out" warning.

Battery Swapping

Okay, we know electronic vagabonds are going to have lots of batteries to worry about charging and are probably going to be too busy to remember what battery had how much of a charge when you last used it. However, if you want each battery to last as long as possible and you don't want to get caught short because a battery you thought was charged isn't charged, follow these rules.

Make sure all your batteries are numbered and dated. For the purposes of this example, we'll assume you purchased two extra batteries when you bought your PowerBook (giving you a total of three batteries). Start with battery number one. Run it all the way down before inserting number two. Try to avoid recharging any battery until it has been run completely down. If you're only halfway through battery number one's charge when you reach your hotel, you can continue to operate off it until it is discharged, then plug in the PowerBook. Make sure when you plug in your battery for a charge that there will be enough time to fully charge it; this will usually mean leaving it plugged in overnight. The next morning, store battery number one and move on to battery number two.

Use batteries in number order only; that way, when you add more batteries to your collection, you'll be sure they outlive your older ones (if you were to use a newer battery a lot more than your older ones, you could prematurely age the new power pack).

If you need to use more than one battery before you have a chance to recharge (if this wasn't a possibility, why would you have invested in three batteries in the first place?), just recharge your packs in number order. If you don't have time to fully recharge all your drained batteries, don't worry. Just charge the ones you have time for and move on to the next fresh power pack in your collection. As long as you charge by the numbers, the lifespans in your battery collection should stay balanced.

The same holds true for quickie charges between flights. Obviously, the battery won't be fully charged after just a half hour in a janitorial outlet (whatever Battery DA says). Just charge whichever battery is already inside your PowerBook as much as you can. As long as you remember to rotate the power pack later, shallow charges should balance out evenly over your entire collection. And, if you run down your NiCad or NiHy battery at the end of the day, you will avoid power memory problems.

Danger, Will Robinson!

So, maybe all this battery talk is starting to get a little scary. After all, you don't want your PowerBook keeling over from an electricity deficit in the middle of an important spreadsheet that you haven't saved because you're trying to conserve power!

Your PowerBook does have an early warning system that will let you know when you're nearly at the end of a charge. It will display three alert messages before putting your portable to sleep automatically. According to Apple, the first warning (Figure 3) displays when you've got about fifteen percent of the battery's charge left (the PowerBook cheats a little by dimming the screen to extend the time). However, as you can see in our test above (Figure 2), the actual time that fifteen percent represents can be very brief indeed!

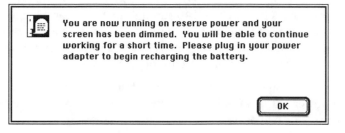

Figure 3. The First Sign

You can usually ignore the first warning, but you should try to bring whatever you're working on to a close at that point. It's when the second warning (Figure 4) displays that you need to take action.

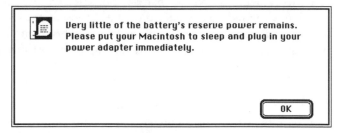

Figure 4. The Second Warning

When you see warning two, it's time to save whatever you're working on. You may want to quit all the applications you're in, just to make sure you have saved all your documents. Most applications ask you if you want to save your unsaved work before quitting; it's a good shortcut when you're in a rush.

Whatever you do, don't push the envelope on this warning, because the next dialog box only gives you ten seconds to respond (see Figure 5)!

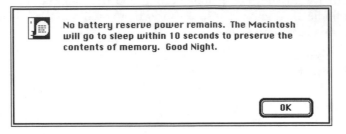

Figure 5. Abandon Hope!

As long as you've saved what you're working on, just let your PowerBook put itself to sleep. Then, if you have a 100 or a Duo, you can swap batteries. If you have a PowerBook 140 through 180, you can plug a Utilitron, Inc. PowerSwap into the back of your computer, so you won't lose what's in memory when you change batteries. The PowerSwap uses a 9-volt transistor battery to protect the contents of RAM while you change power packs.

See the
Digital Nomad
note below.

▼

If you don't have a spare battery, don't sweat it. There's still quite a bit of power left in a depleted battery—enough to protect memory contents for at least two days.

The Hidden Reserve

Just out of curiosity, we wanted to see how much power was left in a supposedly depleted NiCad battery. So, after we got the ten-second warning, we wired up the NiCad to one of those battery-operated halogen lights used on camcorders. Usually, a one-hour camcorder NiCad, fully charged, will drive this particular light for 30 minutes. Yet our "empty" PowerBook NiCad had enough juice left to keep the bulb burning for the same length of time, about a half hour!

This is why we recommend using a third-party discharger to condition your battery, instead of following Apple's instructions (see "I Remember When" below). We *don't* suggest using the video light method to drain your battery.

I remember when...

Power memory is an affliction of NiCad and, to a lesser extent, NiHy batteries, causing them to "think" they have less electrical capacity than they actually have. The result is that the battery charges only part way and stops, no matter how long you leave it in the charger.

The way to prevent this problem is to regularly deep-discharge or condition your battery by sapping almost all of its stored power and then recharging it to 100-percent capacity. According to Apple, if you allow your PowerBook to run down the battery to the ten-second (final) battery-out warning and then fully recharge it, that's all you need to do to condition your battery. However, as we've seen even at this point your PowerBook battery may still have a substantial charge left. If the battery is already showing signs of power memory, Apple's guidelines may prove insufficient to remedy the problem.

There are two ways to fully deep-discharge your battery. First, follow Apple's instructions, but instead of immediately recharging the battery, leave it inside your unplugged PowerBook for another day (make sure your portable is asleep and not shut down—this will draw more power). After sitting for another 24 hours, the battery should be closer to being fully discharged, and you should be able to fully recharge it.

The other way is to buy a battery conditioner. We recommend Lind's External Battery Charger/Conditioner. A device like this can drain your battery until it's almost empty and then recharge it for proper conditioning (you never want to completely drain any battery, it could be damaged). When recharging your battery after deep-discharging, you should always let it recharge overnight.

Conditioning doesn't always "take" the first time. If your battery still shows signs of power memory after being conditioned, try deep-discharging it again. Better yet, condition your battery once a month to prevent the problem from occurring in the first place. Apple recommends that you run down your battery once every 90 days, unless you have a Duo, in which case they suggest doing it every 30 days. However, if you follow either Apple's procedure or one of the other two outlined above, you shouldn't have any problems when you condition your battery more often.

The Last Hurrah

When your battery has breathed its last—when all the charging and discharging and overnight therapy sessions with the power supply fail to garner more than a trickle of electricity—it's time to take the power pack on that last, long walk down to your Apple dealer for immediate disposal. Apple recycles many of the metals in your battery, so even if your municipality allows you to throw away batteries, do your planet a favor and make sure the battery is recycled.

If your battery cracks, wrap it up in a couple of rags and make arrangements with the local trash collector to have it properly disposed of. Your Apple dealer will not accept damaged batteries for recycling.

Be very careful when handling a cracked power pack. PowerBook batteries are filled with all sorts of toxic and potentially hazardous materials, including sulfuric acid (lead-acid batteries), potassium hydroxide (NiCad batteries), and sodium hydroxide (NiHy batteries), any of which could leak from a cracked case and cause severe burning and skin irritation. Don't try to incinerate dead or damaged batteries, they may explode. This is also true of lithium backup batteries. Furthermore, lead-acid batteries emit hydrogen when heated, which could make for some really spectacular fireworks, if you aren't careful.

A Party for Batteries

Lind Electronic Design offers a whole line of PowerBook battery products, including: Automobile Power Adapter, a 12-volt DC auto-lighter adapter that comes complete with a 5-foot cable; the Auxiliary Power Pack, which uses a large, external sealed lead-acid battery to provide power for up to five times longer than a standard PowerBook power pack; and its External Battery Charger/Conditioner. Lind's conditioner can also act like a standard recharger, so you don't always have to deep-discharge a battery when you use it. Lind recently introduced PowerBook Duo versions of its auto adapter and auxiliary power pack, as well as a special emergency power pack that runs on alkaline D cells. The cells are stored in a 11.4-by-2.75-by-1.5-inch case and, according to the company, supply four times the life of a standard PowerBook battery.

Newer Technology Inc. offers an eight-D-cell power pack that the company claims can run a PowerBook for up to twelve hours using alkaline batteries. Either of these external packs could be a real life-saver for those times when you don't have access to either an outlet or a charged power pack (you can usually find D cells in any airport gift shop or gadget store).

Lind is the leader in PowerBook power add-ons, although there are other companies, too numerous to mention here, that offer quality PowerBook battery and power products. However, there is one in that crowd too quirky not to highlight.

For those of you into renewable sources of energy, there's Microtech International's recently shipped SolarPOWER, a solar-cell panel that uses the sun's rays to extend battery life and recharge power packs. It works with the 100 through 180 PowerBook models, and, while you probably can't run your PowerBook off the strongest sunlight, it will help extend battery life on those sunny afternoons in the park. The panel measures 11 by 10.5 by $1/8$ inches and weighs about two pounds.

The Four States of Power

Now that you've probably read a lot more than you ever wanted to know about PowerBook batteries and power supplies, it's time to discuss how to extend the lives of those systems when you're away from an outlet.

The PowerBook itself can operate in one of four states of declining power usage: *Run, Rest, Sleep,* and *Shut Down. Run* is when the computer is executing instructions from an application, driving a communications session, or attached to a server. *Rest* is almost indistinguishable from Run, except that things happen more slowly when the PowerBook enters this state. *Sleep* allows you to shut off almost all power systems (the drive, screen, trackball, speaker, etc.) while maintaining power to RAM. And *Shut Down* turns everything off. You know what it means to have your PowerBook running or switched off, so we'll limit our discussions to Rest and Sleep.

Just a Quick CPU Nap

When processor cycling is engaged (it is by default), your PowerBook's CPU will slip into a semi-dormant state in which it will draw less power and generate less heat. The PowerBook enters Rest mode anytime a few seconds pass without program activity or user input. The CPU "wakes up" almost instantly when activity picks up again, which does not happen when your hard drive or system goes to sleep.

There really is no reason to disable this feature, as you're unlikely to see any performance degradation as a result of processor cycling. You may see things like SuperClock!'s seconds indicator slow down, but that's normal. However, if programs running in the background (literally behind the active program) start running unacceptably slow, or if an application seems to hesitate before executing commands, try turning processor cycling off and see if that helps. Just remember, your PowerBook eats through a battery charge even faster when processor cycling is disabled.

To turn processor cycling off under System 7.1, just go to the Power-Book control panel and click the "Options..." button. Then click the radio button next to "Don't allow cycling" to disable Rest mode.

Turning off processor cycling under System 7.0.1 using the Portable control panel is a bit trickier. Hold down the Option key and click on "Minutes until automatic sleep." A dialog appears—just click the "Don't rest" radio button and then click *OK* (see Figure 6).

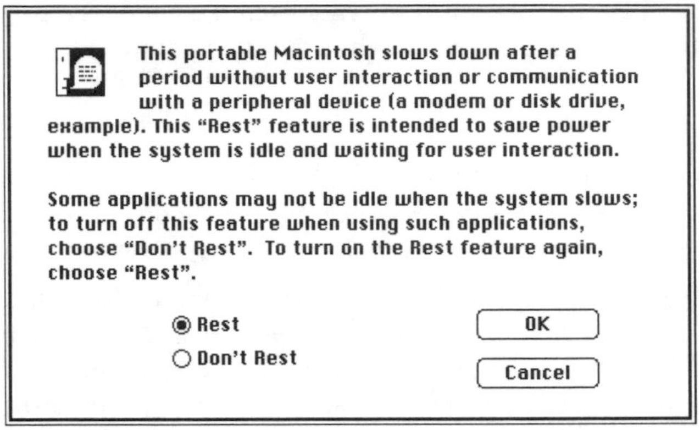

Figure 6. Processor cycling is well-hidden in the old Portable control panel.

More Restful Sleep

There are actually two kinds of sleeping your PowerBook can do: internal drive sleep and system sleep. You can set these discretely under System 7.0.1's Portable control panel; but with the new PowerBook control panel, the two types of sleep have been consolidated into one slider. (Consult Figure 5 in Section II, *Start Your Engines*, Part 1, for a chart that shows what each of the unified settings in the PowerBook control panel equates to in the Portable control panel.)

A PowerBook that is in system sleep is an amazing thing. In Sleep mode, your portable turns off virtually everything but still retains a snapshot of what was happening when it went to sleep (you can think of it as an electronic bookmark). As a result, your computer can, for all intents and purposes, be switched-off; yet at the touch of any key (except Caps Lock), it comes back to life in a matter of seconds and picks up where you and it left off.

Because of its ability to sleep, it is conceivable, and perhaps even advantageous, never to shut down your PowerBook. For example, if you were running your PowerBook off a RAM disk to save power, by putting your computer to sleep instead of shutting it down, you'd avoid setting up the RAM disk again when you start up. (System 7 clears the contents of the RAM disk every time you shut down, unless it is running on a PowerBook 100 or you have installed Connectix's Maxima.) In fact, because you can usually get right back on a network you disconnected from while your computer was asleep, the only time you absolutely have to shut down is to change the extensions you have installed in memory. Duos are the unfortunate exception to this: Apple's tiniest PowerBook must be shut down before it can be docked (see "Docking Trauma" below).

Sleeping on a Drive

In order to save considerable amounts of power, your PowerBook's internal hard drive can spin itself down and park the heads when not in use. The drive automatically spins back up whenever a program requires access to the data on the disk (it will also spin up again when you insert a floppy diskette).

There are two ways to spin down your hard disk. The first is to set it to spin down after a predetermined "idle" period; for drive sleep, idle time is how long it's been since the hard disk was last accessed. This can be tricky with System 7.1's PowerBook control panel, which will, for example, force you to set the whole system to go to sleep in *four* minutes, even if you want the drive to go to sleep after *two* minutes of idle time. With the Portable control panel, it is possible to set the hard drive to go to sleep after two minutes of idle time, while system sleep isn't engaged until the whole computer has been idle for fifteen minutes.

The second method for spinning down the hard drive addresses this first problem. Using the Control+D key sequence that QuicKeys for Nomads installs on your PowerBook, you can manually choose to spin down your hard disk whenever you want. Best of all, if you have the *Guide*, you've already got this useful little utility! With this key sequence, you can set the PowerBook control panel based on when you want the system to go to sleep and use Control+D to downshift the hard drive whenever you want to.

One final note on hard drive sleep. If you're going to be accessing the hard drive every few minutes, it takes more power to spin it up than it does to let the drive run. So, set hard drive sleep accordingly and use the spin-down QuicKey judiciously. Also, be aware that some applications, such as HyperCard, autosave and therefore keep the hard drive spinning almost constantly. These kinds of applications make lousy PowerBook programs, and trying to use the spin-down QuicKey to counter their wanton ways is an exercise in futility. Access-prone programs, on the other hand, can be effectively controlled with QuicKeys for Nomads. You can use Control+D to stymie programs, like Microsoft Word, that like to occasionally kick your hard drive in gear for no apparent reason. This is why it's important to know your software's drive access habits.

The system dozes off.

There are several ways to put your PowerBook to sleep. The first is to let it go to sleep on its own after an idle period that you set up in the Portable or PowerBook control panel. For system sleep, idle time is the period since the last occasion the user interacted with the computer—that includes moving the cursor.

You can knock out your PowerBook by selecting *Sleep* from the Special menu in the Finder, or you can click the Sleep button hidden under the mailbox flag in the Battery DA (see Figure 7). You can also hold down the option key and click on the battery icon in the Battery DA. If you have AppleTalk turned on in the Chooser, all these sleep methods will display a dialog box warning you that putting your PowerBook to sleep may cause you to lose some network services. You have to click *OK* to finish the sleep process. The warning just means that you'll have to use the Chooser to re-mount your AppleShare server when you wake the computer. To bypass this warning, hold down the Shift key when you click the Battery DA button or press the Shift and Option keys as you click the battery icon.

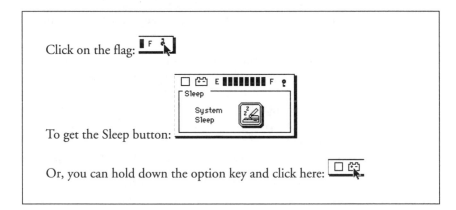

Figure 7. Putting Your PowerBook to Sleep

You can also use SuperClock! to put your PowerBook to sleep. Just hold down the Control key and click SuperClock!'s battery icon; you'll get the network warning dialog if AppleTalk is on. You can also use the Control+S key sequence in QuicKeys for Nomads to put your PowerBook to sleep. This QuicKey automatically bypasses the network warning dialog. Unlike either the Battery DA or the Sleep command in the Finder, you don't have to leave the application where you're working in order to use QuicKey's or SuperClock!'s sleep options.

System Insomnia

Here are the situations that will keep your PowerBook from going to sleep on its own:

- You're using an external monitor, which you can only do when plugged in with a PowerBook 160 or 180.

- AppleTalk is on and the computer is plugged in (your computer will go to sleep if the power plug isn't plugged into the back of your PowerBook).

- You've got a shared disk on your desktop.

- You're accessing a printer or modem.

- You've got "Don't sleep when plugged in" selected in the Power-Book control panel ("Stay awake when plugged in" does the same thing in the Portable control panel) and you're plugged in. Selecting the "Stay awake" option will display a dialog warning you that if you leave your PowerBook screen on for more than 24 hours without dimming the screen's brightness, may cause temporary problems such as shadows. These will go away if you shut your computer off or put it to sleep for a bit. Of course, if you're using Screen Dimming in System 7.1's PowerBook Display control panel, you don't have to worry about this particular problem at all.

Docking Trauma

If you're a Duo owner, you'll have to make sure you've shut down your PowerBook before attempting to dock it. You also won't be able to put it to sleep while it's in a dock (see Figure 8).

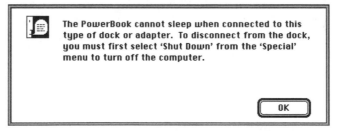

Figure 8. No Rest for a Weary Duo in a Dock

Besides the fact that you won't be able to retain the contents of your RAM disk, this inability to dock a sleeping Duo can cause some stress for users unaware of the limitation. This is because you can actually insert a sleeping Duo into the Duo Dock normally; but when you try and turn it on, the Duo Dock just spits it out without further explanation.

Waking-up your Duo will display a message explaining what happened (see Figure 9).

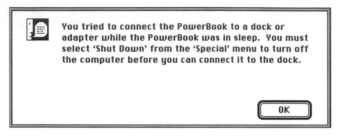

Figure 9. Duo to user: That was a dumb thing to do!

What makes this Duo sleep limitation especially frustrating is the fact that closing the Duo's clamshell is all it takes to put the machine to sleep (and you have to close the Duo to put it in a Duo Dock). We do believe that the Duo design team would have liked to enable the ability to sleep a docked Duo, but it was just too big a job to rewrite system software in time for the Duo's debut. Perhaps they'll have time to remedy this shortfall sometime in the future (hint, hint)?

The Battery-Killer Gang

A better name for PowerBooks would have been "Power Vampires"— they're always sucking current, even when they're shut down!

Different subsystems in your PowerBook drain battery life at different rates. The rate at which each subsystem discharges a battery may differ slightly from model to model, but overall, backlighting draws a lot of current, while trackballs draw only a little.

What follows is the power-sapping Most Wanted. Not every Power-Book subsystem that draws electricity is listed here; instead we've only included those with the most vampiric tendencies, along with the steps you can take to reduce their unquenchable thirst.

Backlighting

Yes, the healthy glow of your PowerBook screen is Public Enemy Number One. Depending on how bright you have it set and what else is drawing power at that moment, backlighting can account for over 50 percent of the load on your PowerBook's battery.

Luckily, backlighting is the easiest of the battery-killer gang to put on a diet. With System 7.1-equipped PowerBooks, Apple includes the Power-Book Display control panel. The panel controls screen dimming, which

See the
Digital Nomad
note below.

can be set to fade out backlighting after anywhere from one to five minutes of idle time. The control panel also includes the "Don't dim when plugged in" option. But unless you have a compelling reason to have backlighting on all the time (it comes back up the instant you move the trackball or hit a key), we recommend you leave this box unchecked.

We've found that the two-minute setting gives us the best battery conservation with the least disruption. If we leave our PowerBooks idle for that long, it's usually okay to have the screen fade out.

You should also manually adjust the backlighting with the brightness switch set to the lowest comfortable level. This can be difficult with some PowerBook models, as the sliding switch seems to go directly from "bright" to "off." Avoid darker desktop patterns; they don't drain any more power than a white desktop does, but they might cause you to turn up backlighting to compensate for the darker cast of your screen.

Also, don't worry about the bit-depth setting on your PowerBook 160, 180, or Duo's built-in screen. Although 4-bit grayscale does take more power than 1-bit, the difference is negligible.

Blind Trust

A trick we've learned for making the battery last hours more than it normally would is to turn backlighting off altogether. We only do this when we're taking notes (something we often do with our PowerBooks); we don't really need to see the screen to know whether what we're typing is going in accurately.

You can switch backlighting off in one of two ways—just turn it down all the way with the controls on your PowerBook's clamshell or use QuicKeys for Nomad's backlighting toggle (Control+B). The advantage of using the key sequence is that you don't have to fool around with the switch, turning backlighting up and down every time you want to look at your work. The toggle keeps backlighting off until you hit Control+B again—you go from on to off with a single keystroke.

Between leaving the hard drive asleep (a great reason to use Spiral as your primary note-taking tool) and keeping the backlighting off, we've managed to make it through five-hour seminars without once having to change our batteries.

Another nice thing about typing with the backlighting off is that there's no chance someone's reading your work over your shoulder! And in the right lighting, you can position the surface of your PowerBook screen to reflect enough light to let you read the screen without backlighting.

Hard Drive

As we mentioned above (see "Sleeping on a Drive"), keeping the power drain from your hard drive to a minimum is a matter of balancing the time and electricity wasted while the drive spins up and down against just leaving it spinning. But manually shifting your drive in and out of gear or letting System 7 automatically spin the drive down aren't your only power-saving options.

Adding RAMjets

You can set up a RAM disk using the Memory control panel (see Section II, *Start Your Engines*, Part 1, "A Quick Walk Down Memory Lane"). Depending on how much RAM you have installed, you can put your most-accessed files on the RAM disk or perhaps even load your System Folder on it and use the RAM disk as your startup device.

If you can spare even more memory, build a larger RAM disk and move a whole application to it. Should you be among the lucky few with lots of memory to spare, open a RAM disk large enough to accommodate your System Folder *and* the application you'll be working with. Once the RAM disk is set up, just copy your System Folder and the program over to it, go to the Startup Disk control panel, and select it (see Figure 10). Now, restart your PowerBook; you'll be running off your virtual hard drive in moments and saving tons of battery power, as your portable will only need to spin up your hard disk to save documents to it.

Figure 10. Select the RAM disk as your startup device after you've installed a System Folder on it.

You may find that you'll have to create a special "trimmed-down" version of your regular System Folder to fit it onto the largest RAM disk you can create. Just follow the guidelines in Part 1 of Section II, *Start Your Engines*, and you should have no trouble creating a System Folder small enough to fit on a 2-Mbyte RAM disk. Of course, you may have to give up some niceties, such as outline fonts, to make this work. Don't worry about having to reconstruct your RAM disk's System Folder every time you want to set it up again. Just keep a copy of the RAM disk System Folder on your hard drive—but don't call it "System Folder" (you wouldn't want to replace your main System Folder with the trimmed-down version, would you?). You can also use a program like Aladdin Systems Inc.'s StuffIt to compress the folder when it's not in use. This way, it'll take up less space.

See the
Digital Nomad
note below.

According to Apple, you can set up a RAM disk with a System Folder on it in as little as 6 Mbytes of RAM. We can only assume they intend you to squeeze System 7 onto a 2-Mbyte partition. Leaving yourself less than 4 Mbytes of RAM to run programs could lead to a lot of memory-out dialog boxes. Well, at least System 7 tries to help by suggesting that you quit one program to make room for another.

A RAM Jam

Okay, so you Intentional Tourists who opted for a 100 are probably beginning to tire of all the snobs who own those big, expensive Power-Books and snicker every time you pull out your little portable. Well, the next time someone pokes fun at your PowerBook, just ask them why their RAM disk won't survive a shutdown and yours will! (Don't forget to snicker when you see their dumbfounded expressions.)

If you've got System 7.0 (the 100 is the only PowerBook that can run 7.0), look for the RAM disk controls in the Portable control panel. If you've got 7.01 or 7.1, you'll find RAM disk settings in the Memory control panel. By the way, you shouldn't need to initialize a 100's RAM disk when you set one up.

You can use Connectix's Maxima to give more expensive PowerBooks the 100's ability to preserve the contents of a RAM disk after shutdown. The only bad part of using Maxima (besides the fact that you're paying for something that Apple should have included when it added RAM disk capability to the OS) is that it's difficult to configure.

CPU

Besides leaving processor cycling on, there really isn't much you can do to reduce your processor's power appetite. If you have a 25- or 33MHz '030 CPU in your PowerBook, you can crank down the processor's clockrate to 16 MHz. While this will save you some power, it'll also make your 160 perform like a 140. Depending on what you're doing, this may not bother you. For example, running a terminal emulator probably won't stretch your computer's processing muscles very much.

If you're running a 170 on System 7.0.1, you cut the processor clockrate by turning on the Power-Saver in the Battery DA (pull down the mailbox flag to see this option; it's only visible on a 170). If you're using the Power-Book control panel from System 7.1, or if you're using any of the other PowerBook models that can have their processor power cranked down (the 160, 180, Duo 210 and 230), just click the Options... button and then click the "Reduced speed" radio button under *Processor Speed* (see Figure 11). But don't go right back to work. You'll need to restart your PowerBook before a change in CPU clockrate will take effect.

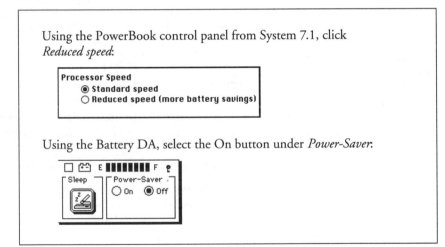

Figure 11. Crank down the processor.

AppleTalk, the Modem, and the Mouse

Although it doesn't require huge amounts of power, if you leave AppleTalk switched on while running off the battery, you will be drawing more current than if you switch it off. This is true even if you aren't hooked to a network. Considering that when you're most concerned about battery life you'll probably be far from the nearest network, turning AppleTalk off is a cheap way to preserve useful power.

Any time a program that accesses the internal modem is running, the modem will be sucking power, even if it isn't involved with a communications session. To prevent this frivolous drainage, make sure to quit any communications programs you're not using.

Finally, avoid ADB devices that aren't marked as low-powered. (Look for the low power symbol to the right of the serial number on Apple's ADB mouse.) They may be draining more current than you realize!

Video-out

Driving the PowerBook 160 and 180's video-out circuitry does consume copious amounts of current. However, this won't be a problem for users of those PowerBook models, because the 160 and 180 won't let you run an external monitor unless the computer is plugged in.

But this isn't true of the Duos. For example, If you connect a MiniDock to the Duo and then connect an external color monitor to the dock, the computer will drive both the MiniDock and the video-out circuitry off the battery—if you let it. So, when you're looking to get the most out of your Duo's battery, it's probably a bad idea to run an external monitor off the computer when it isn't plugged in.

Sample Power Settings

Controlling power consumption on your portable is a very personal thing. You may not want to give up the time it takes to wake the hard drive from sleep, even if you can extend your computing time significantly. So you'll leave the PowerBook control panel set to maximum performance and use the Control+S QuicKey to put your PowerBook to sleep when you're ready, not when some preset period of time has passed.

On the other hand, you may not want to be bothered remembering to spin down the hard drive.

What follows are some brief suggested power configurations for the three main user types. Use these as guidelines for determining how you want to set up your PowerBook when away from a power source.

Intentional Tourist

Note-taking and searching your calendar for the next appointment don't tax your CPU much, so when you're away from an outlet you leave your PowerBook's processor on the slower 16 MHz setting. You also set backlighting to dim after only a minute; it doesn't bother you to wake up the screen after it fades out.

Stretching each battery's life is your primary concern, especially on long plane flights, so you have the Battery Conservation slider set three-quarters toward max conservation (that's system sleep in four minutes and hard drive sleep in two minutes under the Portable control panel). You've selected your applications especially because they don't require hard drive access until it's time to save. You also make it a point to turn off AppleTalk after those rare file-sharing sessions with your desktop Macintosh. There's no point in wasting power on networking that you can't use on an airliner anyway.

Mobile Commuter

You don't worry about power consumption much, because you only need to run off batteries for those short periods of time when you want to access your PowerBook between the office and home. So, you leave the Battery Conservation slider set to maximum performance, which only spins down your hard drive or puts your computer to sleep after fifteen minutes of idle time. As for processor speed, the maximum your PowerBook can produce is what you want for those complex spreadsheets and for working in Adobe Photoshop.

You also don't worry about AppleTalk; it's not worth the bother to turn it off when you'll just have to turn it back on the next morning upon returning to the office. You do have backlight dimming set to five minutes; the power consumption doesn't worry you, but image shadows on your PowerBook's screen do.

Road Warrior

You also leave the Battery Conservation slider set to maximum performance, not because you don't care about battery life but because you want to control hard drive and system sleeping yourself. You may crank down your 180's processor to 16 MHz to help save power when running your Rolodex, but it's a painful sacrifice.

Backlighting you set to switch off after two minutes; you doubt your PowerBook will ever be left idle for much longer than that without you putting it to sleep. You'll probably switch backlighting off manually to take notes anyway.

Disabling AppleTalk is part of your pre-travel ritual. But you always make sure to turn it back on once you reach your destination. You never know when you'll be called on to jack into some PC network!

PART

3

ROAD-PROOFING YOUR POWERBOOK

Don't Do It Yourself

We've talked a lot about what this book isn't. Well, here's another thing to add to the list: it's not a Chilton's repair guide for your PowerBook.

The reason why you won't find in-depth instructions on how to take your PowerBook apart in the *Guide.* is the authors' deep-felt opinion that the inside of a PowerBook is no place for the uninitiated or the uninsured.

Your PowerBook has delicate components inside—even more delicate than a desktop Mac. Once the cover is off, it doesn't take much more than a dirty look to damage your portable's static-sensitive parts. And even if you don't blow up your PowerBook by delving inside, repairing most hardware failures requires replacement parts not available to most people. In fact, opening your portable may void the Apple warranty, meaning that after exploratory surgery, you'll pay for repairs if you decide to send the computer in.

As for upgrading your PowerBook, you can save money by installing RAM or a hard drive yourself. But if you damage the sensitive CMOS circuitry, it could cost you more than you saved. And while accessing the RAM inside your Duo is relatively easy (just remove the keyboard), accessing other areas inside your PowerBook are not. For example, there are nine steps you have to take before reaching the Duo modem slot. You must remove the main battery, keyboard, clutch covers, display assembly and top case, hard drive, backup battery, trackball assembly, the magnesium frame, and the logic board before you can install a modem.

All-in-all, it's probably easier and safer to pay a dealer to do it for you. If you bought the RAM board, modem, or hard drive from a dealer, you can probably get them to install the upgrade for free, which is a good argument against buying mailorder upgrades.

Getting Help

When problems do occur, just dial Apple's toll-free service line at (800) SOS-APPL. Commit that number to memory, because if trouble strikes while you're on the road, it'll be the most important number you know. Apple's technical support engineers man that line from 8:00 AM until 5:00 PM Pacific Time, Monday through Friday. As a result, we're sure your PowerBook will break down only when the support engineers are gone for the day. For those times, Apple also has another number you can call, (800) 538-9696, where you can get the name of the authorized dealer nearest you. Many dealers have service hours more accommodating than Apple's, so if you need help right away, call this number. It's only good for

North America; elsewhere you'll have to consult the local listings for a dealer.

When you need to return your portable for repairs, Apple SOS will arrange to pick it up. You can have your laptop returned to you anyplace in the U.S.; so if your PowerBook dies in Peoria, you can have it fixed and meet up with it again in Pasadena a few days later.

AppleCare

If you live in the U.S, Canada, or Australia, you can extend your warranty up to three years. Prices vary by the model but are usually reasonable, especially considering that PowerBooks are more susceptible to failure than a desktop Mac, due to the mileage they log. It's best to purchase AppleCare when you buy your computer; if you choose to purchase the plan later, you'll also have to pay an inspection fee.

User Groups

We can't say enough good things about the intrepid Mac users who have banded together in search of support and solidarity. These Mac user groups are an inexhaustible resource of information about your PowerBook; many even have special meetings just for people interested in portable Macs.

User groups maintain extensive libraries of software you can copy as a member. Many groups have also made deals with local resellers to give their members special discounts. If you're adamant about getting inside your portable, these folks can tell you how and may even be willing to walk you through the disassembly process.

The biggest Mac user group is the Berkeley Macintosh Users Group (BMUG) Inc. These folks are great! Just give them a call at (510) 549-2684 to find out where their next meeting is or, if you don't live in the San Francisco Bay Area, how to locate a group near you.

PowerBook Care and Feeding

Maintenance

Your PowerBook is a hearty beast. It was designed to take a lot of punishment and our personal experience is, if you treat it with respect, it'll treat you the same.

There is, in fact, very little you need to do to keep your PowerBook in top working order. To keep it clean, occasionally wipe the case and keys with a damp (not soaked), lint-free cloth. Just make sure the computer is switched off and unplugged before cleaning.

To clean dust off the display, spray a little Windex onto a lint-free cloth and gently wipe the screen; don't spray the cleaner directly on the display; it could run off and get inside your portable. The PowerBook's display is a dust magnet, so you may find yourself doing this often. If it really becomes a problem, you can try using one of those screen cleaners, sold at computer superstores, that claim to be anti-static. Our experience is that they're only moderately effective.

The only other part of your PowerBook that could stand a regular cleaning is the trackball. To get at it, rotate the locking ring that surrounds the trackball counterclockwise. It may stick a little, so be firm but don't force it. The ring should come off once you've unlocked it. Just tip your Power-Book over to make the ball roll out into your hand.

Wipe off the ball with a damp cloth. You may want to use the hose from a canister vacuum cleaner to suck any dust out of the trackball assembly. You can also use a little rubbing alcohol on a Q-Tip to clean the metal rollers that the trackball sits on, but *don't touch the rubber rollers.* They control the movement of the cursor and are extremely delicate.

In fact, the rollers will rarely need cleaning, especially if you occasionally pop out the trackball and clean it. A dirty trackball is how the rollers get contaminated.

The Difference Engine

Making sure your PowerBook has the most current version of your files is a critical part of road-proofing your machine. Making sure you've got current backups is also vitally important. In fact, considering that your Power-Book is more likely to be lost, stolen, or damaged than a desktop computer, it's even more critical that you run backups as often as possible.

There are lots of ways to back up a PowerBook. One way is to copy your most important documents to floppy diskettes and store those away. You may also want to bring backups of your critical data and applications with you when you travel. However, backing up files to floppies can be tedious and consume a lot of diskettes, especially with some of the larger capacity hard drives Apple now puts inside the PowerBooks.

See the
Road Warrior
note below.

⬇

There is software you can use to ease this chore. Dantz Development's DiskFit Direct is an easy and inexpensive backup utility that can be used to intelligently back up the data on your drive. Once you've done your initial archive, DiskFit Direct only copies the files that have changed since the last time you backed up. For more sophisticated backups, including unattended archiving and backups over the network, Dantz offers DiskFit Pro.

If you don't want to bother with floppies at all, you could invest in a tape streamer, removable cartridge, or DAT drive. These devices store data on large-capacity media, saving you the trouble of swapping floppies.

Your system administrator may also have made some arrangement for backing up over the network. Retrospect, which also comes from Dantz, is the number-one network backup software on both PC and Mac (even though Retrospect is currently only available on the Mac). This software will back up your drive over the network automatically, to tape or another mass storage system, based on a schedule programmed by your administrator.

It should be noted that network backup programs do have problems with sleeping PowerBooks. When you put your PowerBook to sleep, it goes off the network, meaning that a program like Retrospect can't access your portable to archive the data. However, according to Dantz, if your PowerBook goes to sleep on its own, it stays on the network and Retrospect can access it. This is the first time we've heard of there being two kinds of PowerBook sleep; we'll keep you posted in our newsletter, *Nomad Notes*, as we find out more about this duality and what it might mean for you.

You can also use synchronization programs, like No Hands Synchro, to copy files automatically to another drive on the network. Just drop the file into a folder that's been paired with a folder on another part of the network and ask Synchro to synchronize them.

Wire Your Data

E-mailing a file to yourself while you're on the road is a great way to be absolutely assured that a working copy of a program or a document will be available when you reach your destination.

Compress your most important files and then mail them to your online address (all the online information services we've tested will let you do this). Then, if something amiss happens to the file in transit, just get to your online account when you arrive at your destination and download working copies of your files.

Bootable Diskettes

Another important tool to have handy is a bootable floppy, in case your PowerBook won't start up off the internal drive. The best bootable diskette to have is the emergency floppy that comes with disk utilities like Symantec's Norton Utilities for Macintosh or Central Point Software's Mac-Tools. Not only will these diskettes let you get your PowerBook to boot up, they have software capable of repairing all but the most catastrophic drive failures.

If you own one of the new PowerBook models, be sure to get a utility that has both System 7.1 and the System Enabler for your PowerBook installed on the emergency floppy. You'll find the enabler file in your System Folder; it tells the operating system what's different about your particular model Macintosh. Apple started using enablers with the new models introduced in October, and we expect them to continue using them to make future Macs work with System 7.1.

Without both the appropriate enabler and 7.1, your PowerBook 160, 180, or Duo won't boot off the recovery diskette. At press time, none of the disk utilities we worked with had System 7.1. And even if we had installed 7.1 and the enabler ourselves, there wouldn't have been room left over for the recovery software.

The system disks that come with your PowerBook include a bootable disk. It's called Disk Tools and contains a minimal System Folder, plus Apple HD SC Setup and Disk First Aid, a basic disk recovery utility. You can make a copy of this diskette, throw out the two Apple applications, and replace them with your own software to make a custom bootable disk (that's the easiest way). Or you can build your own disk from scratch. To do that, make a copy of your PowerBook's System Folder and begin ripping files out, following the guidelines in Section II, Part 1, until you can fit it on a diskette. You'll probably have to remove almost everything—all the Apple menu items, extensions, control panels, and fonts—to fit the System Folder and another program on a single floppy.

Viruses

Viruses are nasty little programs written by nasty little people, and they can infest your computer. They usually get to your PowerBook via a program you copied from a floppy or downloaded from an online bulletin board.

Luckily, there are fewer viruses on the Mac than there are on DOS, and the ones we have seen rarely destroy data. Despite the relative passivity of Mac viruses, they can still be a nuisance: locking up your computer, causing programs to crash, or making your PowerBook beep for no apparent reason. To avoid these problems, you can purchase anti-virus utilities from developers like Central Point Software, whose anti-virus software comes with MacTools or can be purchased separately, or you can buy Symantec's Anti-Virus for Macintosh (SAM). Both programs come with extensions that automatically check diskettes and generally watch out for and prevent viruses from infecting your PowerBook.

You can also get a program called Disinfectant, a free anti-virus utility distributed by most user groups and online services. Symantec, Central Point, and the Disinfectant folks do a good job keeping their programs up to date on the latest viruses. All three of these solutions can also be used to cure virus infections without damaging the afflicted software.

Rebuilding the Desktop

Your PowerBook writes things like the name and location of files and what their icons look like to special, invisible files. These files get modified every time you add or delete a file and after a while can get a little confused. If you can't start a program by double-clicking one of its documents or if files in the Finder are displayed without their custom icons, you may be seeing symptoms of disorientation.

To fix this problem you need to rebuild the desktop file. To do that, start up your computer, holding down the command and option keys. Wait until you get a dialog box that says you'll lose the comments in the info windows of your files if you rebuild the desktop (see Figure 1). Ignore it and click *OK*.

It'll take your PowerBook a few minutes to finish the process. When it's done, your icons should display correctly, and double-clicking a document should once again launch a resident application. You may also notice a slight increase in your PowerBook's performance.

It's a good idea to rebuild the desktop on your PowerBook from time to time.

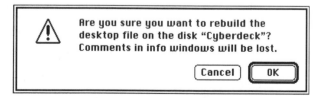

Figure 1. To rebuild your desktop, hold down the option and command (Apple) key and restart your PowerBook.

Red-Hot and Road-Ready

Making backups, installing a good anti-virus utility, and keeping an emergency disk handy is about all it takes to road-proof your PowerBook.

Most of all, rely on your common sense to keep your PowerBook in top condition. If you spill water on the keyboard, shut the computer down, wipe it off and let it dry out. If you spill something stickier than plain water, try the keyboard out to make sure it hasn't gotten stuck before you turn the PowerBook on again. If some of the keys are sticking, bring it to your dealer for a cleaning.

That's all there is to solving most problems. Just think it through and when in doubt, call SOS-APPL or your nearest authorized dealer.

SECTION IV

EXPLORING CYBERSPACE

You discover the real power of networking the first time you receive a message from a newcomer to Cyberspace.

"I don't know if I did this right, but if you get this message I'd sure like to hear back from you," the note on my monitor reads. It's an attempt at connection that echoes the moment a panicked young Alexander Graham Bell called for Watson, initiating a new era in communications.

This time, the message is etched in light on a computer screen rather than uttered in a scratchy murmur over a makeshift speaker; and the conduit through which it travelled is constantly growing, sprouting hundreds of tendrils a day. My computer connects to a network. That network connects me to a dozen other computers in my office; it also connects me through gateways to other computer networks like the one I work on. And it connects me to networks totally unlike mine: large, diffuse systems with millions of computers connecting and disconnecting in a machinated dance. Each computer is controlled by a person, someone like me, living on a network somewhere in the world. Yet each of us can reach out in the time it takes light to get from Barcelona to Burbank, and talk—exchange mail, documents, and programs. We can match wits in the network's imaginary firmament or form friendships and sometimes, more than friendships.

This is Cyberspace, a by-product of our need to keep in touch; the first frontier of our own making.

Cyberspace is a buzzword that describes a territory we don't fully understand. It's the telephone network, the place where telephone calls happen, according to John Perry Barlow, who serves as a philosopher on this frontier. But it's also all the LANs (Local Area Networks) and WANs (Wide Area Networks) that wire computers together like pearls on some enormous string. If it can send a message from one person's address to another, then it's a part of the formless mass of Cyberspace.

None of that matters to the newcomer, whose message desires only acknowledgment. Later, she may want to know the metaphysical parameters of the place. For now, there's only communication between me and someone whom I've never seen and may never meet, except in Cyberspace's theoretical corridors.

Cyberspace is the e-mail reply button, it's the network that delivers the message, but most of all it is the tremendous energy of the millions of people who work and play there.

"Got your message. So tell me more about your interests..." I type, and something begins.

A network is growing across the country and around the world. Called *The Internet*, it is actually a network of networks. Some people refer to it as Cyberspace and know it as a new environment in which they meet and build friendships and communities. It connects government agencies, university libraries, and research institutions and is growing, by some estimates, at the rate of 500,000 new users a month. It has also reached the desktops of office workers and home computer users, expanding through private and commercial networks, like CompuServe and Prodigy. If the Clinton Administration has its way, all these data highways may be joined to create an interstate-international infrastructure on which information can flow.

The Internet is the data highway that a digital nomad can use to keep in touch with company, coworkers, friends, and a world of information. There are many levels of Cyberspace (the term was coined by author William Gibson to describe the internal landscape of a data network). It's possible to play quite comfortably on the commercial surface, in the graphical interfaces of CompuServe or America Online (AOL), or to dive into a vast sea of data that flows deep inside the network, where you may feel as though you're being led on a tour by Captain Nemo. You'll discover extended debates on subjects ranging from technology to touring San Francisco; libraries of great books and software, including huge archives of Mac applications; and even the card catalogs of the Library of Congress and most major research universities. Indeed, there are other cultures with grand traditions living at the bottom of this data sea. Move over Jules Verne, the future is now.

The future is global, too. The whole of Europe and now large parts of the former Soviet Union are linking into The Internet. Soon it will be possible to exchange ideas and information, and perhaps even to do business, on any corner of the human sphere, without ever leaving your desk.

All of these wonders are the product of electronic mail and file transfer capabilities, the simple stuff that enhances life on your company's network. You are in a unique position to pioneer and thrive in this new territory, because it is accessible from cities large and small and allows you to log on and collect electronic mail messages sent to your network address.

With a few commands, you can reach back to your mailbox from almost anywhere on the planet. Whether you're having a discussion with a friend via America Online or browsing the legal archives on the Electronic Frontier Foundation's computers, you'll be relying on the same concepts you learned in *Setting Sail on the Network Clipper*. However, because the structures are so much larger, there are added layers of complexity to deal with, and you'll need to polish your telecommunications skills—but only a little. The fact is, The Internet and its commercial offshoots are easy to use.

The telecommunications revolution extends to less august technologies, too, including fax and voice communications. The idea that a letter must necessarily be sent through the postal system perished when people, from ministers to grandmothers, began using the fax machine as a fast, efficient means for communicating in print. Apple helped PowerBook users take the paper out of the fax equation when it bundled fax software with its internal modems.

If your PowerBook has both an internal speaker and microphone, you can use it in place of your wired or cellular telephone. During the next two or three years, the rigid differentiation between the telephone and computer will vanish. Rising volumes of information have led people to demand a more intelligent interface to the telephone network, as well as a more uniform interface for the personal computer. These two trends are destined to meet somewhere in the middle—PowerBooks may be the first to arrive there.

See the Road Warrior note below.

We cannot hope to do justice to the cavalcade of connections, services, personalities, and archives that are available on The Internet. Several recent titles have impressed us with their complete coverage of the user interface and resources available on the networks: "The Whole Internet User's Guide and Catalog," by Ed Krol, "The BMUG Guide to Bulletin Boards and Beyond," by Bernard Aboba, and "The Internet Companion," by Tracy LaQuey. Check out these titles for more detailed information.

So how do you get to Cyberspace? What do you do once you've stepped into it? Where is all this cool stuff and how do you get to it?

Call Waiting

Screen-based telephony is a hot topic in the Mac market these days. Cypress Research Corporation recently introduced a scripting language that lets you control how a voice modem-equipped Mac processes telephone calls. Experienced Road Warriors can use Cypress's PhonePro software to create sophisticated response scripts, such as one that has your PowerBook receive a call and fax a price list to the caller at their request. But almost anyone can use PhonePro to build a PowerBook-based answering machine.

If you want to take PowerBook telephony a step further, you can combine Applied Engineering's DataLink PB internal voice/data modem (which includes answering machine software) with the company's internal cellular transmitter and an ingenious little device recently announced, but not yet available, from Norris Communications Inc., called the EarPhone. *(continued)*

Call Waiting (continued)

A combination speaker/microphone that fits in the ear, the EarPhone uses low-power radio waves to exchange voice signals with a transceiver that connects to your PowerBook.

Instead of using a regular microphone that picks up sound in the air, the EarPhone uses a unique conduction technology that senses vibrations in the bones of your neck and throat. The EarPhone allows you to speak under your breath in public while still being heard clearly on the phone.

However, wireless PowerBook telephones aren't problem-free. First, because your computer has to be running before the modem will function, trying to make a call could include waiting for your computer to boot up and then launching the software that lets you dial. That's a lot more trouble than lifting a receiver. For this reason, using a cellular phone interface, like Applied's Axcell Portable Cellular Interface, might be a preferable choice (see "So Much for Wires" below).

Another reason to use your cellular phone is that while running (and it will need to be running to answer a call), Applied's internal cellular transmitter may shorten the PowerBook's battery life significantly.

Radiation also concerns us. When Norris introduced the EarPhone, Mitch asked if the radio waves created by the device were safe, because, after all, they are broadcast from inside the ear. The Norris spokeswoman looked a little shocked and replied that the company had not thought about the potential for harm.

It is not clear yet whether low-intensity radio waves are really harmful. Two studies within the past year have pointed to a link between electromagnetic radiation created by high-tension power lines and household appliances and an increased incidence of childhood cancers. More studies need to be conducted to answer these questions before folks surround themselves with more devices which emit electromagnetic radiation.

It all begins with the lowly modem.

A modem lets your computer talk on the phone. When computers talk to one another over an Ethernet connection, they speak in digital pulses that represent ones and zeros; you can't hear it, nor can you see it. The phone system, at least as most of it stands today, was made for people and their noisy languages; it's a brick wall to digital communications. Your computer must use a modem (*modem* stands for MOdulator/DEModulator) to convert its digital thoughts into sound and back again when it is receiving a message.

The best of breed among third-party modems for the PowerBook, in our opinion, is PSI Integration Inc.'s PowerModem IV. A 14.4-Kbps internal modem for the 100 through 180, it stands out for its combination of speed and bundled software capabilities, including faxing with optical character recognition. The PowerModem's OCR capabilities can convert an incoming fax into a Microsoft Word, MacWrite II, or other popular word processing format. OCR is a boon for Road Warriors who, though verging on a paperless lifestyle, still have to deal with information faxed by the paperbound public.

Our experience with Global Village Communications Inc.'s PowerPort Gold and Silver modems has also been very good. The Gold, a V.32bis data modem, delivers up to 14.4 Kbps throughput and 9,600-baud Group III fax capabilities, while the Silver modem comes in a close second with 9,600-baud data and fax. Both install inside a PowerBook and include fax software that lets you schedule late-night transmissions to save on phone bills (you have to leave your 140, 145, or 170 turned on to use this feature; the other models can wake when the software says it's time to transmit).

AppleTalk Remote Access users should definitely go for the Gold or the PowerModem IV. There is no substitute for 14.4-Kbps speed when logging onto a network; overall performance is much better, and transferring large files is a breeze. Of course, your network ARA server will also need to be running a 14.4-Kbps modem to support those lofty speeds.

See the Digital Nomad note below.

⬇

Both the PowerModem and the PowerPort come with software, similar in function to Apple's Fax Sender software (see Figure 1), for sending and receiving faxes.

Digital to Paper

Apple's Fax Sender software, which ships with the company's internal PowerBook modems, is a convenient way to put your work in the hands of non-computer users. It installs as a Chooser document, which allows you select a fax machine rather than a printer as your default output device (your PowerBook is the fax machine, by the way). There's also a Fax Monitor application that tracks the progress of a fax job and Fax Cover, a program for building your own cover sheets (we suggest that you keep the use of graphics in cover sheets to a minimum, because they slow performance).

Once you've selected *Fax Sender* in the Chooser, a Fax command will appear in the File Menu instead of the Print command.   *(continued)*

Digital to Paper (continued)

If you don't want to change your Chooser settings, you can initiate a fax by holding down the Control and Shift keys while selecting the File menu, and *Fax* appears instead of the Print command.

When you select *Fax,* a dialog appears to let you choose from an address book of fax users with whom you communicate frequently, or you can create a new listing by filling in the person's name and fax number in a second window (see Figure 1). If you also include information about the addressee's job and company, that information can appear on your cover page.

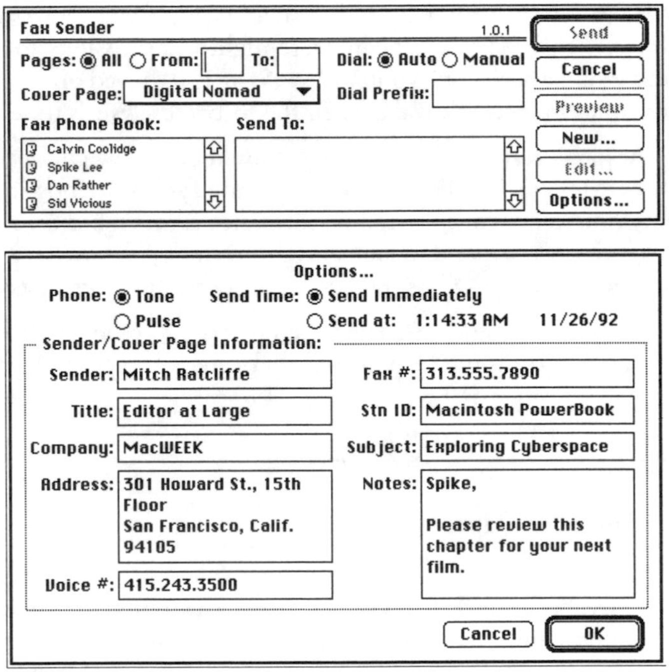

Figure 1. Addressing Options for Fax Sender

So Much for Wires

Nomadic users may disdain hard-wired solutions for connecting to the telephone system, and it seems Apple certainly wouldn't blame them for doing so. During 1993, the company will introduce a digital cellular device that works with the PowerBook to provide users with untethered connections to networks and online services.

Before you rush out to buy the Apple CDPD device, which will fit inside a PowerBook or in a small external transceiver, make sure you can get Cellular Digital Packet Data (CDPD) services from your local cellular carrier. CDPD services will probably be available in most areas, because the regional phone companies have jumped on this bandwagon. What CDPD does differently than ordinary cellular is treat each call as though it were connected to a digital network rather than to the expensive circuit-switched network (on which calls are billed from the moment you dial to the moment you hang up). Over a circuit-switched network, you pay for a lot of dead air when neither PowerBook nor host is transmitting. CDPD will bill only for the amount of data that's sent over the connection, even if you stay on the line all day.

But maybe you already have a cellular telephone and want to use it to log onto your favorite online service. Then Applied Engineering has an answer for you. The Axcell Cellular Interface for the Macintosh Power-Book is a dongle that sits between your PowerBook modem and an AT&T or OKI cellular telephone (among others). It emulates the characteristics of a wired telephone system—for example, it sends a dial tone to your modem even though the cellular phone doesn't produce one—and it initiates a connection once your modem has dialed the number. (Normally you have to push *Send* after dialing a cellular phone; the Axcell does that automatically.) For all your modem knows, it's connected to an ordinary telephone line. The dongle also adds error correction and data compression protocols to those that already exist in your modem, to make up for the low quality of a cellular telephone connection.

Our tests of the Axcell dongle showed good performance when the phone could hold its signal. As we drove along a San Francisco street, which had the requisite hill or two, we lost the signal a couple times for a few seconds and finally crashed a MicroPhone II terminal session. Spotty cellular coverage will be the digital nomad's greatest challenge, whether you are using ordinary service or CDPD.

Tooling Your Modem

With its Macintosh Communications Toolbox, Apple provides the connection between a telecommunications application and a modem. Built into System 7, the Comm Toolbox lets you drop files, known as "tools," into your System Folder (they end up in the Extensions folder) to handle the specific requirements of each type of connection, file transfer, and terminal type. When getting set to log onto an online service, you need to open the Comm Toolbox interface and select the appropriate settings (see Figure 2). Terminal settings must be set so that your application handles text the same way the online host does—otherwise you're likely to be confronted with gibberish. File transfer tools control the way a file is transmitted to and from your PowerBook and what becomes of files when your telecommunications application receives them.

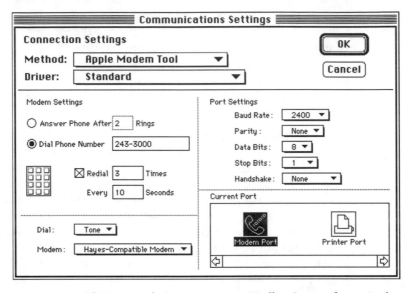

Figure 2. The Macintosh Communications Toolbox Settings for an Apple Modem

Some applications also use their own drivers to control a modem. But with Comm Toolbox or a proprietary driver you need to know several things in order to set up the connection. Online systems support different speeds, but you can set your modem to its highest speed and leave it. When you call a system that provides only 2,400-baud connections, your 9,600-baud modem will slow down to conform with the available speed. You must also set the data bits and stop bits to the parameters of the online service; these indicate how many bits will be needed to describe a single character of text and how the two systems, your PowerBook and the remote service, will determine where one character stops and another begins. Parity, the number of bits in a byte of data, is important when you log onto an older system that defines bytes differently. Macs use 8-bit bytes, but some mainframes use 7-bit bytes.

If you are using proprietary software, such as CompuServe's Information Manager (CIM) or AOL, to log on, these settings will be incorporated in the application and you need not give them another thought.

Everybody, into the Pool

See the
Digital Nomad
note below.

Every exploration should begin with a day trip. With telecommunications, you'll sometimes face more complex, very un-Mac interfaces as you dive deeper into the data flow. For beginners, we recommend you try out one of the following services, the software for which is widely available at computer dealers.

CompuServe Information Service

The granddaddy of online services, CompuServe claims a membership of approximately one million and more than 300 forums, where people exchange ideas and tips on everything from economics to Macintosh programming. This is good place to start with online conferencing, as long as you use CIM, the interface that lets you browse the conversations and navigate between forums using icons and menus (see Figure 3). The software is almost a giveaway—you get free online time approximately equal to the purchase price.

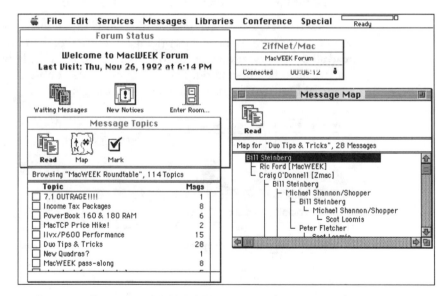

Figure 3. CompuServe's MacWEEK Forum in the CIM Interface

News, sports scores, and an impressive selection of databases are also available through CompuServe. For example, you can browse U.S. census data or archives of full-text articles from many of the leading newspapers in the country. But the real fun is in the forums, including the *MacWEEK* forum, where you can read the top stories each week and participate in discussions with leading Macintosh developers and *MacWEEK* editors and reporters. Also, more than 200 companies offer online support for their products in CompuServe forums.

The big drawback to CompuServe is the cost. 60 minutes of online time at 2,400 baud costs $12.80, exceeded only by AppleLink which runs $37 an hour at 9,600 baud during prime time. (CompuServe costs $22.80 at 9,600 baud.) Many of the value-added services, such as databases and news wires, are subject to surcharges that can double the hourly fee. CompuServe's Navigator software is a graphical scripting environment that lets you automate online sessions. It can cut your online charges substantially.

America Online

For a long time, AOL was the exclusive territory of Mac users. Even though PCs now share AOL with Macs, the service still has a very Mac-like feel. Mac-centricity also fueled development of a wonderful interface that is a natural for PowerBook users on the go (see Figure 4).

Now that PC users have joined in, AOL is expanding its range of services rapidly, without raising its pricing structure. For $5 an hour, you can read all the news you want and also join discussions on the PowerBook, the impact of technology on our lives, and numerous hobbies. There's even a Grateful Dead conference, where people trade concert tapes and tickets.

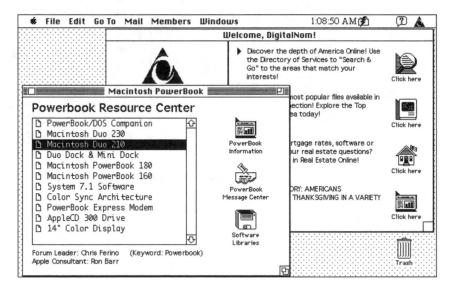

Figure 4. America Online, an Electronic Home Away from Home

One complaint digital nomads might have with AOL is the 2,400-baud limit on modem speeds. It slows reading to a crawl and makes the transition between conferences, while the system downloads the new information, more like a long winter's night than modern living. AOL's administrators claim to have been working on 9,600-baud access for sometime, with no success as this book goes to the printers. Makes you wonder if they're holding things up so they can milk every possible dollar out of 2,400 baud before their members force them to upgrade.

AppleLink

Apple's own online service just recently became available to ordinary users. When you log on, you'll find the heartbeat of the Macintosh industry, with numerous Apple employees, developers, and members of the press discussing new products, software bugs, and marketing strategies. It's a great place to visit if your job description includes Macintosh support, because the latest product announcements, press releases, and pricing are posted here first.

Prodigy

The online version of a commercial interruption, Prodigy was designed to be the first electronic marketplace. Because Prodigy sends all its graphics over the phone line, rather than sending commands to bring up screens that are already installed on your computer, it offers the slowest user interface of the lot, and the frequent advertising and promotional messages slow the user experience to a conceptual crawl.

Prodigy's poor performance won't cost you like the 2,400-baud speeds on AOL—all your online time is covered by a single monthly fee. That's because the advertisers are picking up much of the expense. The mail system gives you only 30 free messages a month, after which you pay a per-message fee. Imagine that the executives at ABC television have seized control of your PowerBook, and that's Prodigy.

MCI Mail

It's not a very friendly environment for PowerBook users, but MCI mail services are the central conduit of information in many far-flung companies. If the sheer numbers of users on CompuServe might sway you to pay for that service, MCI's online corporate population should convince you that this is a good investment.

Commercial Mail: Faster than Federal Express

Choose your commercial online services for their mail capabilities, especially the ability to attach another file to your message. This feature is crucial to extending your working relationships, since great deals are seldom made in a purely textual discussion. Color and animation, if not just plain formatted text, can make a much greater impact on the recipient than an unformatted text message.

AppleLink delivers the best mail services of the lot. It lets you send a message with multiple attached files to many recipients (it even has its own built-in file compressor). We also like AOL's mail interface, but its one-attachment limit is regrettable (you can compress multiple files into a single attachment with a utility like Aladdin Systems' StuffIt). Addressing is easy with both services, because your personal address book listings are available in the mail interface, rather than via a separate window. CompuServe doesn't offer the ability to attach a file to a mail message, but you can send a file as a separate item. Since you have to go through the effort of creating two messages, where you only have to address a single item on AOL and AppleLink, CompuServe is a distant third in our e-mail rankings.

What really lends power to a mail interface is your ability with language. A well-crafted message will speak volumes and go farther than any fancy graphics.

And on to the Deep End

See the Mobile Commuter note below.

As a nomadic user, you'll probably be logging on to The Internet two ways: through your company's local area network and via dial-up connections. The software you'll need will depend upon whether you are using The Internet's native protocol, TCP/IP, or a service that lets you use a UNIX computer in terminal emulation mode.

Personal Accounts

Having an Internet account of your own is probably the most efficient way to guarantee yourself access from anywhere you may travel. Services that sell Internet accounts, such as The WELL (Whole Earth 'Lectronic Link), Netcom, The World, and PSInet, allow you to log into their computers via a local phone number that ties into a national network. That network then connects you to the computer where your mail account actually resides. In addition, many Internet providers allow access via remote login, also known as Telnet. Telnet lets you sign on to another computer, a client's Internet account, for example, and then use The Internet to log on to the computer where your own e-mail account resides—saving you a long-distance charge.

WorldLink, InterCon's personal Internet client software for PSInet, is the best interface to the global network we've seen. It's also the only graphical interface for personal Internet access we've seen, period. If you don't want to endure the command-line interface, send in the enclosed coupon with the *Guide* and try WorldLink for yourself. Dial-up World-Link access is available in most major cities.

Internet sessions are automated by the WorldLink software. You compose and reply to mail messages and set the parameters for searches or file transfers from remote computers using the File Transfer Protocol before logging onto PSInet. At present, the software does not support access to Usenet newsgroups, a quasi-conferencing system that runs over parts of The Internet, in which people carry on lively discussions of the day's events and almost anything else you can imagine. InterCon says Usenet capability will ship with a later version of the product.

Besides commercial services, you can also gain a leg up to The Internet via public-access UNIX systems, such as Panix in New York, Colorado SuperNet Inc. (Colorado only), or The Cyberspace Station in San Diego. Our favorites are conferencing systems and bulletin board services that add local conversation to their Internet access. Such systems include commercial services like The WELL and the BMUG bulletin board in Berkeley, California. The local color alone is enough to merit an electronic visit.

Corporate Accounts

Your entire company will need to get hitched to The Internet if you want to use The Internet to stay in touch with business while on the road. This is not an inexpensive proposition, since a dedicated connection (meaning that the link is always on) can cost more than $1,500 a month. Such accounts are usually obtained from a commercial Internet service. A cheaper alternative is to buy dial-up service, like an individual would use, to provide intermittent e-mail and Usenet connections (the latest messages are downloaded and uploaded to and from your company's computer each time it connects to the Internet). This will not solve the problem of providing Telnet and e-mail services for remote users who may try to make the connection to the computer when it's offline.

Logging into your company's computers will also be difficult if you work in an exclusively Macintosh environment. Remote login support requires that you have a UNIX computer in your office, which acts as mail server and gateway to the larger Internet. While you can run Apple's UNIX, A/UX, it's a task that demands no small amount of familiarity with UNIX. There's also the problem of security. A dedicated Internet connection is an open door on the network, and unless you've installed Security Dynamics' ACE Server, there's no reason someone can't just drop in.

See the
Digital Nomad
note below.

We suggest that it's easier to get a personal account where you send and receive most of your e-mail and restrict corporate Internet activity to things like file transfers.

Brother, can you spare a protocol?

The Internet runs on Transmission Control Protocol/Internet Protocol (TCP/IP), a set of rules for transmitting data between two nodes on a network; it also controls those transmissions to keep messages from becoming scrambled. Apple has developed its own TCP/IP communications stack, MacTCP, to allow Macintoshes to send and receive data over large internetworks. MacTCP acts as the interface between the application and the network, handling the conversion of data to and from IP packet formats (a network packet includes part of your message, addressing information that describes where it came from and where it's going, and control data that assures the packet will be received in the right order).

You can get MacTCP bundled with a third-party application, such as InterCon Systems Corporation's excellent Internet communications application, TCP/Connect II, or through a site-licensing agreement with Apple. In early 1993, Apple is also expected to begin selling MacTCP as a commercial package.

MacTCP must be installed when you plan to use a TCP/IP application over your LAN or through a dial-up connection to a UNIX terminal server that supports the serial line Internet Protocol (SLIP). When you dial into a SLIP server, MacTCP does its work on top of the SLIP protocol. SLIP connections also require that you install a special driver or Comm Toolbox tool to handle the protocol. SLIP extensions are available from Synergy Software, InterCon, Hyde Park Software (send a note to *info@hydepark.com* on The Internet) and over The Internet from Rick Watson at the University of Texas (send e-mail to *macslip@akbar .cc.utex.edu* for information).

It's also possible to use TCP/IP during an AppleTalk Remote Access session. Your ARA server must be connected by a router to a TCP/IP network, and you must have MacTCP installed on your PowerBook.

Heaven's Gateway

E-mail connectivity doesn't have to be limited by your company's refusal to invest in UNIX. Gateways, applications that run on your e-mail server, let PowerBook and Mac users on a local area network exchange mail with Internet users. Besides making the connection to The Internet (a physical connection is still needed), gateways also convert mail from the cryptic format of UNIX-based mail into the familiar graphical interface of your mail system. For example, you can click the Reply button in CE Software's QuickMail when responding to an Internet mail message (which uses the Simple Mail Transfer Protocol, or SMTP, but do you really want to know that?), type your message in a QuickMail form, and send it. The gateway strips away the QuickMail form and adds the appropriate addressing information.

There are shortcomings to gateway access to The Internet. Files cannot be attached to messages sent on The Internet, even if your local mail system lets you do so. Look for gateways from StarNine Technologies Inc. and InterCon Systems, which work with QuickMail, Microsoft Mail, and cc:Mail.

I'm here, but I don't see anything,

Wandering into the desert without a map isn't a good idea, and neither is trekking the electronic frontier unprepared. The Internet is not merely a collection of physical connections, it's a catalog of services. To find your way around, you first have to learn the basic functions available to you.

FTP

See the Road Warrior note below.

The File Transfer Protocol lets you search for and retrieve files from a remote computer, called an "archive" in Internet lingo. Many of the computers on The Internet provide "anonymous" FTP services, which means that you don't have to have a user account to log on and grab a file.

Retrieving a file from an FTP site will take a while, if you don't have the name of the file and its location within the archive's directory structure. Without that information, you will find yourself spending a lot of time shuffling through the electronic stacks in an archive.

FTP can also be conducted through e-mail, if the FTP server supports that capability. Include the filename and directory path for the file in your request. The first step in dealing with any new FTP server is to download the README files that describe that system's special quirks.

For more information on FTP, log on to CompuServe's ZiffNet/Mac forum and download the ftp-primer.txt file, which can also be had by anonymous FTP from the Mac archive at Stanford University (located at *sumex-aim.stanford.edu* on The Internet).

Archie

As electronic librarians, Archie servers catalog all the information on The Internet and point you to files that match your queries for data. Archie returns a list of all relevant files, the names of the FTP servers where they reside, and the directory path you must follow to reach them.

Archie sites are springing up in various locations; you can access the first such server by remote login or via e-mail. As yet, there is no Mac interface to Archie, so you'll have to gain your information through terminal emulation and knowledge of a few UNIX commands.

In fact, why not try Archie for yourself by requesting information about the service? Send e-mail to *archie@cs.mcgill.ca* and include the message: "prog Archie." You'll receive a complete listing of FTP sites that include Archie-related applications and files.

Telnet

Remote login allows you to access your own account on a computer from another computer on The Internet. This can be accomplished by accessing a friend's Internet-connected computer, or through a public data network like the CompuServe Packet Network (no, you don't have to be a member of CompuServe, you only have to pay them for the use of their network). Once you're logged on to your server, you can copy files to or from your PowerBook, read and reply to e-mail, and even jump back onto The Internet to log on to computer after computer in a long string of Telnet sessions (if you had that many accounts, that is).

Chat

This is a little-known feature of The Internet—certainly not one of the most ballyhooed activities in Cyberspace. Internet Relay Chat (IRC) lets you conduct real-time textual conversations with many people simultaneously. Users can be logged onto an IRC server from anywhere on the network, but they will appear to be in the same virtual conference room, their comments appearing in the interface along with their names. Imagine being able to join a meeting from a hotel room in Newark or the south of France.

Information Retrieval

Emerging on The Internet is a new class of services that tries to bring order to the vast sea of data available to you. Wide Area Information Servers (WAISs) and Gopher servers can interact with client applications (available as shareware on the Internet) that run on a PowerBook, helping you identify files you would otherwise have to search for by browsing anonymous FTP archives. These servers are massive archives with intelligent searching capabilities that compare your query with information they store. When there is a match, the relevant file is returned to you via e-mail.

So what's in it for me?

FTP can fill your free time with information, literature, and opinion, as well as a slough of freeware and shareware programs for your Power-Book. Here's a minute sampling of the FTP universe of information:

- **Mac Archives**   On its computers, Apple maintains a large library of technical information, freeware, shareware, and its own system software, which can be accessed through anonymous FTP at *ftp.apple.com* on The Internet.

  Stanford University also provides an extensive collection of Mac software on its computers. The archive, which is open for anonymous FTP at *sumex-aim.stanford.edu*, has been a favorite site for virus-makers to try to unleash their latest bugs to The Internet. Always check files that you download for viruses, whether they come from Stanford or any other archive!

- **Project Gutenberg**   A library of classics is being assembled in Cyberspace. Project Gutenberg provides titles like *The CIA World Factbook*, *Roget's Thesaurus*, *Moby Dick*, and the complete works of Shakespeare by FTP. The Internet address for more information is *hart@vmd.cso.uiuc.edu*.

- **Electronic Frontier Foundation**   Interested in the latest news about in the development of Cyberspace, or computing's impact on the law and civil liberties? EFF has an anonymous FTP archive for you, located at the address *ftp@eff.org*.

Reaching into the Future

The Internet is bound to grow, even beyond the wired infrastructure we know today, to allow digital nomads access from cellular and radio devices. Networking is at the center of almost every major computer industry initiative today, so look for new applications that add more intelligence, multimedia, and video capabilities to PowerBooks and the new personal digital assistants that we are hearing so much about these days.

Only one thing is certain: People will eventually seek out these services, after hearing about them through word of mouth or the press. Directions in national industrial policy, corporate organizational philosophy, and grass-roots networking all indicate that networks are a very compelling technology that captures the imagination of the people, once they use it.

Only a summary of The Internet services could be presented here. As we have said, whole books are being written about this amazing data organism that's spreading from computer to computer around the globe. It would be folly to try predicting what new services will come along in the next few years, because the developer community has only begun to realize and wrestle with the concept of Internet-based applications. It's the opinion of the authors that few people have mined even the outermost surface of The Internet's potential; it will certainly be the richest territory for innovation for the next decade. After that, who knows?

SECTION V

ZONED FOR EXPANSION

"Hiya!" I waved and smiled like an idiot as one of those blonde health nuts California is so famous for trod past me, hands hooked through backpack straps, sweat staining every inch of his "smiling skull" tie-dye tee-shirt.

His pace slowed and he stared at me, slack-jawed. It was obvious from his expression he had decided that what he'd found here was a lunatic. There I was, sitting on a rock on top of Mount Tamalpais, some two thousand feet above anything arguably resembling civilization, overlooking the single most breath-taking view of San Francisco, a city known for its breath-taking views. And what was I doing? I was busy tapping the keys and stroking the trackball of a beeping and buzzing little gray computer. Not exactly what you expect to see squatting on a mountain top.

He stopped, and after a moment smiled and waved back. Apparently he'd decided I wasn't a particularly dangerous lunatic.

The hiker walked over, heaved his pack off his shoulders and dropped it to the ground. "What'cha doin'?" he queried.

"Auditioning for an Apple commercial," I replied.

"Huh?"

"Just kidding," I said, deciding the joke wasn't funny enough to explain. "I'm changing an In Control outline on the server at my office."

"Oh." He replied, eyeing my 180's screen with suspicion.

"I've got this cellular connection to my modem," I showed him my cellular phone and the interface box running from it to the back of my Power-Book. "I'm using AppleTalk Remote Access with my computer's modem and the cellular phone's transmitter to make a standard analog connection to the modem on the Mac in my office. That Mac lets me get access to the server so I can open the outline and make changes."

"It's the same as using a regular telephone only I don't need to be near a wall jack," I added with a smile, "Not much chance of finding one up here."

The hiker's expression was softening. Obviously my explanation was beginning to clear away his doubts. Now he was sure I was a lunatic.

"The only problem is having enough power for a long session. So, I've got this solar panel helping my battery. On a clear day like today there's plenty of power." Surely he must believe me now but he was quiet.

"What don't you believe? The modem?"

"No, I'll take your word." he said. "What I don't get is why you'd spend two hours hiking up a mountain to get away from civilization and then bring the worst part of it with you."

He got up to go. Now it was my turn to stare, slack-jawed.

PART

1

THE ROADSIDE
ASSISTANCE GUIDE

Whether you've purchased the paper or electronic version, your copy of *The Digital Nomad's Guide* should have come with a high-density floppy diskette called The PowerBook Roadside Assistance Kit.

You can think of the Assistance Kit as the not-so-secret surprise at the bottom of your *Guide*. It includes nine programs; four of them are freeware /shareware titles selected because they are especially helpful (or fun) for PowerBook users. The remaining five programs are commercial software contributed to your disk by developers who hope that by using their applications, you'll see the tremendous power locked inside your portable.

The keys to unlocking that potential, in many cases, are third-party products.

Deals for Nomads

The developers of the five commercial programs in the Kit have also included with their programs special offers for owners of the *Guide*. In some cases, these offers allow you to get the "non-demo" version of the product (Spiral and AgentDA are special versions and have some limitations, noted below). In other cases, the developers have included offers to help you get other products they make. The details on these are included in the Read Me files in each product folder on the disk.

No Free Lunch

AgentDA, QuicKeys for Nomads, Spiral, Dynodex, and Synchro are not freeware! You're getting them with this book as part of a special bundle —you are not free to give copies of any of this software to your friends or enemies. We know you've heard about software piracy before, so we won't bore you with another sermon, except to say—don't do it! Remember, every time you give a copy of a program to someone who hasn't paid for it, you're helping support higher software prices. One way or another, developers are going to try to get back the money it cost them to create a program. They can do that by selling a lot of copies at a reasonable price or by selling a few copies at an unreasonable price. Ultimately, the decision is yours.

Installing the Kit

Okay, enough talk, let's get down to business. The first thing you need to do is make sure there's enough space on your PowerBook's internal hard drive to hold the Assistance Kit. Uncompressed, the files will take a total of 2.6 Mbytes, so we'd recommend clearing at least 3 Mbytes of disk space. (You'll want some space left over to store documents, won't you?)

Much of the electronic documentation included with the Kit uses TeachText (although these documents can also be read by some word processors). Make sure a copy of TeachText resides somewhere on your Power-Book. If you can't find it on your drive, Apple includes TeachText on the Tidbits floppy that came with your system diskettes.

Next, insert the Assistance Kit floppy into your PowerBook diskette drive. You should see an icon on your desktop something like this:

Roadside Assistance Kit

If the icon doesn't appear or you get an error message, eject the floppy and try reinserting it. If that doesn't work, try shutting down and restarting your PowerBook and inserting the diskette again. If you still don't get a disk icon, try the floppy on a desktop Mac—PowerBook diskette drives can be very finicky about reading floppies. Whatever you, don't initialize the floppy; that'll wipe the programs off the diskette completely. Once you get the floppy disk icon, double-click, and this window should appear in the Finder:

Ignore the Roadside README file. It's just a copy of these instructions. Instead, double-click the PB Roadside Assistance Kit.sea file.

You'll get a dialog box from the compression software. Click the Continue button. Next you'll get a standard file dialog box.

The dialog box should default to your PowerBook's internal hard drive. If it doesn't, or if you want to put the Kit's software someplace else, use the file dialog box's scrolling window to select a new location. The name of where you want to install the Kit should appear in the pull-down menu. When you're done, click *Save.*

The Assistance Kit will be decompressed and written to your drive. When it's done, the compression software will tell you so; just click *Quit.* You'll have a new folder called PB Roadside Assistance Kit wherever you told the dialog box to put it. Double-click the Assistance Kit folder, and you should have a window in the Finder that looks like this:

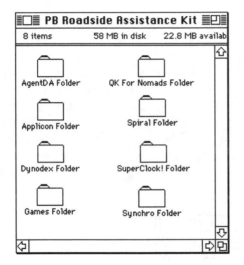

That's it! You've installed the Kit on your PowerBook. See the specific instructions below for installing each program. Included in their Read Me files, you'll also find instructions for installing many of the programs.

Commercial Software

No Hands Software's Synchro

Synchro lets you take any two folders and "synchronize" their contents. Then, any time those two folders appear in the Finder together with Synchro in memory, the contents are matched and updated. You can also ask Synchro to update folders, even if the volumes they reside on aren't available. The program will attempt to mount the volume where the folder was last located, asking you for a password to access the volume once it locates it (unless you used your password when you set up the synchronization).

For example, let's say you synchronize two folders, both called "Sync'd Stuff," on your desktop Mac and PowerBook. You make the connection using System 7 file-sharing by mounting the desktop Mac's hard drive in your PowerBook's Finder and dragging both folders (one at a time) to Synchro. The program will display this panel:

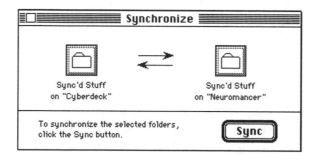

Click the Sync button to finish the pairing of the two folders. If you accessed the folder on your desktop Mac through file-sharing, Synchro will ask for a password that it will use to access the volume automatically in the future. For security reasons, we advise against giving your password to the program; just fill it in any time Synchro asks for it.

That's all there is to it. From now on, when you mount your desktop Mac's volume and Synchro is running, you'll hear a three-tone beep sound letting you know that synchronized folder pairs are available. When you switch to Synchro, you'll be asked if you want to synchronize the folders.

So, why synchronize folders instead of files? There is one big advantage of doing folder-to-folder synchronization: you can use the folder pairs as a kind of automated drop box. When you have a file on your PowerBook that you also want on your desktop Mac, just drop it into a synchronized folder. The next time you connect, Synchro will automatically copy that file over to the folder's mate. By the way, folders don't have to have the same name to be paired.

One last note. After you've set up a folder pair, in both folders you'll notice a new file that looks like this:

Sync'd Stuff«Sync'd Stuff

Don't throw it away! This is a magnet, and it's what makes the synchronization happen.

Installing Synchro

Just put Synchro where you want it and double-click. You'll be prompted to enter your name and company. Also, you'll see a check box in the lower lefthand corner. This puts an alias of Synchro into the Startup Items folder in your System Folder. If you don't want Synchro to boot every time you do, uncheck the box. Synchro requires System 7 to operate. For more information on installing and using Synchro, check out the Read Me file in the Synchro folder.

Opposites attract?

As a digital nomad, you'll quickly get accustomed to relying on Synchro to keep your versions straight. But you may ask, "Is there more? Can I craft my own magnets and do things like automatically reorganize my desktop, do more sophisticated synchronization, or move files around the network based on preset criteria?"

You can, using No Hands' Magnet application. Contact No Hands at the phone number in the Synchro Read Me file to find out how you can get a copy of the program or a paper copy of the full Synchro documentation.

Portfolio Systems' Dynodex

You've heard us talk a lot about being able to track your contacts' most vital information using your PowerBook. Well, here's the program that'll let you do it. Dynodex.

A complete contacts manager, Dynodex is very fast, able to flash through hundreds of records in an instant, without spinning up your PowerBook hard drive. Dynodex has a sophisticated file structure that lets you sort and search on multiple criteria; import and export your data to any other program; mark, select, and merge particular records. You can print cards, labels, and address books, or even dial the phone.

A feature of the program we especially like is the ability to group frequent selections, such as all the restaurants in a database, and install them as menu items.

Another nice feature of Dynodex is that the most-used commands are accessible through icons on the left side of the record window (Figure 1).

Installing Dynodex

Double-click on the program. It's that simple. Dynodex will open a blank database which you can fill, or you can use *Import...* under the File menu to bring in records from another database.

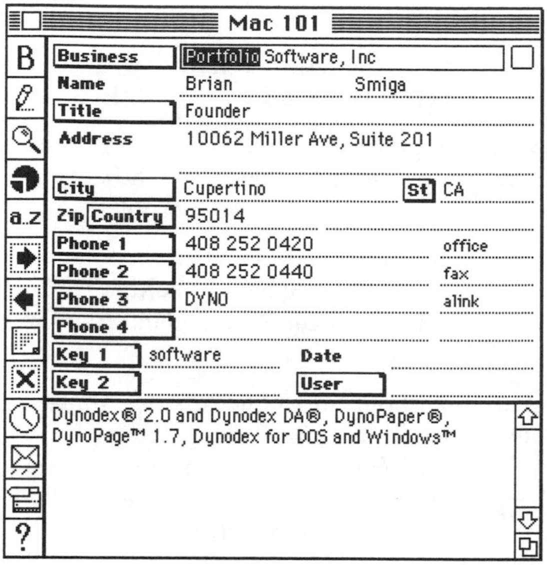

Figure 1. The Mac 101 database included with Dynodex contains the names and addresses of many Mac developers.

We like to double-click our primary database to start up Dynodex, so that all our contacts are available when the program opens. We put the database in a synchronized folder, so Synchro can keep versions of the file on our desktop and portable Macs straight. Aliases on the desktop and in the Apple Menu Items Folder provide quick access.

You can also use the Dynodex DA to access your database. Although you won't be able to do all things you can in the Dynodex application, the DA takes considerably less memory. Use *Preferences...* under the Dyno menu to specify which database you want the Dynodex DA to open automatically. To install the DA, just drag the Dynodex DA file to your System Folder.

For more information on installing and using Dynodex, consult the Read Me First file in the Dynodex folder.

Dynodex Unbound

For a limited time, Portfolio is making Dynodex 3.0, the latest and greatest version of the program, which includes over 100 new features, available to digital nomads at a significant discount. You can also get Dynodex 3.0 and a non-time-locked version of AgentDA bundled together. Read the Special Offer! file in the Dynodex folder for more information.

CE Software's QuicKeys for Nomads

While planning this book, we asked ourselves, what sorts of things do all PowerBook owners need to do a lot?

The answer was simple: sleep, shut down, spin down the hard drive, and switch off backlighting. The only problem was: how could we make accessing these functions easy or, in some cases, possible?

The folks down at CE Software supplied the solution, based on their macro assembler, QuicKeys. They built QuicKeys for Nomads especially to give you control over all those features and more by simply typing a key sequence (see Figure 2).

We've talked a lot about how QuicKeys for Nomads can be used to make your life simpler. Take a close look at Section II, Part 1, *Laying The Foundation of Your Mobile Habitat* and at Section III, Part 2, *The Conservation of Energy* for more information on using QuicKeys for Nomads. Also, consult the Read Me file in the QK for Nomads folder.

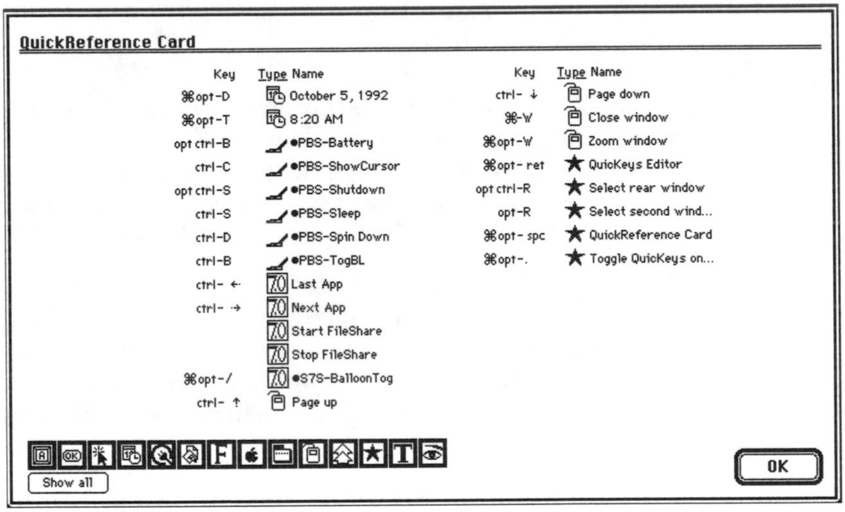

Figure 2. The QuicKeys for Nomad's QuickReference Card

Installing QuicKeys

Open the QK for Nomads folder and then the QK RunTime folder; double-click on the QK Install RunTime file and follow the directions. Don't forget to look at the Read Me file—it contains directions for installing QuicKeys for Nomads.

The Automated Finder

So, maybe we didn't think of a key sequence you'd like? Well, you can build your own key sequences by upgrading to QuicKeys. With it, you can create sequences that mount servers and choose printers or automatically enter often-used text into documents. Just for *Guide* readers, CE Software is offering a special upgrade price. For more information, look at the Read Me file that came in the QuicKeys folder.

Team Building Technologies' AgentDA

Having trouble remembering where your next appointment is? Let Agent-DA remember for you. This program is a dynamic calendar you can use to: schedule appointments, record important facts about where you're going and whom you're meeting, and ask to notify you when it's time to leave for the appointment, even if AgentDA isn't running in memory.

The reason we included AgentDA on the Roadside Assistance Kit disk is that it has the best interface of the smaller calendar programs we've tried. It is extremely easy to navigate through the schedule, to print out calendars, to modify the number of days and weeks displayed, and to quickly jump to any point on the calendar (see Figure 3).

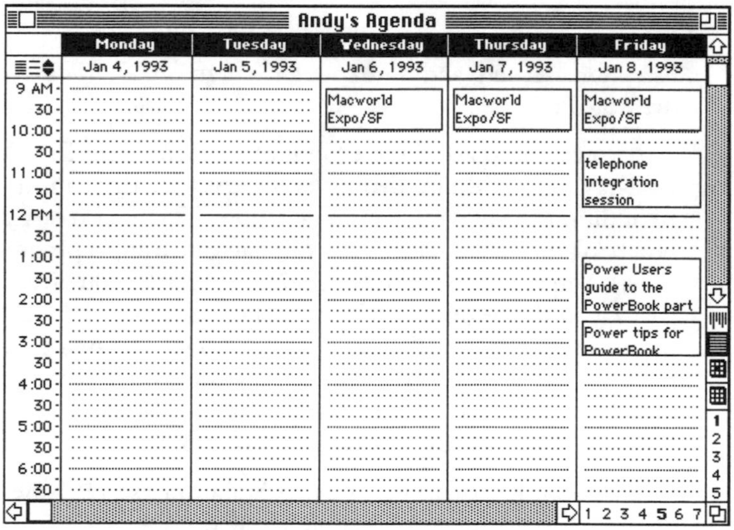

Figure 3. AgentDA makes keeping track of appointments a breeze.

AgentDA takes up a paltry 267 Kbytes of disk space and can run in a modicum of RAM.

Installing AgentDA

AgentDA installs the same way that the Dynodex DA does. Just drag the AgentDA 2.1.2 Trial v. file to your System Folder. You'll be asked if you want to put it in the Apple Menu Items folder; click *OK.* Also, drag the file called The Alarm to the System Folder; if you've asked to be notified, The Alarm lets you know when appointments are coming up.

Now, select *AgentDA* from the Apple menu. You'll be warned that your trial version of the program expires in 90 days. You may want to select the Open Automatically checkbox when you save your calendar, so that Agent-DA will open that appointment book when you start the program.

This Agent will self-destruct.

The version of AgentDA included on this disk is a time-locked demo, good for 90 days from installation. This should give you plenty of time to try out the program and see if tracking your schedule electronically is something you want to do. Complete instructions on how to use AgentDA and how to get upgraded to a non-time-locked version are included in the Teach Text Agent DA and Random House Offer files in the AgentDA folder.

TechWorks' Spiral

There you are, typing along, and, all of a sudden, your cursor hangs! You listen for a second, and, sure enough, Microsoft Word has spun up the disk drive again.

If you want to avoid these kinds of moments, use TechWorks' Spiral, a note-taking application that never hits the hard drive until you want it to. In addition to allowing you to take notes, Spiral also lets you break up a notebook into sections that you can navigate using a progress bar (see Figure 4). You can create tables of contents that take you directly to a particular page at the beginning of each tabbed section of a notebook. Password protection is also available for your notebook. The best time-saving device for notetakers is a menu that creates shorthand entries for often-used phrases. For example, when you type the shorthand cue *exl* (for *existential*), Spiral will automatically extend the word for you.

For more information on using Spiral, please read the "About Spiral demo" file that comes in the Spiral folder.

Installing Spiral

Double-click either Spiral or one of the two notebooks that come in the folder. That's all there is to it.

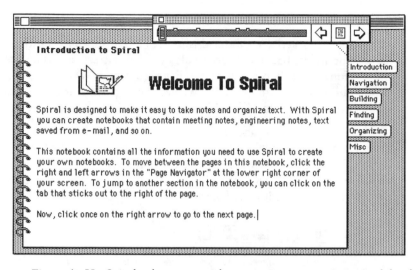

Figure 4. Use Spiral to keep notes without spinning up your PowerBook hard drive.

Spiral Creations

This is a demo version of Spiral. It's not time-locked, like AgentDA; rather, it will only open the files "Nomad notes demo" and "About Spiral demo" that are included with it. You can edit, add, and modify these files to your heart's content but you won't be able to create any new Spiral notebooks. So, use the Spiral demo as a nice to-do list or Notepad replacement. The "Nomad notes demo" file provides information on how to get Spiral.

Assistance Kit Shareware and Freeware

Applicon

If you're one of those people who really misses System 6's ability to switch between running applications by clicking on the icon in the menu bar, you'll love Applicon. It goes System 6 one better, displaying the applications' icons on user-configurable tiles in the Finder. To get to an application just click on its tile (see Figure 5).

Figure 5. Applicon means fast access to applications.

Don't forget to check out the Read Me file for more information.

SuperClock!

We've talked a lot about this useful bantam utility that displays a clock in the menu bar. Its ability to also display battery status and to let you put your PowerBook to sleep by clicking a battery icon make it especially useful to Mac portable users. (We like the stopwatch for timing speeches.) Do consult the SuperClock! Read Me file for more about the program.

One warning about using SuperClock! with newer model PowerBooks: it may occasionally give spurious readouts, such as the battery low icon (see Figure 6). If this happens often, you may want to forgo using SuperClock on your 160, 180, or Duo. In either case, watch CompuServe and AOL closely for an updated version of the program sometime in the future.

Figure 6. SuperClock! sometimes gives inaccurate readings on late-model PowerBooks.

Glider and Klondike

What Macintosh software collection would be complete without a few games? Glider is a reflex game where you try to fly your paper airplane from room to room without crashing. Klondike is more sedentary entertainment. It's Solitaire brought to your PowerBook!

Installing These Goodies

The best place to put Applicon is in the Startup Items folder of your System Folder. That way, the application switcher will be up and running when you need it.

SuperClock! is a control panel and must be located in the Control Panel folder of the System Folder before it'll work.

As to the games, we'd keep them handy for times when you need a quick break. Maybe put them in a folder called "Fun Stuff"?

PART
2

JUST GOTTA HAVE IT!

We've talked about a lot of goodies throughout the *Guide*. Products were included as examples of what you can purchase to expand your PowerBook's talents. That, after all, is the mission of the *Guide*, to help you construct the ultimate mobile habitat for your specific needs.

However, since finding some of these products will take more than calling up your favorite mailorder house or searching the latest ads in *MacWEEK* and *MacUser*, we've included this listing of how to contact developers who have interesting products for your PowerBook. You can also consult the sample database, Mac 101, included with Dynodex in the Roadside Assistance Kit. It contains the names, addresses, and contact information for many more developers than we had space to list here (although we can't vouch for the accuracy of the Mac 101 list).

PowerBook Hardware, Software, and Services

ACI US
10351 Bubb Road
Cupertino, CA 95014
Phone: (408) 252-4444
Fax: (408) 252-0831
4D relational database and server

Adobe Systems Inc.
1585 Charleston Road
P.O. Box 7900
Mountain View, CA
94039-7900
Phone: (415) 961-4400
Fax: (415) 961-3769
*Photoshop, Premier, Illustrator,
ATM and PostScript fonts*

After Hours Software
5990 Sepulveda Blvd.
Suite 240
Van Nuys, CA 91411
Phone: (818) 780-2220
Fax: (818) 780-2666
*TouchBASE contact management
software*

Aladdin Systems Inc.
165 Westridge Drive
Watsonville, CA 95076
Phone: (408) 761-6200
Fax: (408) 761-6206
StuffIt compression utilities

Apple Computer Inc.
Customer Relations
20525 Mariani Ave.
Cupertino, CA 95014-6299
Phone: (408) 996-1010;
(800) 538-9696
Apple Service: (800) 767-2775
PowerBooks

Argosy Software Inc.
113 Spring St., Fifth Floor
New York, NY 10012
Phone: (212) 274-1199
Fax: (212) 431-6567
RunPC DOS emulation software

Asanté Technologies Inc.
404 Tasman Drive
Sunnyvale, CA 94089
Phone: (408) 752-8388
Fax: (408) 734-4864
*SCSI-to-Ethernet adapters,
network hardware*

ASD Software Inc.
4650 Arrow Highway
Suite E-6
Montclair, CA 91763
Phone: (714) 624-2594
Fax: (714) 624-9574
Active Memory to-do list software

Attain Corp.
48 Grove St.
Somerville, MA 02144-2500
Phone: (617) 776-1110
Fax: (617) 776-1626
In Control to-do list and outliner

Banyan Systems Inc.
120 Flanders Road
Westboro, MA 01581
Phone: (508) 898-1000
Fax: (508) 898-1755
Enterprise network software

BMUG Inc.
1442A Walnut Street
Suite 62
Berkeley, CA 94709
Phone: (510) 549-2684
Fax: (510) 849-9026
*Macintosh user group; publisher
of ToonWare*

Cayman Systems Inc.
University Park at MIT
26 Landsdowne Street
Cambridge, MA 02139
Phone: (617) 494-1999
Fax: (617) 349-3811
*GatorLink AppleTalk Remote
Access server*

CE Software Inc.
PO Box 65580
West Des Moines, IA 50265
Phone: (515) 224-1995
Fax: (515) 224-4534
QuicKeys, QuickMail

Central Point Software Inc.
15220 N.W. Greenbrier
Parkway #200
Beaverton, OR 97006
Phone: (503) 690-8090
Fax: (503) 690-8083
*Data recovery and anti-virus
utilities*

Claris Corp.
5201 Patrick Henry Drive
Santa Clara, CA 95052
Phone: (408) 727-8227
*ClarisWorks, HyperCard and
productivity software*

CMG Inc.
1001 Capitol of Texas
Highway South, Building 1
Austln, TX 78746
Phone: (512) 329-8220
Fax: (512) 329-5532
Physical security for PowerBooks

Computer Care Inc.
420 N. Fifth St.
Suite 1180
Minneapolis, MN 55401
Phone: (612) 371-0061
Fax: (612) 371-9342
Internal video cards

Connectix Corp.
2655 Campus Dr.
San Mateo, CA 94403
Phone: (415) 571-5100;
(800) 950-5880
Fax: (415) 571-5195
*PowerBook, Maxima RAM disk
utilities*

Coral Research
P.O. Box 2055
Stateline, NV 89449
Phone: (702) 588-9690
TimeLog time-tracking software

Dantz Development Corp.
1400 Shattuck Ave.
Berkeley, CA 94709
Phone: (510) 849- 0293
Fax: (510) 849-1708
*Retrospect and DiskFit backup
software*

DataViz Inc.
55 Corporate Drive
Trumbull, CT 06611
Phone: (203) 268-0030
Fax: (203) 203) 268-4345
Mac/PC translation products

Dayna Communications Inc.
50 South Main St., Fifth Floor
Salt Lake City, UT 84144
Phone: (801) 531-0600
Fax: (801) 359-9135
*DOS Mounter and NetMounter;
SCSI-to-Ethernet adapters*

E-Machines Inc.
9305 S.W. Gemini Drive
Beaverton, Ore. 97005
Phone: (503) 646-6699
Fax: (503) 641-0946
Duo docks; external monitors

Envisio Inc.
510 First Ave. N., Suite 303
Minneapolis, MN 55403
Phone: (612) 339-1008
Fax: (612) 339-1369
Internal video cards

Farallon Computing Inc.
2470 Mariner Square Loop
Alameda, CA 94501
Phone: (510) 814-5000
*PhoneNET connectors; Timbuktu;
plus lots of other networking
products*

Fifth Generation Systems Inc.
Mac Development Group
124 University Ave.
Palo Alto, CA 94301
Phone: (415) 321-5375;
(800) 873-4384
Fax: (415) 321- 5378
*DiskDoubler, AutoDoubler
compression software*

Future Perfect, a distributor for
Quorum International Ltd.
19672 Stevens Creek Blvd.,
Suite 110
Cupertino, Calif. 95014
Phone: (408) 983-2700;
(800) 995-1206
Fax: (408) 253-5794
Elert alarm

GCC Technologies Inc.
580 Winter St.
Waltham, MA 02154
Phone: (617) 890-0880
Fax: (617) 890-0822
WriteMove II portable printer

GDT Softworks Inc.
4664 Lougheed Highway
Suite 188
Burnaby, B.C. V5C 6B7 Canada
Phone: (604) 291-9121
Fax: (604) 291-9689
PowerPrint print drivers

Global Village
Communication Inc.
685 E. Middlefield Road
Building B
Mountain View, CA 94043
Phone: (415) 390-8200
Fax: (415) 390-8282
Internal modems

Inline Design
308 Main St.
Lakeville, CT 06039
Phone: (203) 435-4995;
(800) 453-7671
Fax: (203) 435-1091
*Inline Sync file synchronization
utility*

Insignia Solutions Inc.
526 Clyde Ave.
Mountain View, CA 94043
Phone: (415) 694-7600
Fax: (415) 964-5434
AccessPC and SoftPC DOS and
Windows emulation

InterCon Systems Corp.
950 Herndon Parkway
Herndon, VA 22070
Phone: (703) 709-9890
Fax: (703) 709-9896
WorldLink and TCP/Connect II
communications software;
InterPrint Unix print drivers

Iomega Corp.
1821 West 4000 South
Roy, UT 84067
Phone: (801) 778-1000;
(800) 777-6004
Removable (Bernoulli) cartridge
drives

James Engineering Inc.
6329 Fairmount Ave.
El Cerrito, CA 94530
Phone: (510) 525-7350
Fax: (510) 525-5740
MacVGA adapter cable

Kensington Microware Ltd.
2855 Campus Drive
San Mateo, CA 94403
Phone: (415) 572-2700;
(800) 535-4242
Fax: (415) 572-9675
Security and input devices

Kent Marsh Ltd.
3260 Sul Ross
Houston, TX 77098
Phone: (713) 522-5625
Fax: (713) 522-8965
FinderBolt and MacSafe II
security software

La Cie Limited,
A Quantum Company
8700 SW Creekside Place
Beaverton, OR 97005
Phone: (503) 520-9000;
(800) 999-1179
Fax: (503) 520-9100
PocketDrive portable external
hard disks

Lapis Technologies Inc.
1100 Marina Village Parkway
Suite 100
Alameda, CA 94501
Phone: (510) 748-1600
Fax: (510) 748-1645
SCSI-to-video adapters

Leader Technologies Inc.
4590 MacArthur Blvd.,
Suite 550
Newport Beach, CA 93660
Phone: (714) 757-1787
Fax: (714) 757-1777
PowerMerge file and folder
synchronization utility

Liberty Systems Inc.
160 Saratoga Ave, Suite 38
Santa Clara, CA 95051
Phone: (408) 983-1127
Fax: (408) 243-2885
Portable external hard disk and
magneto-optical drives

Lind Electronic Design Inc.
6414 Cambridge St.
Minneapolis, MN 55426
Phone: (612) 927-6303;
(800) 659-5956
Fax: (612) 927-7740
Tons of PowerBook battery
products

Lotus Development Corp.
cc:Mail Division
2141 Landings Drive
Mountain View, CA 94043
Phone: (415) 961-8800;
(800) 448-2500
Fax: (415) 960-0967
cc:Mail electronic mail and
Notes groupware

MacVONK USA
313 Iona Ave.
Narbeth, PA 19072
Phone: (215) 660-0606
Fax: (215) 558-4360
InForum network conferencing
software

MasterSoft, Inc.
6991 E. Camelback Rd.
Suite A-320
Scottsdale, AZ 85251
Phone: (602) 277-0900;
(800) 624-6107
Fax: (602) 970-0706
File translation software

MicroMath Scientific Software
P.O. Box 21550
Salt Lake City, UT 84121
Phone: (801) 943-0290
Fax: (801) 943-0299
MMCalc scientific calculator
desk accessory

MicroNet Technology Inc.
20 Mason
Irvine, CA 92718
Phone: (714) 837-6033
Fax: (714) 837-1164
Big, fast hard drives

Microtek Lab Inc.
680 Knox St.
Torrence, CA 90502
Phone: (213) 321-2121;
(800) 654-4160
Fax: (310) 538-1193
Scanners

Microsoft Corp.
One Microsoft Way
Redmond, WA 98052-6399
Phone: (206) 882-8080
Fax: (206) 936-7329
Productivity software; e-mail

Microtech International Inc.
158 Commerce St.
East Haven, CT 06512
Phone: (203) 468-6223
Fax: (203) 467-1856
*RAM, hard drives and a solar
panel for PowerBooks*

Newer Technology Inc.
7803 E. Osie
Suite 105
Wichita, KS 67207
Phone: (316) 685-4904;
(800) 678-3726
*PowerBook RAM, battery
products and replacement
color screens*

No Hands Software
200 Page Mill Road
Suite 260
Palo Alto,CA 94306
Phone: (415) 321-7340;
(800) 598-3821
Fax: (415) 321-2209
Synchro; Magnet

Novell Inc.
122 East 1700 South
Provo, UT 84606
Phone: (801) 429-7000
Fax: (801) 453-1267
*The really big network software
company*

Now Software Inc.
319 SW Washington St.
11th Floor
Portland, OR 97204
Phone: (503) 274-2800
Fax: (503) 274-0670
System 7 utilities

nView Corp
860 Omni Blvd.
Newport News, VA 23606
Phone: (804) 873-1354;
(800) 736-8439
Fax: (804) 873-2153
LCD projection panels

ON Technology
155 Second St.
Cambridge, MA 02141
Phone: (617) 876-0900
Fax: (617) 876-0391
*Meeting Maker group scheduler
and Instant Update workgroup
software*

Orange Micro Inc.
1400 N. Lakeview Dr.
Anaheim, CA 92807
Phone: (714) 779-2772
Fax: (714) 779-9332
Grappler IIsp printer adapter

Pacer Software Inc.
7911 Herschel Ave.
Suite 402
La Jolla, CA 92037
Phone: (619) 454-0565
Fax: (619) 454-6267
*PacerTerm terminal emulation
and PacerForum conferencing
software*

Palomar Software Inc.
2964 Oceanside Blvd.
Oceanside, CA 92054
Phone: (619) 721-7000
Fax: (619) 721-4758
*On The Road offline print spooler
and network remounter*

Panamax Inc.
150 Mitchell Blvd.
San Rafael, CA 94903
Phone: (415) 499-3900;
(800) 472-5555
Fax: (415) 472-5540
Computer surge protectors

Pastel Development Corp.
113 Spring St., Fifth Floor
New York, NY 10012
Phone: (212) 941-7500
Fax: (212) 431-3079
*DayMaker personal scheduler
software*

Peripheral Land Inc. (PLI)
47421 Bayside Pkwy.
Fremont, CA 94538
Phone (510) 657-2211;
(800) 288-8754
Fax: 510-683-9713
Magneto-optical drives

Portfolio Systems Inc.
10062 Miller Ave, Suite 201
Cupertino, CA 95014
Phone: (408) 252-0420;
(800) 729-3966
Fax: (408) 252-0440
Dynodex contacts database

Premier Technology Inc.
1072 Folsom St., Suite 456
San Francisco, CA 94103
Phone: (415)255-9300
Fax: (415) 775-2134
*PowerBook shoulder strap;
lock-down device*

PSI Integration Inc.
851 E. Hamilton Ave., Suite 200
Campbell, CA 95008
Phone: (408) 559-8544
Fax: (408) 559-8548
Internal modems

Qdea
PO Box 19531
St. Paul, MN 55119
Phone: (612) 779-0955
Update! file synchronization utility

Quark Inc.
300 S. Jackson, Suite 100
Denver, CO 80209
Phone: (303) 934-2211
Fax: (303) 377-6327
*Quark XPress desktop publising
software*

Radius Inc.
1710 Fortune Drive
San Jose, CA 95131
Phone: (408) 434-1010
Fax: 408-434-0127
PowerBook SCSI display interface

Safeware The Insurance
Agency Inc.
2929 N. High St.
PO Box 02211
Columbus, OH 43202
Phone: (614) 262-0559;
(800) 848-3469
Fax: (614) 262-1714
Computer insurance

Sigma Designs Inc.
46501 Landing Parkway
Fremont, CA 94538
Phone: (415) 770-0100
Fax: (415) 770-2640
*PowerBook SCSI-based external
displays*

Shiva Corp.
One Cambridge Center
Cambridge, MA 02142
Phone: (617) 252-6300
Fax: (617) 252-6852
*LanRover AppleTalk Remote
Access servers*

Sitka Corp.
950 Marina Village Parkway
Alameda, CA 94501
Phone: (510) 769-9669
Fax: (510) 769-8771
Network and file-sharing software

Software Ventures Corp.
2907 Claremont Ave.
Berkeley, CA 94705
Phone: (510) 644-3232
Fax: (510) 848-0885
*MicroPhone II and MicroPhone
Pro terminal emulation software*

Symantec Corp.
10201 Torre Avenue
Cupertino, CA 95014-2132
Phone: (408) 253-9600
Fax: (408) 252-4694
*Integrated software; anti-virus,
data recovery and PowerBook
utilities*

Synergy Software Inc.
2457 Perkiomen Ave.
Reading, PA 19606
Phone: (215) 779-0522
Fax: (215) 370-0548
*VersaTerm Pro terminal
emulation software*

SyQuest Technology
47071 Bayside Pkwy.
Fremont, CA 94538
Phone: (510) 226-4000;
(800)-245-2278
Fax: (510) 226-4100
Removable cartridge drives

Timeslips Corp.
239 Western Ave.
Essex, MA 01929
Phone: (508) 768-6100
Fax: (508) 768-7660
*Laptrack and timeslips
time-billing software*

Traveling Software Inc.
18702 N. Creek Parkway
Bothell, WA 98011
Phone: (206) 483-8088
Fax: (206) 487-1284
*LapLink Mac III translation
software for Macs and PCs*

Team Building
Technologies Inc.
836 Bloomfield Ave
Montreal, Quebec,
Canada H2V 3S6
Phone: (514) 278-3010
Fax: (514) 278-2874
*AgentDA personal calendar and
appointments program*

TechWorks Inc.
4030 Braker Lane W.
Suite 350
Austin, TX 78759
Phone: (512) 794-8533;
(800) 688-7466
Fax: (512) 794-8520
Spiral; RAM

WestWare Inc.
10148 Diamond Head Court
Spring Valley, CA 91977
Phone: (619) 660-0358
Fax: (619) 660-0233
*Contact Ease contact
management software*

Utilitron Inc.
P.O. Box 811
Allen, TX 75002
Phone and fax: (214) 727-2329;
(800) 428-8766
*PowerSwap, backs-up sleep on
PowerBook 140-180*

WordPerfect Corp.
1555 North Technology Way
Orem, UT 84057
Phone: (801) 225-5000
Fax: (801) 222-5377
*Word processing; groupware;
e-mail*

Online Services and Internet Access

Call for local access numbers.

America Online Inc., AOL
8619 Westwood Center Drive
Vienna, VA 22182-2285
Phone: (703) 448-8700;
(800) 827-6364
Fax: (703) 883-1509

Apple Computer Inc.,
AppleLink
APDA
20525 Mariani Ave.
Cupertino, CA 95014-6299
Phone: (408) 996-1010;
(800) 282-2732

CompuServe Inc., CIS
5000 Arlington Centre Blvd.
PO Box 20212
Columbus, OH 43220
Phone: (614) 457-0802;
(800) 848-8199
Fax: (614) 457-0348

MCI International Inc.,
MCI Mail
2 International Dr.
Rye Brook, NY 10573
Phone (914) 937- 3444
Fax (914) 934-6996

Prodigy Services Co., Prodigy
445 Hamilton Ave.
White Plains, NY 10601
Phone: (914) 993-8820;
(800) 776-3449
Fax: (914) 684-0278

Performance Systems
International, PSInet
1180 Sunrise Valley Dr.
Suite 1100
Reston, VA 22091
Phone: (703) 620-6651
Fax: (703) 629-4586

The WELL, Whole Earth
'Lectronic Link
27 Gate Five Road
Sausalito, CA 94965
Phone: (415) 332-4335
Modem: (415) 332-6106

The World
Software Tool and Die
1330 Beacon St.
Brookline, MA 02146
Phone: (617) 739-0202
Modem: (617) 739-9753

Happy Trails!

We couldn't resist just one more Nomad note.

We hope you get as much out of the *Guide* as we did writing it. After years of writing news stories on painfully slim deadlines, we thought nothing could have challenged our ability to write well and fast—that was before writing this book.

We discovered that a guide to building the perfect PowerBook took more space than we originally planned. With new products coming along every week, it's going to be a big job updating the *Guide* next year, and you probably can't wait that long to get the lowdown on the latest for PowerBooks. That's why we started a newsletter for PowerBook users. You can get the first copy by sending in your reader registration card.

(continued)

Happy Trails! (continued)

To anticipate another question concerning the development of the *Guide*, yes, it was written on PowerBooks (mostly a 170 and 140, although the manuscript did live on a Duo 230 and a 180 for awhile). In fact, a large part of it was written on airplanes, in air terminals, and in hotel rooms around the nation—what you might call proof-of-concept testing. Also employed were a Quadra 900, a Mac IIfx, and an SE/30. We wrote it in Microsoft Word 5.0 and 5.1, not because we especially like Word but because it's what we're used to (it's used at *MacWEEK*). We edited most of the screen shots in Adobe Photoshop 2.0; Nevin Berger used Adobe Illustrator 3.0 to create most of the illustrations, except for the cartoon in the Manifesto (by the way, anyone who likes Nevin's cartoons can get a book of them from BMUG). The *Guide* was laid out in PageMaker.

We also used a myriad of third-party Mac products while researching the *Guide*, many of which appear in it. We stayed in touch using Quick-Mail, AOL, AppleLink, CompuServe, the Internet, and two Motorola cellular phones. This book wouldn't have been possible if it weren't for the PowerBook's incredible support for collaborative work!

That's it! Now get out there; that's why you bought a PowerBook, isn't it?